MW01618399

THE BUSINESS OF GOLF
What Are You Thinking?

A Primer—Third Edition
How to Maximize the Financial Return of a Golf Course

Written for Golfers, Professional Golf Management Students and Golf Industry Personnel Seeking to Strengthen Their Knowledge

By
James J. Keegan

Managing Principal
Golf Convergence, Inc.

ISBN: 978-0-9846268-9-2

Library of Congress Control Number: 2013953827

Printed in the United States of America.

Table of Contents

CHAPTER 5: The Golfer Local Market Analysis 73

CHAPTER 6: The Strategic Planning Summary 85

Section 2—Tactical Planning 95

CHAPTER 7: Technology—The Foundation 97

CHAPTER 8: The Key Financial Metrics 113

CHAPTER 9: Financial Modeling 133

CHAPTER 10: Pricing and Yield Management 151

CHAPTER 11: Golf Course Valuation 169

Section 3—Operational Execution 181

CHAPTER 12: The Playing Field 183

CHAPTER 15: Who Are Your Customers? 247

CHAPTER 16: Creating Customer Loyalty 265

CHAPTER 17: Customers—A Future Perspective 283

Acknowledgments

Every day I remind myself
that my inner and outer lives are based on the labors
of other men, living and dead,
and that I must exert myself in order to give
in the same measure as I have received...

Albert Einstein

When I read a book, I usually skim the acknowledgments thinking they are a never-ending list of meaningless (to me) thank you notes. I no longer have that opinion.

Writing this book has been like putting together a 90,000-piece jigsaw puzzle without the box cover. It has been tedious, time-consuming, and frustrating—a most difficult task—but I have been blessed to avoid many of bullets that life hurls at you while putting all of these thoughts and experiences on the page.

Professional Appreciation

A pleasant by-product of this writing has been remembering and reviewing the past two decades of my life in the golf industry, especially the many wonderful people I have met. With an ACT! Database of 23,178 contacts within the golf industry, 20,724 active email addresses in Vertical Response, over 300 Twitter followers and having had over 700 golf courses across the world as clients, I hardly know where to start to thank each person who contributed to my knowledge of the industry. I have come to realize that I am merely a secretary transcribing the thoughts and best practices of the brilliant minds within the industry.

Therefore, proper credit is due to Joe Beditz, President of the National Golf Foundation, for the outstanding research this organization has undertaken. The quality of the NGF's reports and services has soared during the last several years. Bravo! His willingness to have the NGF check the facts and statistics in this book is deeply appreciated.

While there are those who espouse theory, Stuart Hayden is incredible in his ability to cut the wheat from the chaff. He is a dear friend, a confidante, and an individual whose golf industry insights have greatly influenced my own. The ideas for this book have been largely molded by Stuart's insights. The organization for this book was definitely influenced by Stuart's introduction of the strategic, tactical, and operational divisions for the book's organizational structure.

Serving in this industry for 25 years, I have been impacted by some amazing people whom I hold in deep admiration and respect: Eddie Ainsworth, Joe Assell, Kathy Aznavorian, Mary Pat Black, Ben Blake, John Bond, Marshal Brereton, Jeff Burkle, Frank Cain, John Cannon, Mike Cato, David Clark, Graham Cliff, Jack Crittenden, Whitney Crouse, Cindy Curtis, Mike Cutler, Gordon Dalgleish, Bob Doyle, Tim Eberlein, Christian Faergemann, Craig Farnsworth, Jim Fedigan, Niall Flanagan, Doug Follick, Jeff Foster, Keith Foster, Thomas Frutchey, Ed Gowan, Eric Greytok, Bob Griffioen, Jack Grum, Joe Guerra, Chad Hatch, Doug Hellman, Dr. Brian Horgan, Chantel Jackson, Mike Jamison, Katherine Jemsek, Jim Kass, George Kim, Tom Kensler, Lisa Langas, Walt Lankau, Jeff Levine, Mike Loustalot, Rick Lucas, Dennis Lyon, Doug Main, Troy Malo, Dawes Marlatt, M.J. Mastalir, Ray McGury, Paul Metzler, Alex Miceli, Paul Milholland, Jayne Miller, Nick Mokelke, Karen Moraghan, Tim Moraghan, Greg Nathan, Kevin Norby, Chris Padgett, Joe Passov, David Pillsbury, Warren Pittman, Sandy Queen, Del Ratcliffe, Don Rhodes, Joe Riekena, Jon Rizzi, Marcia Robbins, Rick and Tom Robshaw, Jim Roschek, Dan Scherman, Paul Schock, Kristine Schoonover, Randy Shannon, Richard Singer, Steve Skinner, David V. Smith, Dr. Tim Sommerville, Tom Stine, Jim Stracka, Art Strickland, Michael Tinkey, Dr. Jim Turmin, Rob Waldron, Alan Walters, Brian Whitcomb, Donna White, Andrew Wood, Mark Woodward, and Ben Wright.

About 10 other "experts" involved in the business of golf have had a great impact on the thoughts contained herein, but their contributions were about how to operate incorrectly, how to be rude, and how to be completely self-serving.

Though I often have little discretion, in this case I will exercise some and not list their names save for one obtuse reference. How can a firm who claims its unbiased research in creating clear perspectives be considered of value when it comes with a vitriolic condemnation of the industry at large?

And to the many senior citizens, season pass holders, and members of most golf advisory committees—who usually put self-interest ahead of the best financial interests of a golf course—thank you for indelibly contributing to my opinion that change designed to serve the betterment of a group is always met with resistance by individuals serving their own interests.

Professional Appreciation for Assistance with This Endeavor

Sue Cummins, a fabulous editor whose attention to detail is amazing, repeatedly corrected the same mistakes without commenting. I deeply appreciate her work.

Steve Eubanks advised that writing is a discipline in which you talk to the computer while your fingers listen and type. That was sage advice that got me past the mental blocks that I was having in trying to be too precise as I created the first draft. His further assistance in doing the content edit was invaluable.

Brad Klein is one of the industry's foremost authorities on golf course architecture. His command of English is equally impressive for it was his role to eliminate the double-speak and undertake the line edit of this book. His knowledge is truly admired.

Golf Convergence has been very fortunate to have many marvelous clients. This book was made possible by the inclusion of data and insights from the strategic, tactical and operational reviews performed on their behalf: Alamo City Golf Trail, Bakker Crossings, Bemidji Town and Country Club, Brooklyn Park, City of Ann Arbor, City of Atlanta, City of Becker, City of Bloomington, City of Brookings, City of Casper, City of Charlotte, City of Columbus, City of Durango, City of Grand Rapids, City of Greenville, City of Midland, City of Minneapolis, City of Ocala, City of St. Paul, City of Virginia Beach, City of Winnipeg, Cog Hill Golf and Country Club, Colorado Golf Club, Cougar Canyon Golf Links, Fernie Golf and Country Club, Four Mile Ranch, Island Hills Golf Club, Los Amigos, Merrill Hills Country Club, Naperville

Park District, Oak Creek Golf Club, Oitavos Dunes, Pacific Grove Golf Links, Pine Meadows Golf Course, Prairie Club, Reignwood Pine Valley, Seneca Hills, Tartan Park G.C., University of Minnesota-Les Bolstad Golf Course, Western Illinois University-Harry Mussatto Golf Course, and Willow Run Golf Course.

Personal Appreciation for Those Who Have Influenced My Life

When all is said and done, what really matters is family. To my father who passed over ten years ago, his discipline is now appreciated. The daily support from my 95-year-old mother, Kathryn, and my brother Mark goes beyond appreciation. In silence the strong bonds are felt, recognized, and respectfully remain private as that represents who we are.

To Martha and Michaela for the past that was memorable, and for the potential joys, fellowship, and heartaches that may arise; may we experience all there is in unity.

And to Debra, for your encouragement, understanding, and patience with my foibles, I am in deep gratitude.

Concluding Thoughts

A glow of one warm thought is, to me, worth more than money.

Thomas Jefferson

A poor idea well written is more likely to be accepted than a good idea poorly written.

Isaac Asimov

Attributions

How You Will Benefit from Reading This Book

Industry Research Groups

The Business of Golf is an exhaustive work that brings the world of golf course management under one roof. I highly recommend it. **Joe Beditz, President & CEO, National Golf Foundation**

How many times have you heard, "Boy, I'd like to run my own golf course!" Well, before you do, or if you already do, you should work behind the counter in a pro shop, and read everything you can about the business. You can start with this book. It is well researched by someone who knows how to apply it to a wide range of golf course operations. **Tom Stine, Co-Founder Golf Datatech, LLC**

Golf is a game—but building and managing the courses is a serious business—this book is a welcome injection of serious business. **Colin Hegarty, Chairman, Golf Research, Inc.**

Trade Associations

This comprehensive treatise on *The Business of Golf* by an accomplished and respected industry expert provides a definitive formula for a golf course owner to increase their net income. I highly recommend it. **Michael Tinkey, Deputy CEO, National Golf Course Owners Association**

It is widely recognized that superintendents play a key role in the success of any golf facility. They manage the number one asset at the facility and that is the golf course itself. Avid and influential golfers overwhelmingly acknowledge that superintendents are the key to their enjoyment of the game. Owners of golf courses believe very strongly that superintendents are a key to the financial success of their golf courses. All of this point to the fact that the number one reason golfers choose a particular golf course to play is the conditioning of that course. This is clearly the value that superintendents bring to the game and the industry as emphasized in this book. **Mark Woodward, CGCS, former CEO of the Golf Course Superintendents Association of America**

Outstanding Golf Course Operators

Jim Keegan's unique business and life experience has brought a new level of critical thinking to the golf industry. On the golf course he may be a 7 handicap, but his insights into the business side of the game are no less than "scratch." This book is to the business of golf what the *Rules of Golf* are to playing the game. **Nick Mokelke, CCM, General Manager, Cog Hill Golf and Country Club**

The golf economy in recent years has taught us all the value of building appropriate business models and having realistic goals and objectives. Jim Keegan's work with this book brings these lessons to the forefront. A good addition to the library of any golf course or club operator. **Bob Doyle, PGA Master Professional**

Jim Keegan's comprehensive analysis of the golf business is an extremely enlightening manuscript for the golf business person. Whether you are a 35-year operator like myself, or just getting started in the golf business, each chapter is packed full of useful insight that can be used TODAY to make your golf operation better. **Jim Roschek, PGA, President, Alamo City Golf Trail**

In September of 2008, I took over responsibility for two municipal golf courses that had posted a significant loss. Logic dictates that one does not "operate on themselves," so I hired Golf Convergence to come in and diagnose where we were hemorrhaging money. Through, Golf Convergence's WIN™ Formula we have realized a savings in labor alone of over $175,000.00. I highly recommend *The Business of Golf—What Are You Thinking?* as a roadmap to success for the business of golf. As Jim stated, "Where is your focus?" Is it on the business of golf or on the game of golf? **Ray McGury, Executive Director, Naperville Park District**

To everyone's benefit, especially municipally run courses where stewardship is often inherited rather than based on industry acumen, Jim Keegan has written a diagnostic and repair manual for golf courses operating at all success levels. Jim's three-year study of our courses identified critical financial, player, technological and operational insights. With the City of Ocala not having even moderate industry expertise, Jim involved us in the formulation and implementation of the remedial steps that were necessary to keep our golf programs alive and sustainable. With this book, Jim gives generously of his time and talents by putting twenty years of up-to-date experience into a resource we can all learn from and refer to as we strive to improve and fine tune the golf experiences we offer. **John Zobler, Retired-Assistant City Manager, City of Ocala**

Any municipal operation would benefit greatly from using the tools and expertise that Jim Keegan shares in *The Business of Golf.* Keegan's knowledge and insights on the business of golf are exceptional. His passion and enthusiasm as a person are contagious, making him a great person with whom to work. His comprehension and understanding of customer perceptions is invaluable, making him a great person from whom to learn. **Sandy Queen, CGCS, City of Overland Park, Kansas**

A great book for sure! I am planning on using sections in the book for a class I teach at Kansas State University Professional Club Management. Very worth while statistics for students to ponder over. **David W. Gourlay CGCS, CCM, Colbert Hills**

Golf Course Management Companies

Jim Keegan's inherent strength is his ability to recognize and understand the problems and challenges of a golf club operation, and then having the knowledge, discipline and work ethic to dive into the issues and come out on the other end with solutions. This book illustrates both his technique, and his tenacity towards solving these problems. Very useful in these trying times! **Phil Green, President, OB Sports Golf Management**

Jim has consolidated years of experience, and visits to over 3,000 courses around the globe, into a comprehensive review and guide to the business of golf. More importantly, he shares the tools, techniques, and best practices he has developed and repeatedly implemented to decrease operating costs, drive revenues and improve customer service. Anyone interested in accomplishing any, or all, of these three objectives is sure to find this book insightful and a valuable reference. **Stuart Hayden, Managing Principal, SK&C Management Consulting, former Senior Vice-President, American Golf Corporation**

Well documented, well researched—much like a great manual on golf lessons. It is our goal to become a scratch golfer in the business of golf through the lessons contained in this book. **Jeff Levine, Principal/Senior Vice President of Public Courses, Century Golf Partners**

PGA Professionals

In today's business of golf, this book is a must read to insure you're on the right course. Jim Keegan splits the fairway in this approach to strategic planning! **Eddie Ainsworth, PGA, Executive Director, Colorado Section PGA**

I am confident of one thing. For those who diligently read the book and studiously complete this case study, the vast knowledge gained will place you significantly ahead of your peers in being able to manage the profitability of a golf course. I believe students learn best by doing, and the case study has provided exercises and opportunity to grasp the important Golf Convergence™ formula concepts and their positive effects on financial performance." **Rick Lucas, PGA, MBA, Doctoral Student; Director, PGA Golf Management Program, Clemson University**

I have enjoyed reviewing the Business of Golf. I am creating a course for our students and it may be the perfect textbook for the class. **Mollie G. Sutherland, PGA, LPGA, Director, PGA Professional Golf Management Program, University of Colorado Springs**

This is the most comprehensive and insightful book on the golf business in print. Everyone in the business or interested in the economics of our game should read it. **Steve Eubanks, PGA, author of 21 books including *Playing by the Rules*; *All the Rules of the Game, Complete with Memorable Rulings From Golf's Rich History* by Arnold Palmer with Steve Eubanks**

Trade Publications

Like any how-to manual for a multi-billion dollar industry made up of approximately 16,000 individual case studies (i.e., golf properties) in the U.S. alone, most of which are owned and/or run by people with a distinctly individual and entrepreneurial mindset, *The Business of Golf* is not going to be a 100 percent match for each facility's unique set of challenges. On the other hand, if any of those 16,000 can't find at least a few ideas worth trying, they aren't reading very carefully. **Jim Dunlap, Former Senior Editor, *Golf Inc***

Reading this book has changed my view of how golf courses operate—and how they could operate. I've been looking at golf courses for 30+ years, but in the wake of Keegan's analysis I've already walked into clubhouses and onto courses and seen them very differently, with a much sharper eye for those vital moments of customer contact and business management that can make or break an operation. Golf has always been a great game; but as Keegan shows, it doesn't have to be a lousy business. Owners and operators who heed to finer points of this volume will have a heads up on the competition. **Bradley S. Klein, architecture editor of *Golfweek*, author of thousands of essays and five books on golf design and the golf industry**

Consultants

Jim Keegan has launched a great discussion in *The Business of Golf*. His book is informative, insightful and a 'should read' for everyone who wants to learn more about the golf business. For those who are active in the business of golf, there are jewels of knowledge that add great value. **Henry DeLozier, Principal, Global Golf Advisors**

Jim is attempting to turn what is largely a communistic endeavor into a capitalistic enterprise. Bravo! **David V. Smith, Chairman, Golf Projects International**

The component of a golf course that fails the quickest is the "crop." This book provides the guidelines necessary to ensure the golf course owner as the "leader of the band" can focus on the music and turn his back to the audience (largely industry pundits) which largely serves as a distraction. **Tim Moraghan, former USGA Agronomist, President Aspire Consulting**

In "The Business of Golf—What are you Thinking", Jim Keegan brings together the two very complex worlds of investing in and managing real estate and operating a going concern business. Golf courses are unique in this manner because they represent a business with an intensive use of real estate. Few books have gone as deep into both worlds and tied them together as neatly as Jim has. I've often thought of taking on this project and writing such a book myself but Jim not only beat me to it, he did a great job. Nice work! **Larry Hirsh, CRE, MAI, SGA, President—Golf Property Analysts**

Golf Management Software Vendors

Jim has managed to take such a multi-faceted subject as the golf industry and create an understandable benchmark with which any club can measure themselves and create realistic goals to become more successful. **Jim Fedigan, Chief Executive Officer, Jonas Software**

Most people understand why bars and restaurants have a very high failure rate. Someone who likes to drink or is a good cook opens an F&B operation with no clue how to run a business. After 20 some years in the golf business I see time and again people who have a passion for the game but lack the business skills to be successful. Having a passion for the game does not make you a successful golf facility operator. This book is filled with a systematic approach to running a golf facility. Rarely do you find a complete how-to guide on running an entire operation. *The Business of Golf* covers everything. If you can't turn a positive return on investment using the methods in this book, then perhaps you should be looking to sell your property to a real-estate developer (which is also covered in this book!). **Rick Robshaw, Chief Executive Officer, Club Prophet**

The Business of Golf provides a very structured look at the complex metrics involved in running a successful golf course in challenging times. Along with thought-provoking anecdotes and ideas the book provides the reader with a host of real world solutions sure to improve the success of any operation. **Andrew Wood, Author, *The Golf Marketing Bible & CEO Legendary Marketing***

Introduction

A good plan today is better than a perfect plan tomorrow.

General George S. Patton

Warning

This book is not a simple narrative that one reads in a single sitting. Rather, it is designed as a textbook for understanding the "golf business." It is a reference book in which subsequent review is recommended for full absorption and proper application. Why?

The term "golf business" often seems like an oxymoron. Golf is a game—a fun one people play for a myriad of reasons, but some, at least, to escape the stresses and strains of life. Those who work in the industry, managing and marketing golf courses, understand that golf is far more than a quiet, outdoor recreational pursuit. It is a challenging business in a competitive and unique working environment. Thus, grasping the concepts contained herein mandate a disciplined approach.

You now hold a roadmap for turning a recreational facility into a profit center—for maximizing revenue while increasing efficiency and enhancing customer service.

The seven steps outlined in this plan have been developed by crystallizing the facts, observations, and opinions I have gleaned over 25 years, having traveled more than 2.5 million miles visiting golf courses in over 40 countries. There are things I have observed that are meritorious; things that can be learned, and things that any conscientious golf course operator should want to emulate. There also are many pitfalls that can, and should, be avoided.

There are multitudes of detailed policy, procedure, operational, and best-practices manuals published by the leading trade organizations: The Club Managers Association of America, the National Golf Foundation, the National Golf Course Owners Association, and the Professional Golfers' Association of America. Furthermore, many writers skilled in the business of golf have written numerous articles, pamphlets, and books about the details of the business of golf.

Most people are too overwhelmed to discover and work with all the details. This book boils it downs, sums it up, and puts all the disparate data into an easy-to-follow plan.

Strategic Vision, Tactical Planning, Operational Execution

To build a winning formula, you have to know where you've been, where you are, and where you're going. Then you have to develop plans to get there, and, finally, you have to go—pull the trigger and get it done. In other words, you have to execute.

Phrases like "strategic vision, tactical planning, and operational execution" look great on a Buzzword Bingo Card. Most people's eyes glaze over when you even mention that you're having a "strategic vision planning session."

In reality, these words describe the steps you must take to maximize your income and your profits. And by realizing that you need a strategy, some tactics, and a way to execute, you achieve two goals: (1) You define timeframes in which to achieve benchmarks, and (2) you can use them to differentiate the roles of the course's governing authority, functional departments, and operational staff.

The lines between these distinctions can become blurred, but what is important is not defining precise boundaries, but creating a clear foundation on which solid business decisions can be made.

"Strategic vision" is often thought of as mind-numbing meetings with whiteboards and a lot of blank faces. Actually, your "strategic vision" is like the setup for a golf shot—it accounts for where you are, where you want to be, and the swing you need to make in order to get there. Unfortunately, too many people memorialize the "strategic vision" as a business plan. It is not. It is a dynamic document that evolves based on changing conditions. It is neither a fixed nor a static record, for it contains many detailed recommendations, including short-term, interim, and long-term goals.

Tactical planning, sticking with the golf game analogy, is picking the right club and taking the proper practice swings—making sure you have the right equipment, conditions, and mindset, and practicing to execute the shot you need. In business, your tactics deal with the implementation of your plan—turning strategy into reality.

Operational execution is hitting the shot. In your business, it is the day-to-day and week-to-week work routine, when the primary goal of management is to effectively communicate with staff. Weekly meetings and monthly summaries are the norm.

These tools—strategic vision, tactical planning, and operational execution—blend together in relative proportions to create a profitable formula.

The seven-step process in this book is the "critical path" that moves you from strategy to tactics to execution—from setup, to the pre-shot routine, to hitting the ball. The strategic planning methodology is depicted on this page.[1]

It should be noted that the delineation between strategic, tactical, and operational often is subject to debate. There are no right answers. In writing this book, we have blended the concepts of strategic planning by department and by time horizons to analyze a golf course based on the elements shown in the screen shot below.[2]

The approach of this book is very macroeconomic, but the focus narrows as the text progresses. Industry veterans might find the first five chapters elementary, but the information is good for everyone. No matter how much you know, it never hurts to review and be reminded of some of the basic facts of the golf business. From Chapter 6 on, however, everyone, including the self-proclaimed experts, should read in earnest.

Please keep in mind that to implement this seven-step process, it is recommended that the assistance of such fine firms as the National Golf Foundation,

1 Edward A. Merritt, Premier Club Series, "Leading the Strategic Planning Process," p. 4.

2 Club Managers Association of America (CMAA), "Adapted from the Management to Leadership Model," 2008, http:www.cmaa.org/template.aspx?id=68.

Golf Convergence, or perhaps some of the consulting divisions of the leading golf course management companies be utilized if for no other reason than to acquire independent empirical data, something many golf course owners seem loathe to do, which is required to implement the process precisely.

Also be mindful that this book will provide the greatest benefit to the management of municipal, daily-fee, and semi-private clubs. The lessons in this book, while of value to all golf courses, have a slightly diminished value to resorts, because of their transient customer base, and private clubs, because of their fixed customer base.

The Formula for Success

As Thomas Edison said, "Opportunity is missed by most people because it is dressed in overalls and looks like work."

The creation of a strategic plan requires work. The Golf Convergence WIN™ (what's important now) seven-step process can be viewed as the "critical path" on which the planning and execution occurs.

At a minimum, golf course owners need to undertake the following:

Strategic

1. **Geographic Local Market Analysis.** Age, income, ethnicity, and population within 10 miles of the golf course are predictors for 90% of all golf courses. Only resorts escape precise classification based on these factors. (Chapter 5)
2. **Weather Impact Study.** The axiom that "if rounds are up, it's because of good management, and if rounds are down it's because of bad weather" is a standard joke, but golf is an outdoor sport. Experts estimate that over 90% of rounds are played when the temperature is between 55 and

90 degrees. Monitoring the number of playable golf days in a year compared to a 10-year trend allows an analyst the opportunity to filter the financial information to clearly differentiate between the impact of weather and the impact of management on a course's performance. (Chapter 5)

Tactical

3. **Technology—The Foundation.** The aggregation of data on which a business can be analyzed is dependent upon having an integrated technology solution, properly installed and fully utilized, by the staff. Unfortunately, there may never in the history of man have been more money invested with such a small return as there has been in the acquisition of golf management systems. (Chapter 7)
4. **Yield Management, Key Metrics, Financial Modeling and Course Valuation.** The valuable research data of the National Golf Foundation, Golf Datatech, and PGA PerformanceTrak is contrasted to a facility's performance to determine opportunities for improvement. Statistics like course utilization, revPAT, revPAR, EBIT, technology ROI, cost per round, staffing levels, capital budgets, and deferred expenditures are compared to those of local and regional courses. (Chapters 8, 9, 10, 11)

Operational

5. **Facilities and Maintenance Review.** Ronald Fream, the acclaimed golf course architect, commented to me while we were touring Nine Bridges Golf Course in Jeju, Korea, "A course is only designed by the architect on the day it opens." What he meant is that a golf course is a living organism—not just living in the sense that grass grows, but living in that it is constantly changing. Their two primary constants are the equipment required to maintain a course and the replacement life cycle. Comparing the available equipment to industry standards and identifying deferred capital benchmarks provides valuable information. (Chapter 12)
6. **Management, Marketing, and Operational Review.** The entrance to the clubhouse, staffing, organizational structure, merchandising, food and beverage, accounting and budgeting procedures, information systems, advertising, marketing, and public relations are evaluated and compared to the industry's best management practices. (Chapters 13 and 14)

7. **Customers: Learning Their Preferences and Loyalty.** By utilizing a golf course's database, purchasing an e-mail of local golfers, and employing electronic survey tools, enlightening insights can be obtained. Why aren't the golfers in your area playing more? What are the motivating price points in your region? What is your course's brand image? You'll never know the answers if you don't ask the questions. (Chapter 15) Fifteen percent of the customers generate 60% of the revenues; 25% generate 85% of the revenues; and many daily fee golf courses have at least 50 customers who spend in excess of $4,000 annually. While only half the golfers who played a course one year will return the next, identifying your core customers provides the foundation for your marketing program. (Chapter 16)

This seven-step formula creates a tapestry of sound principles and common-sense solutions for the golf course operator.

The Audience

In writing a book, the first question is: Who is the audience?

That was easy. Just check out the following chart:

Category	Target Audience
Golfers	26 million
Industry Personnel	2 million
PGA Professionals	28,000
Golf Course Owners	14,000
PGM Students	1,000
Multi-Course Operators	200
Golf Course Associations	91

Not everything in these pages fits the needs of each potential reader, but hopefully everyone will find it interesting, and there will always be some nugget that makes you say, "Wow, I didn't know that."

The greatest benefit from this book will be derived by those not satisfied with the status quo, but for those committed to positive change—those who seek to improve their current operating methods, for the benefit of the game. It is not for the average manager. As Yogi Berra says, "The average person is average." Golf courses, to survive, must be raised to something higher.

My Goal

As author Anna Quindlen stated, at a speech given at the University of Denver's "Pen and Podium Series," "I hate writing. I love having written."

I feel the same way. This has been an arduous process, but one that has been, for me, very worthwhile. As I wrote, I was often reminded of the folly of Hlade's Law, "If you have a difficult task, give it to a lazy man—he will find an easier way to do it." I have truly found that the old cliché, "If you desire to master a subject, teach it" is true. Having invested a good portion of my life assimilating this knowledge and undertaking the necessary research, committing the resulting thoughts to paper is clearly the hardest thing I have ever done; not getting a BBA, not earning an MBA, not passing the CPA exam, but writing this book.

As human beings, we process information in three primary ways: through verbal skills, through images, and through intuition. Of these processes, the most powerful is the image. Words have opposites; images do not. Therefore, my goal was to present as many images—tables, charts, graphs, and photos—as possible.

Golf represents what is best about our society. Nearly all of the 26 million who play the game represent ideal role models. In my 50 years of playing the game, I can think of very few people whose company I did not enjoy during a round of golf.

Part of the game's allure is that golf is an elitist sport and therefore unlikely to be adopted by the masses. In 1899, Thorsten Veblen wrote, "Golf is a game of the leisure class."[3] Golf will remain an elitist sport, for it is far too expensive to be adopted by the world at large. However, golf is a great game, and the business of golf can generate a sizeable investment return for those who can compete successfully. It is a sport that is simply marvelous, and it should be enhanced and nurtured.

3 Thorstein Veblen, *Theory of the Leisure Class* (Oxford, Oxford University Press), 1899. http://en.wikipedia.org/wiki/The_Theory_of_the_Leisure_Class. Veblen argued that, while sports could be advantageous to the community, the true reason for the popularity of sports were their usefulness as means of displaying conspicuous leisure.

Ensuring that each golf course uses best practices to adroitly balance the business of golf with the game of golf is the goal of this book.

Concluding Thought

Tell me and I'll forget. Show me and I'll remember.
Involve me and I'll understand.

Confucius

SECTION 1

Strategic Vision
Chapters 1 through 6

To create a strategic plan, a broad vision must first be defined. In Chapters 1 through 6, we progressively narrow the focus on the uncontrollable factors that influence the financial success of a golf course.

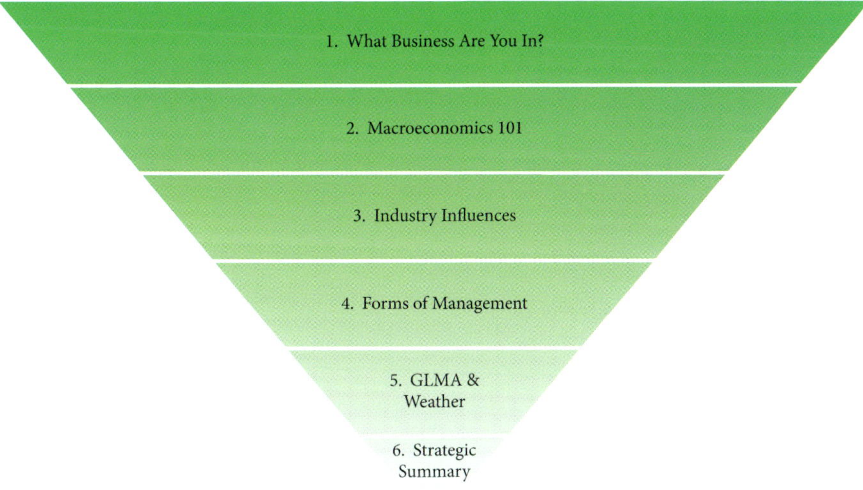

An understanding of what a golf course can't directly control frames one's ability to create a plan that can be successfully executed.

If you don't know where you are going,
you might wind up someplace else.

Yogi Berra

The chains of habit are too late to be felt
until they're too heavy to be broken.

Blaise Pascal

Chapter 1

What Business Are You In?

Our task is not to fix the blame for the past, but to fix the course for the future.

John Kennedy

Chapter Highlights

This chapter will introduce the first strategic elements that help you decide what role your business provides the golfer.

Is your facility meant to be the entry door to the game for the masses, a park to entertain the taxpaying citizens, a forum for businesspeople to meet and greet, a private enclave, or a resort that attracts a certain clientele?

What is the economic, societal, and business impact of golf in your area? What is the current environment? What are the opportunities to grow the game? What are the barriers to increasing play?

The mantra that golf is a business in which an investment return is required is a fundamental precept on which the entire strategic planning process is based.

This chapter is the first of four that discuss the environmental factors, often beyond the control of the golf course owner.

An Industry Under Siege

From an historical participation perspective, the game peaked in 1999. Since then, supply has exceeded demand. Leading research firms forecast that it will take at least 15 years before these market forces are again balanced. It takes too long to play. The game is too difficult and too expensive for the majority to enjoy. Individuals have more demands on their time. Lifestyles have changed. All of these factors have a direct impact on golf. Whatever worked in the past no longer sustains the operation.

Reduced to its essentials, the business of golf is about creating entertainment for customers in a venue that generates profit. With that as the goal, the industry faces many challenges:

- The heart of the golf industry's woes lies within the ***average*** golf course owner's inability **to consistently execute,** providing a customer experience that equals or exceeds the price, ensuring value.
- Few in the golf business realize that they are principally in the entertainment and leisure industry.
- Supply will continue to exceed demand for the foreseeable future.
- Operating a golf course is a small business endeavor.
- Revenue generation programs targeting age, gender, or ethnic segments have little short-term impact.
- The attitude and the aptitude of most staff can be enhanced.
- Many golf courses that are losing money make tactical changes that lead to strategic failure.
- Technology (Web sites, tee-time reservation systems, Point of Sale, e-mail tools, social media, accounting) is an investment that often produces a low return due to insufficient training and improper use.
- Golf course owners' marketing efforts are more reactionary than proactive.
- Many courses believe marketing solely comprises offering tee times at a discount, participating in coupon books, and utilizing last-minute, online, third-party vendors to liquidate inventory.
- Few courses identify or retain successful core customers.

- Few courses identify defectors and attempt to re-solicit their business.
- Many golf courses are in need of renovation but lack the required capital and/or are unable to secure debt financing.

If you focus on just the private club market, the challenges expand:

- Declining guest and member spending have driven revenue declines.
- Waiting lists have turned to resignation lists, impacting transfer-fee income.
- Dues are at the top of the market, with increases not keeping pace with rising costs.
- Assessments, as they rise to cover operating expenses, accelerate attrition.
- Deferred maintenance is mounting.
- The club's nonprofit tax status limits outside play to 15% of gross revenue.
- Large, inefficient clubhouses are becoming out-of-date.
- Competition from championship premium public courses is providing viable alternatives.

The list of challenges is endless. It can become overwhelming. No golf course plans to fail, but many simply fail to plan. To succeed, understanding the economic impact of golf is vital.

The Economic Impact of Golf

Capitalism creates. Capitalism destroys. The average company lasts less than 20 years before it fails or is purchased. Of the Top 100 companies in 1970, only 30 remain.

So, what image does the word "Golf" conjure for you—the PGA Tour and its celebrity players, the latest in equipment, your home course, a course you grew up on, or merely a pastoral setting?

Golf is a major industry that generates employment, economic development, commerce, and tax revenues, but few people think of the game in those terms. Understanding the vast scope of the industry's core, including its supporting and interrelated industries, helps define the boundaries of the business of golf.

In a study conducted by SRI International for Golf 20/20, the economic impact of golf as measured on the U.S. economy was valued at $68 billion, as reflected in the following table.[1]

Golf's Economic Impact

Size of the U.S. Golf Economy by Industry Segment in 2000, 2005 and 2011 ($ millions)

Core Industries	2000	2005	2011
Golf Facility Operations	$20,496	$28,052	$29,852
Golf Course Capital Investment	$7,812	$3,578	$2,073
Golfer Supplies	$5,982	$6,151	$5,639
Endorsements, Tournaments & Associations	$1,293	$1,682	$2,045
Charities	$3,200	$3,501	$3,900
Total Core Industries	**$38,783**	**$42,964**	**$43,509**
Enabled Industries			
Real Estate	$9,904	$14,973	$4,745
Hospitality/Tourism	$13,480	$18,001	$20,555
Total Enabled Industries	**$23,384**	**$32,974**	**$25,300**
TOTAL GOLF ECONOMY	**$62,167**	**$75,939**	**$68,809**

Note: Columns sum based on rounding of individual estimates. Numbers also have not been adjusted for inflation but are expressed as nominal dollars.

Source: Golf Course Industry, February, 2013 ©2014, Golf Convergence Inc.

Golf is a meaningful contributor to the nation's economic engine, supplying approximately 2 million jobs.

However, from 2006 through 2012, 499.5 golf course have closed. It is predicated that an over 1,000 more golf courses will need to close before supply and demand are in balance, presuming no further increase in the golfers.

Rounds have fallen from 518.4 million in 2000 to just under 470 million in 2012.[2] Since 1994, the supply of golf holes has increased 25% as measured by the increase in the number of U.S. golf facilities, rising from slightly over 12,000 to 15,619 in 2012. During that time the demand for golf has increased only 8%, as measured by the increase from 24 million golfers in 1994 to nearly 26 million golfers in 2012. This trend has created a supply/demand imbalance of 10%; hence the current dilemma faced by the golf industry.

Interesting Times

While golf does not escape the basic forces of capitalism and the laws of supply and demand, it is unclear if golf course owners are unwitting accomplices to the industry's woes. We live in a world bombarded by pessimism and bad news. It is easy to be consumed by the disaster du jour.

The following examples illustrate our information environment and the impact media has on our thinking:

---

1 http://golf2020.com/media/31526/2011_golf_econ_exec_sum_sri_final_12.17.12.pdf, pg. 5.

2 National Golf Foundation, "State of the Industry," April, 2011, slides 4, 8.

- "Most Stocks Down, Energy Up: Last Monday, the stock market retreated under the pressure of record oil prices, a slumping dollar and worries about rising prices for imported oil."
- "White House Urges Fed to Lower Rates in Light of Data on Inflation, Housing"
- "Home Builders Hurt by Credit Crunch"

These headlines were extracted from the Chairman's Commentary from the December 2007 Fennimore Assets Mutual Trust Fund Annual report.[3]

Here is the punch line. The Chairman's letter continued, "These headlines are typical of today's news items, yet they are taken from newspaper archives. The first is from *The New York Times* in 1979 during the post-oil embargo years. The second and third headlines are from newspaper articles written in 1990 during the Savings and Loan crisis and subsequent housing recessions."

Do we use these negative themes as excuses for our lack of accomplishment in our business and personal lives? A multitude of convenient excuses is available.

Despite the turmoil of business in general, being a part of the golf industry does have a security blanket attached. The underlying value of golf course real estate more than likely exceeds the present value of discounted future cash flow stream at 10%.

As Lao Tzu stated, "The journey of a thousand miles begins with a single step." Let us begin.

Welcome to the Entertainment Business

Golf is a game that is expensive to start, difficult to learn, and frankly, may not be a lot of fun, unless you are competent or are playing with friends in a social setting.

Many within our industry have lost sight of this fact, having become seduced by the "game" of golf at the expense of their success in the "business" of golf. Many individuals in the golf business presume that everyone who

3 Fennimore Assets Mutual Fund Annual Report, December, 2007, p. 1.

plays golf is like them, watching golf on TV, and enjoying learning, practicing, and playing. These individuals have become seduced by the game and believe that financial success will be assured by teaching golfers to play better on more challenging courses and by selling game improvement equipment.

However, the new driver that promises greater distance, the new course heralding the ultimate test, the eye-grabbing video technology that offers to change your swing forever—these appeal to only 15% of those who play.

While everyone would like to play better, few do. Golf is a difficult game that requires tremendous perseverance, skill, and some athletic ability if one desires to become even marginally successful. The game is too difficult.

That begs the question: Are the expectations of those entrenched in the business of golf realistic?

Eighty-five percent of individuals who play golf don't have a handicap—the benchmark that measures ability. Seventy percent drink alcohol, principally beer, while playing. Thirty-three percent of a course's revenue is from tournaments and outings, which largely represent golfers who are playing in corporate or charity events. This may well be their single annual visit on a course.

Who is the "real" golf consumer? The "real" golf consumer is the recreational player—an average everyday Joe or Jo who wants to challenge the course, drink a beer, have some conversation, and forget the client complaints of that morning or the hectic week at work.

Golf is not principally about competition, athletic challenge, or individual accomplishment. Golf is simply entertainment, and golf courses are like theme parks—no two courses are identical, and each one offers a different thrill ride every time you play.

Therefore, the success of a course is measured by how much fun the customer has, and how his or her perception of personal service was met or exceeded. By understanding and exceeding each customer's unique needs and desires, we can create customer loyalty and lead to the thrill ride of operating a business: financial success.

The Assembly Line of Golf

The golf course is a meeting place for businesspeople who work hard and want to be catered to and made to feel special in a beautiful setting. Golf provides families with a place to bond, friends with an opportunity to extend and deepen their camaraderie, juniors a venue to learn the values of discipline and ethics, seniors a well-earned hobby, and men's and ladies' groups the opportunity to meet and compete. Today's savvy businessperson knows the golf course is an office, a lunch meeting, a conference room—it is common ground.

Retention is critical to enhancing revenue. Opportunities to impress (or entertain) your customers are limited, and you must create interest (preferably something that differentiates your course from others) that causes them to return.

Retention starts by realizing what golf is not. It is not a game that starts at 1 and leads through 18 holes in which there are typically 4 par 5's, 10 par 4's, and 4 par 3's. Depending on the type of golf course, the number of opportunities to favorably impress a golfer can vary from 6 to 15. As expected, the higher the price per round of golf, the greater the number of anticipated touch points a golfer will experience. Thus, the exclusive private club, the high-end daily fee course, or exclusive resorts are likely to take advantage of many opportunities and continued efforts to enhance the overall impression.

The table on the next page illustrates the "Assembly Line of Golf."

Each golf course operation is a series of interconnected processes, the end product of which is a challenged, entertained, and satisfied customer. Every game is a "story," and you can create a place for your customer to tell it. Course personnel, just like those who work at Disneyland, should be viewed as "cast members," with roles to play in order to meet and exceed customers' expectations.

Excellence is shown in many ways, but consistent attention to detail is one of the discriminating marks of a golf course, that is, steel, bronze, silver, gold, and platinum. By understanding and exceeding your customers' unique needs and desires, customer loyalty can be created and financial success achieved.

Touch Point	Municipal	Daily Fee	Resort	Private Club	Military
Reservations	X	X	X	X	X
Club Entrance	X	X	X	X	X
Bag Drop		X	X	X	
Cart: GPS		X	X		
Locker Room Before Round			X	X	
Pro Shop	X	X	X	X	X
Range	X	X	X	X	X
Starter & Marshalls	X	X	X	X	X
Beverage Cart Attendant		X	X	X	
Halfway House			X	X	
Cart Return—Club Cleaning			X	X	
Locker Room After Round			X	X	
Bar/Restaurant	X	X	X	X	X
Likely # of Contact Points	6	9	13	12	6
Note: Each golf course is unique. While the number of contact points may vary slightly from facility to facility, the concept that each course has only a certain number of opportunities to make a favorable impression is consistent between facility types.					

Why Do Golfers Choose One Course Over Another?

In surveys conducted by NGF and Golf Convergence asking, "What is the primary reason you choose one course over another?", the results are very consistent, as shown below:

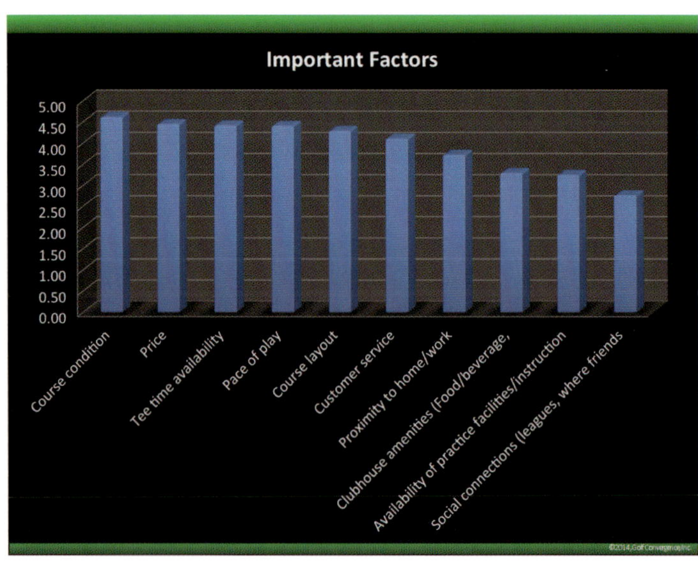

Those criteria remain important today. In multiple golfer surveys conducted by Golf Convergence over the past decade, conditioning and price are among the highest rated categories.

What Are the Barriers to Playing?

Historically, time has been the largest constraint to increased play in the United States.

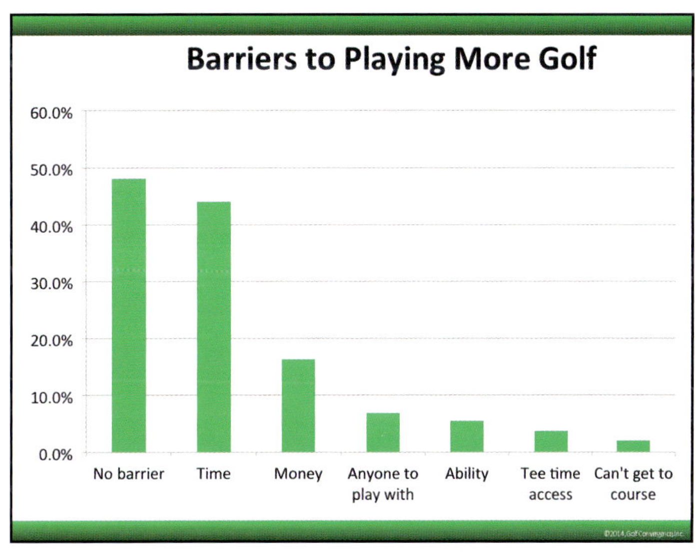

Beginning in 2011, when conducting a survey, Golf Convergence added an additional option "no barriers" when asking golfers the question, "What are the primary barriers that prevent you from playing golf more often?"

In responses from California to Florida the results are nearly identical. Overwhelming majorities cite either no barriers or time as the primary constraint to playing more golf as illustrated in the chart. No barriers is a troubling answer as it implies demand for golf is satiated. Let's examine in greater detail, time as a factor in adversely impacting golf.

Time Culture Crunch

Time, not money, has become our scarcest commodity.

At the Annual Golf 20/20 meeting, Madeline Hochstein of the DYG Group gave a compelling presentation regarding the DYG Scan, which provides insight into the culture of the United States by identifying critical social, lifestyle, and consumer trends. The goal of DYG is to analyze the impact of these changes on business, marketing, communications, HR management, strategic planning, and public policy.

Hochstein said that "most powerful social change occurs when different types of trends converge."[4] She cited that in 1960, the United States experienced the medical breakthrough of birth control, the demographic change of the largest number of singles leaving their parents' homes in history, and the lifestyle change to a more independent society. The mixing of those factors led to the sexual revolution of the 1960s.

She cited a major American culture change that occurred in 2003, one that she labeled as "The Time Crunch Convergence," which was manifested by the following emerging trends:[5]

1. The technology trap of endless improvements; the more empowered technology makes you, the more you are expected to do.
2. The update mandate compels us to constantly update our information; our devices (phones, e-mail), our knowledge (events, education), our values (tolerance to risk, work, etc.). We have dramatically increased our "work cycles." Employee productivity is up 24.2 percent in the past 10 years.
3. The marketplace gives us endless choices (47 car manufacturers, hundreds of models, thousands of choices). Shopping takes a lot more energy, thought and time.
4. We have become an experience economy; Starbucks to see it made, Krispy Kreme to watch it bake, Harley to gather on weekends to participate.
5. Lifestyle integration; we insist that everything be efficient, and we can do many things at the same time. This has caused the erosion of the barriers between home, work, and commuting.
6. Child centeredness; our focus on wants, needs, and desires have transferred from ourselves to our children. There is now a social status attached to the "child first" attitude. Our parents put themselves first. We put our children first.
7. Conspicuous activation. Status is now achieved by being involved in the most activities.

Since the Golf 20/20 presentation, these trends have accelerated. It makes one ponder if our entire society isn't suffering from attention deficit. The results of

4 Golf 20/20 annual meeting, October 2003, DYG, Power Point Presentation, Slide 7.

5 Golf 20/20 annual meeting, October 2003, DYG, Power Point Presentation, Slides 10, 13, 18, 21, 24, 28, and 32.

these changes are that each individual's day has taken on 24 hours, where the lines between home and work are now permanently blurred.

The Hand Dealt

Today's operators of facilities find themselves in a difficult environment. What are the options?

The formula for success is actually quite simple. The value created is measured by the customer's experience less the price paid. To the extent that the experience exceeds the price paid, customer loyalty is created. The reverse is also true. To the extent that the price paid exceeds the customer's experience as measured by their expectations, customer attrition occurs.

Why does this occur? The common thread in virtually every troubled company is the lack of disciplined management. As Napoleon Hill stated, "85% of all failures result from not having a clear purpose." Failure comes from management creating expectations that exceed the asset base, as measured by the capital assets and the investment made in human resources.

To correct this, the creation of a definitive strategic vision with precise detail provides an economic roadmap for a golf course to (1) maximize its revenue, (2) increase its operational efficiency, and (3) enhance its customer service. The successful implementation of that triad results in increasing a golf course's investment return.

Strategic Vision—The Aim of Your Golf Operation

A golf course owner should have a clear vision of a course's strategic plan. Is the strategic vision for Seminole, Sand Hills, Pebble Beach, Reynolds Plantation, Cog Hill, Bethpage, and Crandon Park the same? Not even close. While each of these facilities has a superior golf course, their revenues, the depth and breadth of their customers, their management, their customer experience, and their projected investment return vary widely.

What remains common among these facilities is that before the first shovel of dirt was turned, each had a vision, perhaps only in the mind of the owner, as to how the facility would evolve, the niche it would serve, and the experience that it would create.

"Unique" is the most useless word in business. Everything is unique. Your garbage is nothing like your neighbor's. In golf, every course is unique. No two provide the same experience. But rather than be satisfied with your "uniqueness," it is important that you understand how your facility is different, and how you can capitalize on those differences.

The first key to increasing the net income at a golf course is to understand the big picture. Is your facility meant to be a platinum, gold, silver, bronze or steel golf course? Clearly understanding your target market ensures consistency in tactical planning and execution, for what is being compared is the experience sought by the customer versus the fees assessed.

Definition of Market Segments

	Platinum	Gold	Silver	Bronze	Steel
Vision	Rolls Royce	BMW	Volvo	Chevrolet	Hyundai
Examples	Pine Valley, NJ Cypress Point, CA	Cherry Hills, CO Pebble Beach, CA	TPC Clubs Bay Harbor, MI	Lakewood, CO Bethpage, NY	Brookhaven, TX City Park, Anywhere
Cost	Over $250 per round	$175 to $500 per round	$75 to $200 per round	$50 to $100 per round	$50 or less
Carts	Caddies Mostly	Caddies + Electric Carts	Caddies Rare: Electric Carts plus Pull Carts	Electric or Gas Carts plus Pull Carts	Gas Carts plus Pull Carts
Access	By Invitation	Waiting List	Available	Seeking	Open Access
Style	Formal	Professional	Relaxed	Very Casual	Loose
Social Status	Generational Wealth	Upper Class	Upper Middle Class	Middle Class	Anyone

This chart highlights some of the important distinctions between the classifications.

Other criteria to differentiate the experience might include whether the course is ranked in national magazines, the architect, championships hosted, slope, conditioning, cart policies, amenities provided, customer touch points, cell phone usage, dress code, smoking, other activities, use of computers, tipping policies, gift policies, whether reciprocity is granted, gender/ethnicity barrier whether express or implied, whether members hold multiple memberships at other clubs, and whether the facility attracts individuals who are first-time members or golfers.

Delineations, while arbitrary, serve as points of conversation in which a strategic vision can be determined, because a golf course should be looking to differentiate itself by establishing a clear brand image in the mind of the customer and ensuring that the investment in capital assets and personnel are sufficient to achieve the strategic vision.

Differentiation is important. Can you think of a time at a golf course where the check-in experience was not just perfunctory but added value? I can't. Think

Apple stores, where store representatives walk around with wireless devices and check you out anywhere within the store and then e-mail you a receipt. Quick, fast, and very friendly. Empower the starter with this capability. You just saved your customer 5 to 10 minutes. Cash customer? No problem, swipe the driver's license and bill the customer. You might get stiffed, but consider this relevant example from Stephen Covey's book, *The Speed of Trust*:

> "Jim, a vendor in New York City, set up shop and sold doughnuts and coffee to passersby as they went in and out of their office buildings. During the breakfast and lunch hours, Jim always had long lines of customers waiting.
>
> Finally, Jim simply put a small basket on the side of his stand filled with dollar bills and coins, trusting his customers to make their own change. Now you would think that customers would accidentally count wrong or intentionally take extra quarters from the basket, but what Jim found was the opposite. Most customers responded by being completely honest, often leaving him larger-than-normal tips. Also, he was able to move customers through at twice the pace because he didn't have to make change."[6]

Covey's formula is simple: "The less the trust, the slower the speed of the transaction and the higher the cost."[7] All bad.

Successful storied golf clubs all have one thing in common: a rigid discipline to adhere to the strategic vision for the club. Thus, in crafting this strategic plan, a broad vision of the bold initiatives must be established first. Meticulous (and often overwhelming) details come later.

The centerpieces of a strategic plan are the Vision and Mission Statements that guide all decisions regarding the operation of the facility. These statements serve as a lighthouse, providing a frame of reference for the owner, membership, management, and staff.

The Vision Statement is perhaps the most fundamental of all of elements in strategic planning. It must be future-oriented and should tell the world what your golf course is about. It infuses the club with a sense of purpose, direction, and destination.

---

6 Stephen M. R. Covey, *The Speed of Trust* (New York, Free Press, 2006), 16.

7 Ibid, 13.

Thus, the strength of the Vision Statement, which is about ideals and not the current environment, is that the golf course knows what it represents and, as importantly, what it does not. By defining its vision, the golf course has the ability to align its infrastructure, facilities, and labor resources to match the service ideals envisioned through innovative thinking.

End Notes

The lessons of this chapter are:

1) A golf course is a venue that creates entertainment for the purpose of generating a profit.
2) Who the targeted customer is and what experience will be provided at which price point are three factors that need to be ascertained.
3) The industry is undergoing many challenges.
4) The customer's leisure time is being constricted.
5) A course owner needs to carefully reflect on who is their target market.
6) The creation of a strategic plan will provide a definitive roadmap and benchmarks to achieve financial success in the operation of the golf course.

Concluding Thought

A path without obstacles usually leads nowhere.

Defalque's Observations

Chapter 2

The Macroeconomics of the Golf Business

What is actual is actual only for one time.
And only for one place.

T. S. Eliot

Chapter Highlights

Before a vision statement can be created, it is necessary to understand the environment in which the golf course operates.

Macroeconomics is a big-picture look at the game: worldwide supply of golf courses vs. demand; the convergence of rounds, courses, and players; and factors influencing the current client, along with profiles of golfers and retention rates.

The Current Outlook

Golf is a recreational sport that consumes the disposable income of its patrons. Golf competes for the entertainment dollars of its consumers. The financial prosperity of golf is indirectly correlated to the world economy.

The National Golf Foundation conducts ongoing industry research. At the 2011 National Park and Recreation Congress, they reported on the dilution of rounds over the last 25 years which is shown in the chart below:[1]

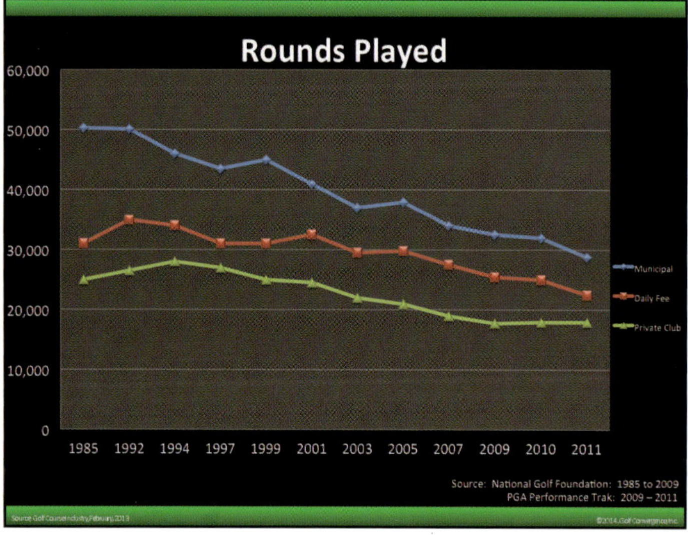

Golf courses can be segmented into varying categories: price (under $40 green fee), value (green fees between $40 and $70), and premium (green fees over $70). With the median private and public green fee at $47, a decline of 6,000 rounds equates to a loss of $282,000.

With the average earnings per golf course (before interest, taxes, and depreciation) historically benchmarked at $200,000, it is no wonder that many golf course operators are financially squeezed as they see their course utilization plummet.

The extent and seriousness of the problem was studied by the National Golf Foundation in an extensive survey on "The Future of Public Golf in America."[2]

1 National Golf Foundation, "Maximizing the Potential of Municipal Golf Course," November 3, 2011, Slide 25.

2 National Golf Foundation, "The Future of Public Golf in America," April 22, 2009, Slide 18.

In that survey of 1,100 golf courses, 15% of the golf courses rated their financial health extremely poor. Of those golf courses sampled, 56% of daily fee golf courses were considering closing and selling, and 26% of municipal golf courses were evaluating the same alternatives. Uniformly, with rounds and revenue off, losses increased, maintenance standards deteriorated, capital investments were deferred, and discounting practices were employed to boost rounds. The NGF projected that from 500 to 1,000 golf courses will close or be sold during the next five years.

The depth of the financial challenges faced by these golf courses is such that on a rating scale of 1 (extremely poor) to 10 (excellent), only 9% rated their financial health as excellent.[3]

The NGF identified that those golf courses at risk were:

- 9-hole facilities
- Lower price points
- Alternative facilities
- Those in less populated areas[4]

The National Golf Foundation's formula for success is clear, and it is evidenced in the following information that indicates what successful golf courses were doing.[5]

The Right Things

	Success (7-10)	At-Risk (0-3)
Customer service emphasis	73%	52%
Have strategic plan	69%	48%
Structured player development	59%	41%
Customer surveys	49%	36%
Promote other revenue centers	43%	26%
Pace of play	43%	24%

Maintaining customer databases, engaging in e-mail marketing, and the publication of newsletters are the additional traits of successful facilities that have been widely recognized over the years. The wrong things,

3 National Golf Foundation, "The Future of Public Golf in America," April 22, 2009, Slide 20.

4 National Golf Foundation, "The Future of Public Golf in America," April 22, 2009, Slide 21.

5 National Golf Foundation, "The Future of Public Golf in America," April 22, 2009, Slide 26.

according to the NGF, consist of discounting, lowering maintenance standards, and delaying capital expenditures.

Because golf is largely a leisure activity of the wealthy, the impact of the national economy is not as likely to be as severe as experienced in other industries. The NGF concludes that while every golf facility will feel the impact, existing demand is stable, latent demand exists, and the current climate is good for golfers and bad for facility operators. However, well-managed courses in populated areas are most likely to thrive.[6]

In April 2008, the National Golf Foundation completed a similar study for private clubs and concluded:

- For every private club that has closed its doors during the past decade, another 10 have converted to public courses.
- The number of private golf clubs in the United States today (4,400) is equal to the number that existed on the eve of the Great Depression.
- After home relocation, financial reasons top the list of why members are leaving clubs.[7]

The Business of Golf

In theory, business is actually very simple. It is balancing supply against demand. By establishing the price that correctly balances the brand promise offered and the value delivered commensurate with the market demand, net income is maximized.

Business can be made very complicated. The permutations of operating a successful golf course increase quickly when one considers the factors that shape supply (the number of golf courses) or those factors that influence demand (course conditioning, price, weather, service, and customer demographics and preferences).

In a perfect market, customers purchase products that satisfy their needs or desires at prices they determine to be the best value. Golfers purchase a round of golf for the price that creates the social status they seek, for the networking

6 National Golf Foundation, "The Future of Public Golf in America," April 22, 2009, Slide 38.

7 National Golf Foundation, "Inside the Ropes," April 2008, p. 1.

they want to achieve, for convenience to home or business, and for the recreational and leisure experience.

Unfortunately, capitalism is not about perfect markets. Inadequate information, undisciplined decision making, misleading marketing, and government intervention can create aggregate failure. The essence of capitalism is for the successful entrepreneur to gain a strategic advantage over competitors within an imperfect market.

In bridging the business of golf and the game of golf, the goal of the course owner should be to blend superlative information, disciplined decision, and crisp execution, as illustrated in the chart.

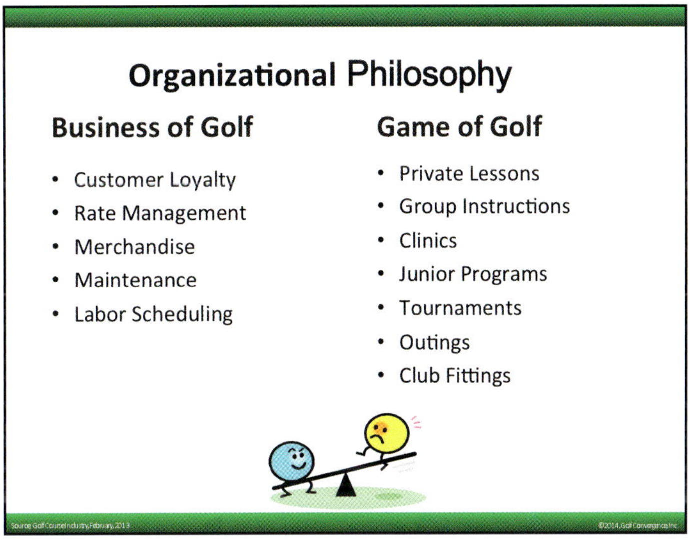
Organizational Philosophy
Business of Golf
Customer Loyalty
Rate Management
Merchandise
Maintenance
Labor Scheduling
Game of Golf
Private Lessons
Group Instructions
Clinics
Junior Programs
Tournaments
Outings
Club Fittings
Source Golf Course Industry, February, 2013
©2014, Golf Convergence Inc

Worldwide Supply

How pervasive is golf around the world? For those reading this book, the game probably holds an amazing allure. As you read *Golf Magazine*, *Golf Digest*, or *Links Magazine*, you see photographs of some incredible golf courses throughout the world. The list of "must play" courses in just Scotland, South Africa, South America, South Vietnam, Spain, Sweden, or the United States seems never ending. Great golf courses are abundant.

While golf started in 1454, the popularity of the game has more than doubled in the last 40 years. The following chart shows the supply in golf courses.[8]

8 National Golf Foundation, "Golf Around the World—International Database Project," April, 2013, Slide 9.

Since 1999, 63% of all new courses opened and 55% of courses under construction or in the planning phases are outside of the United States.

With respect to the United States, nearly 60% of golf courses during the past decade have been built contiguous to a real estate development project. Why the tie of real estate to golf construction? While roughly only 9% of all individuals play golf, nearly everyone identifies with the lifestyle. The ability to live next to a golf course with its open vistas, manicured fairways, and upscale culture imbues in these homeowners a feeling of success by association.

As the slide above indicates,[9] we can deduce that the sport of golf is correlated to income if we look at the number of courses in various parts of the world.

Continent	Number of Courses
North America	18,410
Europe	7,014
Asia	4,425
Oceania	2,014
Africa	865
South America	603
	33,331

Those continents and countries where golf courses prevail have all thrived from capitalism. Golf is one of the by-products of economic success; 59 percent of the courses are in North America, and 19 percent are in Europe.

9 National Golf Foundation, "Golf Around the World—International Database Project," April, 2013, Slide 9.

US Golf Courses by Type of Facility: 2012		TYPE			Total
		Daily Fee	Municipal	Private	(by size & length)
SIZE	9 holes	2,879	717	670	4,266
	18 holes	5,573	1,481	2,846	9,900
	27 holes	453	152	204	809
	36 holes	261	88	176	525
	45 or more holes	66	13	40	119
	Total	9,232	2,451	3,936	15,619
LENGTH	Regulation Only	7,997	2,066	3,681	13,744
	Executive Only	624	177	117	918
	Par 3 Only	403	110	78	591
	Regulation & Executive	83	41	23	147
	Regulation & Par 3	112	52	36	200
	Executive & Par 3	12	3	0	15
	Regulation, Executive & Par 3	1	2	1	4
	Total	9,232	2,451	3,936	15,619

What is confusing is differentiating between 18-hole equivalents, facilities, and number of golf courses. Roughly, 18-hole equivalents represent 90% of the facilities that exist, including 9-hole, 27-hole, 36-hole, and 45- or more hole complexes.[10] The chart reflects the number of U.S. golf facilities by type.

Worldwide Demand

With golf courses worldwide, the capacity for the sport exceeds 2.788 billion rounds of golf every year. But only 0.86% of the world's population plays golf, as calculated across the following parts of the world:[11]

Continent	Number of Golfers
North America	32,300,000
Europe	7,663,560
Asia	16,174,000
Oceania	1,789,400
Africa	800,850
South America	148,450
Caribbean	44,600
Central America	12,750
Middle East	11,500
	58,945,110

10 National Golf Foundation, "Golf Facilities Report for 2011", p. 5.

11 Colin Hegarty, Golf Research Group, "Golf 20/20 Presentation," November 2005, Slide 8.

A Closer Look at Demand

The financial health of the business of golf can be measured by many numbers. Three of the most effective are the relationship between the number of golf courses, the number of golfers, and the number of rounds played.

Many factors influence those three components.

In order to compute the number of golfers and the number of rounds, we first need to define "golfer." The National Golf Foundation defines a "golfer" as an individual, age 6 or older, who has played at least one round. "Core golfers" are defined as adults 18 or older who play between 8 and 24 rounds per year. The term "avid golfer" is used for those golfers who play more than 24 rounds per year. Other industry research groups use 12-year-olds as the starting point for calling a person a golfer. Since our industry's methods of gathering statistics are not standardized, results vary, sometimes wildly.

Another word that causes much debate is "round." When you play a "round," of golf, have you played 9 holes or 18? The most common use of the word "round" merely means "a start." In other words, golfers teed off on at least one hole, whether they paid or were provided complimentary access.

Further, counting starts is an inexact science. Paper tee sheets (used on perhaps 20% of the courses) are notoriously inaccurate. But the decline in rounds is also due, in part, to the fact that many golf courses have installed golf management software that tracks rounds more accurately. A computer count trumps a hand count any day.

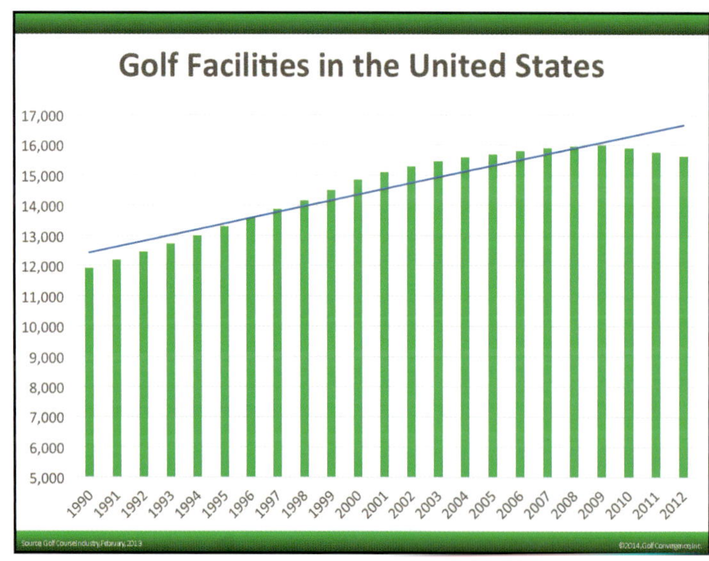

As imprecise as all these statistics may be, by measuring these three key benchmarks (number of golf courses, number of players, and number of rounds), we can determine the financial health of the game.

The chart on the previous page is highlighting the growth in golf courses in the United States since 1990.

The growth is impressive, but there are even more dramatic changes in the underlying composition of the golf courses that have been built.

In 1950, 62% of all golf courses in the United States were private. Municipal courses accounted for 15%, and 23% were daily fee.

By 2013, daily fee golf courses accounted for 62% of all golf courses while private golf clubs accounted for 27% of the courses (4,400). This shift came when high-end, daily fee courses created the same experience as private clubs without the initiation fees and dues. The market share for municipal golf courses remained constant at 15% during that 55-year span.

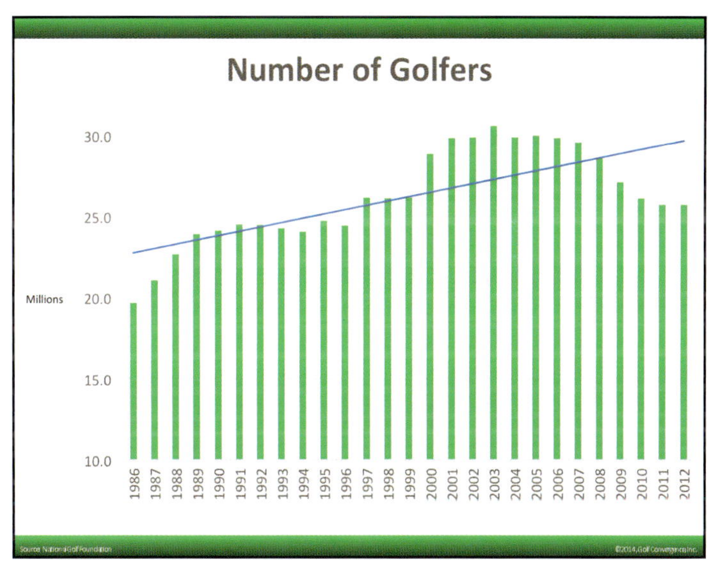

Though golf has become a game readily accessible by the public, the number of individuals who play, about 26 million people, hasn't changed much since the later 1990s, as reflected in the graph.

Is the future of golf bright? Is it America's favorite pastime? Taking a wide perspective of a half-century, that conclusion would be yes. Taking a more narrow view of the past two decades, the game is wounded by such rosy "self-proclamation."

Golf, as measured by rounds played, has largely remained stagnant, as highlighted in the graph on the next page.

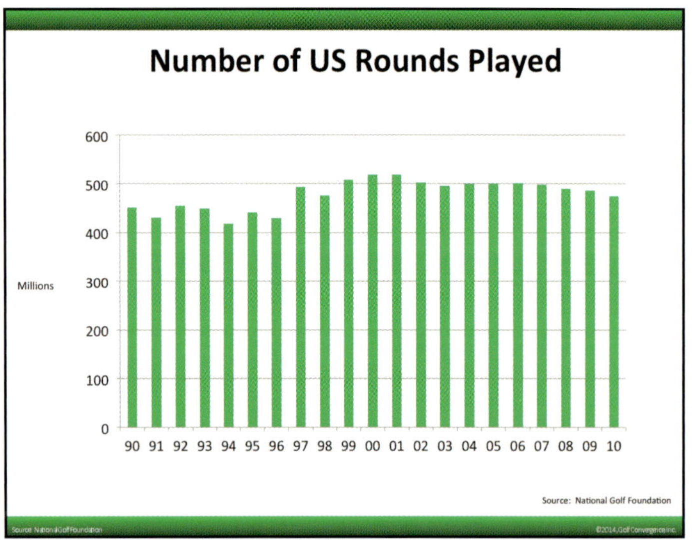

The increase in supply coupled with stagnant demand has created a reduction in the number of rounds played at each facility.

Interpreting the Numbers—Caught in the Death Spiral

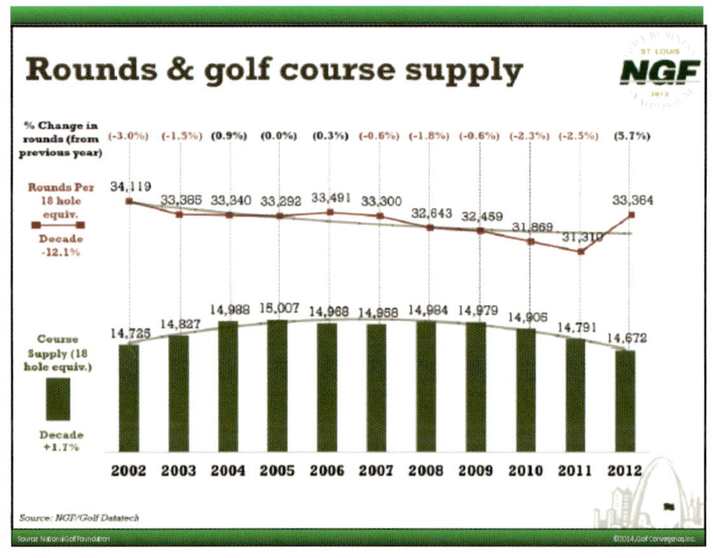

The increase in the supply since 1986 coupled with stagnant growth in demand means that the golf industry is overbuilt by nearly 10%. With the golf market oversupplied, and if the annual growth in new courses is less than 1%, based on growth of the population, it is estimated that it will take more than a decade for the excess supply to be mitigated. As a result, as shown above, the number of rounds played has fallen over the past decade.

What has caused the decline? There are many reasons.

The disparate factors of supply exceeding demand, golf's lessening popularity, and changes within our societal framework have created what might be called a "death spiral" for golf courses. Before 1990, golf course operations were profitable and course demand exceeded supply.

Then began four distinct phases:

- Phase 1 (1991–1998): Expansion. New courses were added, creating an oversupply, while existing courses tried to boost revenue by attracting customers through discounted green fees.
- Phase 2 (1999–2003): Erosion. With low interest rates and loose monetary policies, new courses continued to be added in excess of demand. Courses began to lose money, resulting in general reserves being tapped. Green fees and revenues fell as competitors matched prices, forcing the reduction of expenses and the deferral of capital expenditures.
- Phase 3 (2004–2009): Depletion. With financial reserves depleted, government subsidies were required for municipal facilities. For other golf courses, additional borrowing or the deferral of capital expenditures was required. This led to a decrease in course maintenance and service levels. The quality of courses declined, accelerating the decrease in rounds.
- Phase 4 (2010–?): Privatization, Sale, or Closure. Deferred capital expenditures, which were typically more than $2.5 million per facility, became critical and forced owners to borrow in a tight lending market or liquidate. As many as 5% of all golf facilities are in or entering this final phase.

To reverse this cycle there are two scenarios. In the managed scenario, the NGF believes that latent demand exists that could be stimulated from:

- Millions of high-interest golfers who want to play more (for example, baby boomers who are now in their prime working and family rearing years).
- Millions of former golfers who are open to trying again (for example, people who were turned off by slow play, embarrassing situations, or cost of entry).
- Millions of never-evers who want to start (recent NGF research shows that 4% of 200 million never-evers are very or somewhat interested in playing golf).

The unmanaged scenario (the hope and pray strategy) is hopelessly flawed. Understanding the data of the industry is important, but understanding the underlying causes for the decline in golf is vital.

Beyond the Societal Factors—Why Is Golf in Decline?

The game is becoming marginally less a part of popular activity, as measured in the graph below.

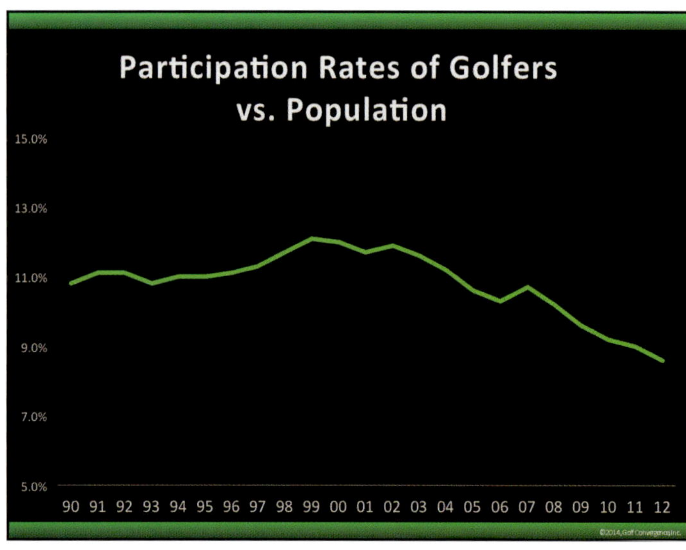

The game is experiencing attrition as the participation rate and the frequency rate are both decreasing.

The participation rate is declining for many reasons, including the fact that almost 50% of population growth is Hispanic, a population that plays less golf than other ethnicities. Only 4% of Hispanics play golf. Thus, as the population increases, the participation rate will automatically decrease, even if the same percentage of Caucasians and Asians play.

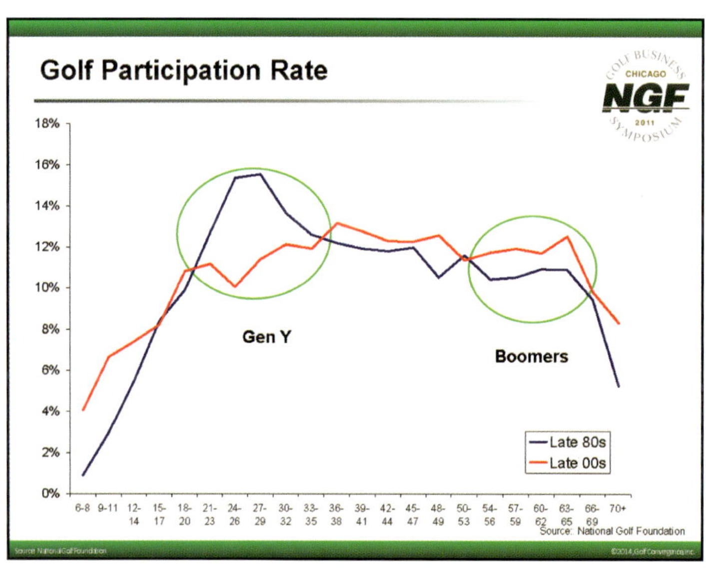

With respect to the frequency rate, generations X and Y are playing far less and illustrated in the chart to the left:[12]

The average golf participation rate of 18-34-year-olds in the late 1980s was 13.5%, vs. 10.8% in the late 2000s. Combining this lower participation

12 National Golf Foundation, "Generational Risk," April, 2011, Slide 20.

rate with population change has resulted in roughly a 1.8 million drop in the number of golfers age 18-34.

Many thought the baby boomers would have an offsetting positive effect. While most new demand will come from golfers over age 55, that growth comes at a significant cost. With the senior citizen receiving an average 27% green fee discount from the rack rate at municipal and daily fee golf courses, the aging of the population has the potential to actually decrease gross revenue at a golf course.

Currently, 68% of all rounds are played by those over the age of 43. Soon, the majority of rounds played will be played by those over 50. This has serious ramifications for course owners, as the majority of their customers will qualify for discounted senior rates. Plus, the old assumptions about 50-year-olds working less and playing more may not hold true for the future. According to the AARP, 65 percent of people over age 45 (all the boomers) planned to postpone retirement. Not only that, a report issued by McKinsey Global Institute found that two-thirds of boomers have failed to adequately prepare for retirement, and few of those even realize it.

The challenge the game of golf faces is not only attracting new players but also curbing the attrition among the golfer base. Because of demographic and situational factors, less than 54% of men and 27% of women introduced to the game continue to play after five years.

On July 8, 2008, Conde Nast ceased publication of *Golf for Women*, despite the magazine's award-winning journalism and visionary design. The press release from Conde Nast read, "We came to this decision because we feel the magazine will not support our long-term business objectives."[13]

Of course, one of the reasons for the scarcity of women golfers may be that many male-dominated pro shops create a harsh and unfriendly environment that makes women feel unwelcome.

The demographics of American society make clear the reasons for the shift from golf.

13 Golf Press Association Press Release, http://www.golfbusinesswire.com/releases/132574/ Conde Nast, July 8, 2008.

USA Today in September, 2007[14] reported a dramatic change in the daily routines of Americans. They affect the entire spectrum of everyday life, from family schedules to TV ratings to restaurant hours.

- 15 million drivers, 12.9% of the population, go to work by 6 a.m., altering workers' relationships with their families.
- 18.9 million people are considered "house poor," as 37% of the population spends at least 30% of income on their house. One-third of unmarried American men between 25 and 34 are still living at home with their parents, the highest rate ever recorded.
- 20-somethings say, "I don't" to marriage.
- Women outnumber men at colleges 56% to 44%.

Combine these factors with even more dramatic numbers: 43.7% of custodial mothers and 56.2% of custodial fathers were either separated or divorced,[15] 50% of all families are divorced, and 80% of existing families have dual wage earners.[16] The concept of available leisure time has been redefined, as has the country's dress standards, which are now inconsistent with the traditional dress standards in golf. Jeans on a golf course are an exception found usually only in few rural areas.

If the dress standards were changed, would the game attract or lose players?

Evan Rothman opined, "But jeans, serious golf doesn't go there . . . It's the class war, stupid."[17] Is golf restricted to a certain class? Should golf change its dress standards to attract the masses and bolster profits, or does golf define and defend its traditions to retain the culture of the sport?

Hence, another contributing factor is that golf is expensive. To even begin playing, you need clubs, shoes, golf balls, and more. It's not uncommon to invest between $500 and $3,000 to start. Participating in golf consumes approximately

---

14 *USA Today*, "Life in America," March 6, 2007, p. 1.

15 Divorce Magazine.com, "US Divorce Statistics," 2008, http://www.divorcemag.com/statistics/index.shtml.

16 Beverly Baskin, "Dual-Career Couples Facing the 'Stress of Success'—How Families Cope," http://www.selfhelpmagazine.com/article/node/796.

17 Evan Rothman, "The Cultural Divide—It is Class Warfare", *Golf Week*, April 9, 2007.

3% of an individual's discretionary income; the national average household disposable income is $45,301.[18]

What Is the Solution?

Credit, loan, and employment indicators are putting pressure on golf's Achilles heels: discretionary money and time. Recent tax law changes factor into this equation as what were once previously business expenses deductions, i.e., entertainment, are far more restricted and no longer deductible.

To prosper during these difficult times, golf course managers and owners need to increase participation of current customers and attract new participants through player development programs.

There are some quick fixes that should address the game's primary barriers.

- Time—Create more opportunities for alternative forms of play (Stableford scoring, among families, Scrambles, reward pace of play, emphasize range programs for the severely time-compressed).
- Money—Find creative ways to make frequency more affordable (don't discount, but pay for volume; offer couple or family rates; offer season passes only on a restricted basis during the slowest playing times, usually weekdays from noon to 3). Also educate the aspirational golfers; encourage them to practice more with the latest equipment. Keep in mind the statistic reported by the NGF that "half of golfers who have quit cite money reasons."[19]
- Skill—Facilities should focus on playable options with multiple tees, easier pin positions, and eliminating those elements of "penal architecture" found within their courses. Course renovations should emphasize "fun" over difficulty.

But these fixes only are temporary. What follows is the formula to address these woes permanently. For the golf course creating a strategic plan, the

18 Tactician Corporation, "Mapping and Reporting Service", http://www.mapscape.com/MapscapeV3/1033/ReportWizard2.asp?WizardType=PR&App=001&Meth=001&Ind=001&Geog=, December, 2011.

19 National Golf Foundation, "Golf Industry Report—The Future of Private Golf Clubs in America," Summer 2008, p. 4.

environmental economic factors present a gloomy picture. It is vitally important that a golf course owner has a clear delineation, as reflected in its mission statement, as to its course's market niche.

End Notes

The lessons of this chapter are:

1) The exact number of golf courses in the world, based on a National Golf Foundation survey, is 33,331.

2) Growth of the game is international, not U.S. based.

3) Supply for golf in the United States exceeds demand by 10%.

4) The number of individuals who play golf in the United States has remained flat for the past decade at about 26 million golfers.

5) Soon 50% of the rounds of golf will be played by those over 50.

6) Golf is losing relevance.

7) Golf is losing its middle-class appeal.

8) Sports that are time-consuming are losing market share.

Concluding Thought

The pessimist sees difficulty in every opportunity.
The optimist sees the opportunity in every difficulty.

Winston Churchill

Chapter 3

The Players: Associations and Equipment Manufacturers

We are inclined to believe those we do not know, because they have never deceived us.

Samuel Johnson

Chapter Highlights

This chapter concentrates on the trade associations that influence the business of golf: the National Golf Course Owners Association, the National Golf Foundation, the Professional Golfers' Association of America, and the United States Golf Association. How these organizations could effectively serve their constituents and the game better is explored.

Also, the role of leading equipment manufacturers in attracting golfers to the game is examined. Is the process of purchasing golf clubs, which is embedded with arcane and highly technical descriptions, too foreboding?

Why is this information important to the golf course owner? Golf associations and equipment manufacturers influence golfers. Their efforts promote entrance to the game and perhaps also create barriers.

You Need a Scorecard

Each industry has trade groups. Golf is no exception.

The game has the PGA Tour, the PGA of America, the Royal and Ancient Golf Club, The First Tee, the World Golf Foundation, Golf 20/20, the Ladies Professional Golf Association, Golf Course Architects societies, Golf Course Builders associations, the Executive Woman's Golf Association, the Junior Golf Association, as well as many golf unions; state, city, and club amateur golf associations; PGA sections; golf course owners associations; club management chapters; and many others who serve a role for their constituents.

Seven associations or foundations have the most influence over the business of golf. They are:

Association	Headquarters	Focus	Mission Statement
Club Managers Association of America, founded in 1937 (CMAA)	Alexandria, Virginia	General Managers at Private Clubs	The professional association for managers of membership clubs
Golf Course Superintendents Association of America, founded in 1928 (GCSAA)	Lawrence, Kansas	Superintendents	Dedicated to serving those responsible for maintaining the golf course by advancing their profession, and enhancing the enjoyment, growth, and vitality of the game of golf.
National Golf Course Owners Association, founded in 1979 (NGCOA)	Charleston, South Carolina	Course Owners and Operators	To enhance the lives of golf course owners by making their business more profitable, more efficient, better managed, and more stable.
National Golf Foundation (NGF)	Jupiter, Florida	Industry Research	To help golf businesses succeed by providing marketing, research, customer targeting, and other consulting services.
Professional Golfers' Association of America, founded in 1916 (PGA)	Palm Beach Garden, Florida	Professional Golfers	Experts in growing, teaching, and managing the game of golf.

Association	Headquarters	Focus	Mission Statement
The Royal and Ancient Golf Club (R&A)	St. Andrews, Scotland	Clubs, Courses, Rules	International governing body of golf outside U.S. and Mexico.
United States Golf Association (USGA)	Far Hills, New Jersey	Clubs, Courses, Qualified Practice Facilities, and Schools; conducts US Open, US Women's Open, US Senior Open, 10 National Amateur Championships, and the State Team Championships	U.S. governing body of golf for the United States, its territories, and Mexico.

No single association claims leadership in the golf business. Instead, many associations serve in ways that, by the invisible hand of capitalism, blend together (sometimes smoothly, sometimes awkwardly) to support the business of golf. Some have an implied monopoly power in their domain, others seek that influence.

Of these associations, those doing most of the heavy lifting with respect to the business of golf are the National Golf Foundation (providing valuable research), the National Golf Course Owners Association (representing the owners' investment interests), and the PGA of America (providing qualified staff to play, teach, and manage the business end of the game).

Just as golf is a gentlemanly sport, the business of golf has a competitive aspect as golf associations often subtlety protect and respect each others' loosely defined territories.

What Is the Role of These Associations: To Educate or to Lead?

One of the great benefits of these trade associations is that they can influence an industry by representing their members' more enlightened interests.

A diverse range of professional talents is found within these organizations—from the very skilled and progressive to the bureaucratic and turf-protecting. If they fulfill their charter by serving the narrow interests of their members but adversely impact an industry, then are they good stewards of the game?

At its core, what are the essential components required for the golf industry to thrive? The industry would include individuals who:

- Are financially sound, providing recreational entertainment to their customers and stable employment for their management and staff. (NGCOA)
- Understand the business of golf and can maximize the investment return of the facility. (CMAA)
- Understand the game of golf and can provide the instructions and programs to enhance the customer's enjoyment. (PGA)
- Are able to create, maintain, and enhance the grounds on which the customers play. (GCSAA)
- Provide guidelines by which individuals can compete. (R&A and USGA)

In theory, these roles could be provided by a single association. In reality, the lines are blurred as individuals and associations perform, on occasion, tasks within each of the core components required for the successful operation of a golf facility. However, is the golf industry served well in the following examples?

1. A golf course owner who has financial resources but lacks the business skill to maximize the investment return at a golf course or to teach the game chooses not to hire a general manager or a PGA professional to assist him.
2. An individual who understands the business of golf but not the game of golf fails to retain qualified personnel to fill that void, thereby reducing the investment return received by his employer.
3. An individual who is skilled in the game of golf but assumes the responsibility for managing the business of golf with few asset management skills in finance, human resources, or maintaining the facility's physical assets.
4. An individual who creates the standards for an industry but so narrowly defines the guidelines that they effectively create deterrents for the masses embracing the activity as participants.

We all like to classify individuals and associations into well-defined categories to give us a frame of reference. That provides security so that when advancing our personal interests, we understand the motivations of those with whom we interact.

The PGA's Influence

Five percent of PGA club pros serve as general managers.[1] Though the general manager's job closely mirrors that of a chief operating officer of a business, the cornerstone of the PGA's emphasis for its membership historically has been the game of golf, not the business of golf. In fact, you can have 20 years of experience, but if you can't shoot a low enough score to pass the player's aptitude test, you cannot become a PGA Professional.

Brian Whitcomb's ascendancy to the presidency of the PGA of America (a post he held from 2007 to 2009) was not surprising. Brian fully realized that the PGA Professional must become financially and operationally astute to remain a viable component at a golf course—something that he practices at the course he owns, Lost Tracks Golf Club in Bend, OR.

The PGA of America continues to expand career opportunities for its members. Few individuals outside of the PGA of America realize that the association has many member classifications. The PGA of America's Certified Professional Program offers certification in six fields (general management, golf operations, instruction, retail, executive management, and ownership/leasing).

With the 19 Professional Golf Management programs adding 500 to 700 new PGA members annually, there is an overabundance of PGA Professionals. As a result, wages are depressed.

The Importance of Education and Experience

Finding educated talent to operate a golf course is essential for success. Any business is dependent upon qualified management and staff.

1 Josh Sanburn, *Golf Magazine*, "Joe Golf Pro, COO," August 2008, p. 42.

Like any industry, golf attracts a wide range of talents—from the very sophisticated to those with basic business knowledge. A course owner asked on NGCOA's listserv,

> "We just purchased our golf course last year and my bank is wanting to see a balance sheet. Does anyone have one that I could look at to get ideas on how to create one?"[2]

Can you imagine someone owning a golf course, getting a loan from a bank, and not knowing about a basic financial statement? That is unfathomable. But a lack of financial sophistication is perhaps more widespread than we would care to admit in the golf industry.

Another course owner queried,

> "What is a loyalty point program?"[3]

Started by American Airlines in the early 1980s, the program is so widely studied in the business world that it's impossible to know how someone can be unfamiliar with the concept 29 years later?

What is important is not the moniker with which one is associated but their education, experience, and commitment to serve with passion in a role for which they are qualified.

How the Associations Can Better Serve the Business

The two largest and most prestigious golf associations are the Royal and Ancient Golf Club and the United States Golf Association.

The Royal and Ancient home Web page states,

> "Based in St. Andrews, The R&A is golf's governing body and organizer of The Open Championship. The R&A is committed to working for golf and operates with the consent of 136 organizations from the amateur and professional game and on behalf of over 30 million golfers in 123 countries.

2 NGCOA Listserv, "Balance Sheet," November 7, 2007.

3 NGCOA Listserv, "Balance Sheet," November 8, 2007.

> The R&A takes its name from The Royal and Ancient Golf Club of St. Andrews, which has continuous records dating back to its foundation in 1754, and although the Club continues its long history with 2,400 members throughout the world, The R&A has become a separate entity to focus on its governance role."[4]
>
> By developing The Open Championship as one of the world's great sporting events and as an outstanding commercial success, the R&A is able to invest an annual surplus through the R&A Foundation into grass roots development projects around the world.
>
> Particular emphasis is placed on the encouragement of junior golf, the development of the game in emerging golfing nations, coaching, and the provision of open-to-all courses and practice facilities.
>
> The R&A also provides best practice guidance on all aspects of golf course management, with specific reference to ecological and conservation issues, to help the growth of the game in a commercially and environmentally sustainable way."

The role of the United States Golf Association is similar. Its Web page states,

> "The Association sponsors a variety of programs that benefit everyone who plays the game, from conducting 13 national championships each year, to writing and interpreting the Rules of Golf, to funding turf grass and course maintenance practices, to supporting grassroots programs through its "For the Good of the Game" initiative."[5]

These golf associations do a superb job protecting the history and tradition of the game. From formulating detailed specifications for balls and equipment, formulating biennially the rules of the game, and creating a platform to ensure equitable competition, these organizations and their volunteers play a laudable role in promoting the game of golf.

However, the game of golf and the business of golf are not synonyms, and in fact they directly compete.

At the PGA Merchandise Show in 2000, the PGA of America sponsored an amazing conference on the "Business of Golf" and attracted a distinguished panel that included the following: Bob Wood, Nike; Ron Drapeau, then of Calloway; Mark King, Taylormade; Tom Fazio, Architect; Pete Dye, Architect;

4 R&A, St. Andrews, http://www.randa.org/home/TheR%2526A

5 http://www.usga.org/about.aspx?id=7881#show=d1615101-00df-42fe-97f1-bb9cd1de416c

Peter Dawson, Royal and Ancient; David Fay, USGA; Kerry Haigh, PGA Tour Official [he's with PGA of America]; Dick Ebersol, NBC Sports; Sean McManus, CBS Sports; Marv Lazerus, Turner Sports; Mike Hulbert, PGA Tour; and Judy Dickinson, LPGA Tour.

In reporting on comprehensive studies that had been conducted, panelists presented data indicating that the technology explosion in golf was not benefiting the average players:

- The #1 fear in golf is getting the ball airborne.
- Only 17% of golfers have handicaps of 20 or less.
- Golfers play to hit 5 to 15 good shots a round. At fewer than 5 good shots, they quit. With more than 15 good shots per round, they become avid golfers.
- The average woman golfer hits the ball the same distance now as she did 30 years ago—129 yards.
- The most gullible consumers in America are golfers, who will buy anything that gives them any chance of improving their enjoyment or score.

We further learned at that conference that 85% of the 26 million golfers in the United States are recreational golfers. Only 3% maintain a single-digit handicap and are thus classified as accomplished golfers.

The challenge to growing the participation in the game of golf was clear from the dialogue among the panelists. Pete Dye stated, "In basketball, football, and baseball, there is different equipment, rules, and playing fields for the pros, college, high school, and junior athletes. Golf needs to adopt similar diversity in the game." Pete Dye felt strongly that the game should start offering different golf balls to players of differing abilities. Golf is the only major sport in which an entrant and a professional athlete use essentially the same equipment with the same ball under the same rules on the same athletic field.

This theme was echoed again in 2006, when James Achenbach wrote in *Golfweek*, "Do we really want the game to grow? Or do we want to preserve the integrity of par in an era of more gifted, more dedicated athletes? With one set of equipment rules, we can't have it both ways."[6] Achenbach believes that the rules are too confusing and too confining and are largely constructed in reaction to

6 James Achenbach, *Golfweek*, "From My Perspective," February 4, 2006, p. 54.

touring pros. He concludes that the governing bodies are too focused on regulation rather than innovation.[7]

But just as the equipment manufacturers were adamant that they could create recreational entertainment that would attract people to the game and make the sport fun, the governing bodies, represented by David Fay for the USGA and Peter Dawson for the Royal and Ancient Golf Club, were firm in stating that a central tenet of the game is that all people play with the same equipment, that it is "from the innate difficulty of the game that enjoyment emanates," and that the rules needed to be consistently applied. Such thinking constrains growth, and by extension, the business of golf.

Arnold Palmer clearly sees this vision. He stated is his book *Playing by the Rules*, "I'm sure that I could watch the golfers at one of my clubs for a while on any given day and be able to disqualify half of them for this or that infraction. But why would I want to? Golf should be fun. And those of us who love the game should be encouraging fun and recreation, not building roadblocks for future golfing generations. The USGA would be well served by adopting that attitude."[8]

The lines that were drawn then—advances in technology for the average player to make the game more enjoyable, or adherence to the rules of one standard for all—remain largely in place today. However, a crack in the regulatory bodies' firm position on equipment standards occurred in August 2008 when the following press release was issued:

> "FAR HILLS, N.J.—The United States Golf Association (USGA) announced revisions to the Rules of Golf, placing new restrictions on the cross sectional area and edge sharpness of golf club grooves.
>
> The revisions are designed to restore the challenge of playing shots to the green from the rough by reducing backspin on those shots. The initial focus of the new rules will be competitions involving highly skilled professional golfers and will have little impact on the play of most golfers.
>
> The rules apply to clubs manufactured after January 1, 2010, the same year that the USGA will enforce the new regulations through a condition of competition for the U.S. Open, U.S. Women's Open and U.S.

7 Ibid, p. 54.

8 Arnold Palmer, *Playing by the Rules* (New York, Pocket Books, 2002), p. 240.

> Senior Open and each of their qualifying events. All USGA amateur championships will apply the new regulations through the condition of competition, after January 1, 2014.
>
> 'The PGA TOUR supports the decision of the United States Golf Association and The R&A regarding new groove specifications, and we plan to implement the rule change as a condition of competition for our events across the three Tours beginning January 1, 2010,' PGA TOUR Commissioner Tim Finchem said in a statement.
>
> Clubs manufactured prior to January 1, 2010 that conform to current regulations will continue to be considered conforming to the USGA Rules of Golf until at least 2024. This includes clubs purchased after that date from manufacturers' existing model ranges. So long as these clubs continue to be conforming they may be used for establishment and maintenance of a USGA Handicap Index."[9]

This is a start. If golf, and especially the USGA and the R&A, were to adopt the diversity in the game offered by other sports and start with offering different golf balls and other equipment to players with differing abilities, the game, economically, would grow dramatically. The bifurcation of equipment would create "tiered" levels of excellence that would first encourage the growth of the game and then, in turn, the business of the game.

Does a golf course owner really care if a guest pays $50 to play a course, uses nonconforming equipment to shoot a 65, has fun, and returns again and again?

Nope. The game versus the business of golf remains an oxymoron as some focus on traditions while other focus on profits.

Hence, the game of golf and the business of golf remain largely disconnected. Only by making the game fun is there a chance for growth and, in turn, long-term financial success for operators.

Equipment Manufacturers Are Limiting, Not Encouraging, Participation

Many people in the industry believe that equipment manufacturers, perhaps inadvertently, reinforce through their advertising the idea of golf as an elitist sport.

9 http://www.pgatour.com/2008/r/08/05/usga.rules/index.html

Equipment manufacturers sell $5 billion of golf equipment annually.[10] They invest untold millions in research development and advertising. But it seems that with the arcane and technical product descriptions used, making informed decisions on what club is right for each golfer is all but impossible.

Need proof? Look at the ads certain manufacturers run on television. Their engineers and designers are touted as modern-day Isaac Newtons, complete with algorithms dancing whimsically around their heads. To think that the average golfer understands the technical nuances of design is folly. Following are some of the exact product descriptions from the November, 2013 Golfsmith On-Line Catalog:

- **Callaway RAZR X HL 4H, 5H, 6-PW, AW Combination Iron Set with Steel Shafts.** The **Callaway RAZR X HL Combo Iron Set** takes accuracy, distance and foregiveness (sic) to new highs. Each iron in this set has a low center of gravity so golfers can launch shots higher, even on impacts low on the face, so golf balls fly consistently farther and land softer on the greens. This low center of gravity makes the sweet spot more accessible at lower impact locations, where many amateurs strike the ball, meaning more accuracy and consistent distance. **RAZR Technology** shifts the center of gravity lower and deeper by redistributing weight in the back cavity; providing the power and forgiveness of a wide-sole iron with the precision and playability of a thin-sole iron. A **Solid Impact Sole** creates smooth turf interaction for better distance, accuracy and consistency. The **VFT Power System** is a fully integrated clubface/undercut cavity system that enables engineers to precisely position the center of gravity and engineer the face of each iron to maximize ball speed. A **Multi-material Medallion**, constructed of aluminum and thermoplastic polyurethane fine-tunes sound and enhances feel off the clubface.
- **Ping i20 4-UW Iron Set with Steel-Black Dot.** The **Ping i20 Iron Set** is multi-metal iron set that offers optimized performance through progressive set design. The forgiving, high-launching long irons blend into more-penetrating mid- and –short irons, offering control for precise shot making. A dense tungsten toe weight provides forgiveness across the face for accurate results as well as a high-launch, low-spin trajectory. Distance control and a solid feel come from a thicker hitting area and stabilizing bars in the cavity and a low moment of inertia about the shaft axis gives golfers the ability to shape shots with confidence. The set is finished off with a non-glare chrome finish and black-and-silver color scheme, offering a players'-style contemporary look.

10 SRI International, "The Golf Economy Report," November 2002, p. 1.

- **Mizuno JPX EZ Iron Sets.** Max Pocket Cavity (4-7): Massive sweet area, tightest dispersion, and effortless launch characteristics. Deep Pocket Cavity (8-PW): For increased accuracy and launch control. Hot Metal Face: Thin multi-thickness design for maximum COR to deliver long, consistent distance. Harmonic Impact Technology (H.I.T.): Feel and sound tuned through cavity frame design.

From those descriptions, could you tell which club was best for your game? Probably not.

Shouldn't it be easy to find the "perfect" club? It isn't. I ponder whether many golfers abandon their search for new clubs because there are so many choices and they can't differentiate among the various clubs. If so, it is costing manufacturers millions in lost revenue.

While all club makers maintain that PGA Professionals and off-course store representatives should educate and custom-fit golfers, such practices violate rule number one of the basic principles of Marketing 101: The customer doesn't like to look stupid and thus, if the answer isn't obvious to them, they will rarely ask a question because they don't want to appear to be an idiot.

We yearn for simplicity, yet the golf industry gives us complexity.[11]

The Historical Role of State Golf Associations

State golf associations, which are private 501(c)(3) nonprofit organizations, are principally governed by volunteers representing distinguished members of the community from a cross section of golf courses and are usually weighted to the more prestigious golf clubs. In addition to conducting as many as 40 tournaments per year, the associations also sponsor rules seminars, calculate course ratings, provide a handicap and tournament management software service, and assist in the redistribution and implementation of USGA policies, programs, and championships.

For those on the periphery, there is often confusion about the differing roles of the USGA, the PGA, and the PGA Tour. The difference between the motivations of individuals affiliated with an amateur state golf association versus those affiliated with the PGA is easy to explain: The amateur associations are

11 *Golf Magazine*, "Buyers Guide 2008," June 2008, p. 192.

motivated to preserve tradition. The PGA and the PGA Tour are focused on the business of golf—earning money.

To sustain themselves, state golf associations usually rely upon handicapping accounts for in excess of 75% of their gross revenue, based on the following revenue model:

The Economics of Handicaps	Cost
Software providers' charge to state golf association	$3.05
State associations levy golf courses who provide service to their players	$12.00–$20.00
Golf course assessment/upcharge to player	$25.00–$65.00

On January 1, 2006, the USGA sanctioned the use of Type 3, Internet-based handicap clubs in which the members had no prior affiliation and which solicitations of members is done via public advertising. These handicaps provide state golf associations the opportunity to attract further interest in the game of golf by attracting the casual player, from whom loyalty to the sport can be built. In contrast, the members of a Type 1 club are located at a single specific golf course, playing where the club's *scoring records* reside. Members of Type 2 clubs are affiliated, or known to one another, via a business, fraternal, ethnic, or social organization.

By creating online communities, state golf association Web sites could become a central focus for golfers. One of the services that could be provided might be online tee reservations on behalf of their member golf courses. State associations would earn a small fee per transaction for creating additional rounds.

The state associations' credibility as supporters of member courses will be reinforced by assisting them to sell their tee times at the "rack rate." Every golf course owner would appreciate the opportunity to have their available inventory posted to an interested audience representing at least 15% of the golfers within the state.

Why is this important? A lot of independent third-party companies are serving as intermediaries between golf courses and their customers, thereby creating rate instability within the golf industry.

Golf associations, with their extensive customer databases, could stem the discounting that is occurring within the industry to the benefit of the associations and the course owners. But that would require a paradigm shift in the thinking of associations. Currently, they view the clubs as their constituency rather than focus on providing services to golfers.

Further, state golf associations need to expand their world view to include golf course owners as part of their customer base. If state associations would provide access to their customer databases, it would mutually benefit their members, themselves, and golf course owners. As a result, the golf industry would be on firmer footing.

End Notes

The lessons of this chapter are:

1) There are six trade associations that largely influence the policies of the industry and create brand recognition for the sport, heavily influencing the masses' perception of the game.
2) Many people do not trust the motivations of these organizations because they sometimes work at conflicting odds.
3) The PGA of America's educational programs leading to certification are properly balancing their members' affinity for the game of golf with the business of golf.
4) Some would argue that the bifurcation of the rules of golf would stimulate new entrants to the game, making one of the traditional barriers to entry, difficulty, an obstacle that could more easily be overcome.
5) Equipment manufacturers limit the growth of the game with arcane descriptions of technology.
6) State golf associations have many opportunities to stimulate the growth of the game by leveraging their core constituency to create relevant social networks that provide services far beyond handicapping, including tee time reservations, Facebook, YouTube and other social media functionality.

For the golf course owner, it is imperative to realize that the brand of their facility can be impacted, both positively and negatively, by trade associations that are beyond their control.

Concluding Thought

You can't handle the truth!

Actor Jack Nicholson as Colonel Nathan Jessup in the 1992 film *A Few Good Men*

Chapter 4

Ownership and Governance: A Privilege or Burden?

The mass of men never comes up to the standard of its best member, but on the contrary digress itself to a level with the lowest.

Henry David Thoreau

Chapter Highlights

This chapter discusses the forms of ownership of golf courses: municipal, daily fee, resort, and private, and the great divisions in structure, philosophies, and operating policies among these different types of ownership.

While these ownership groups all serve the golf industry, the divisions between them can be quite bitter, with daily fee operators often loathing their municipal brethren, citing significant cost advantages and crying for a level playing field in the land of capitalism. Presumed cost advantages are often offset by bureaucratic burdens of government, but the hostilities still exist.

Finally, there is the evolving role of management companies. Whether or not management fees are justified by the increased profits they supposedly lead to, the intangible benefit of an owner not having to worry about day-to-day management is fair compensation itself.

Public and Private

The average golfer thinks of golf courses in two ways: public and private.

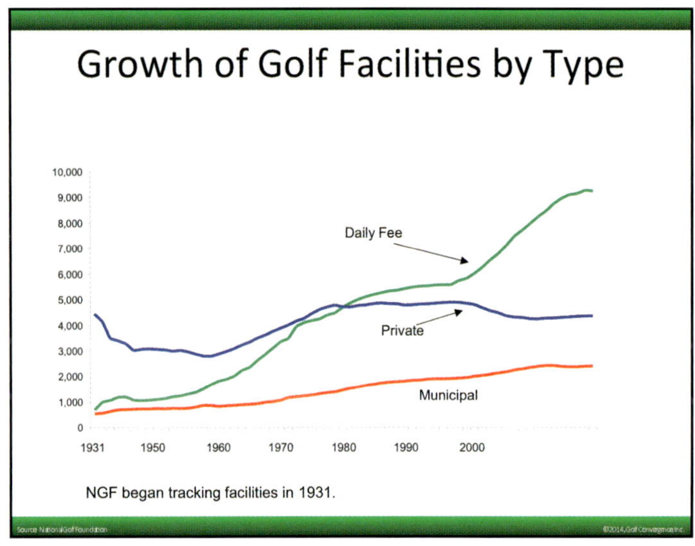

Within those divisions are sub-categories that include municipal, daily fee, semi-private, resort, private equity, private non-equity, and military golf facilities. No matter how we classify a golf course, the changing nature of supply within the golf industry has been dramatic during the past 58 years, which is depicted on this page.[1]

Why does the type of ownership matter? It impacts every aspect of the operation, from course conditions to pricing and from rules about access to the depth and breadth of staffing. The type of ownership conveys a strong brand image in each golfer's mind prior to arrival at the course.

Municipal golf courses are often viewed as the entry door—the stereotype of inexpensive, affordable golf. Average course conditions, small clubhouses, and limited food service cater mainly to seniors, juniors, season pass holders, and new golfers. During the past decade, this stereotype has changed, as many municipal courses now offer high-quality experiences.

While looking to provide a recreational experience to its citizens, municipal golf encompasses a number of goals and functions:

- Generating the largest possible return on investment in order to divert profits to support other nonrevenue-supporting park activities.
- Providing an appropriate return on investment with a value-based recreational activity for the citizens.

1 National Golf Foundation, Golf 20/20, November 2005, Slide 10.

- Enhancing the lifestyle of constituents by catering to the perceived needs of niche groups—ladies, senior citizens, etc.
- Appealing to and facilitating the formation of core values among children, adolescents, and teens.

Regardless of the charter or operational framework of a municipal course, the pricing it sets becomes the "buoy" on which all prices in the market are set. As municipalities raise their prices, based on perceived increases in value, the prices at other courses in that market adjust accordingly.

Reed Myers, president of a 501(c)(3) nonprofit entity that is astutely named "The Alamo City Golf Trail," assumed in 2008 operation of the City of San Antonio's golf courses. Having received a $10 million grant to extricate the City's Parks and Recreation Department from massive losses, Myers has an enlightened perspective about the responsibility of municipal golf courses.

> "It is our responsibility to set the prices fairly in order to earn not only a satisfactory return on investment for our municipal golf courses but to also provide our friends in the industry who operate the other golf courses an opportunity to profit also," he said. "We cannot subsidize golf for the benefit of a few citizens at the expense of our fiduciary responsibility to the City and to the industry."

In contrast to the varying mantra of a municipal golf course, the mission of the daily fee course owner is clear—maximize net income while providing a living for the owner and accumulating an investment return that secures the owner's future. That mission only becomes slightly tempered amongst a few golf course owners whose philanthropic interests result in their donating access to their facilities for charitable causes or to attract major golf championships.

For resorts, a golf course is one of the most important amenities offered. While it may be viewed as a profit center, its major contribution is to fill the hotel and restaurants, especially by attracting large corporate and social events.

Private clubs range in form and function. In small towns, they tend to serve the upper-middle class. Private clubs may be exclusive, and offer membership only to those for whom membership provides prestige, a designation far beyond the value of the experience offered by the club.

For example: Would you join an expensive private club in a temperate southeastern U.S. climate with only 18 regulation holes; a club that is closed all summer, and is virtually unplayable for several premium weeks in the spring? When described that way, the answer is probably "No." But that is a fair description of the Augusta National Golf Club, a private club that every serious golfer would jump at the chance to join.

At St. Andrews, Scotland, the following definition of the purpose of a private club is displayed:

> *Is a haven of refuge and accord in a world torn by strife and discord.*
> *Is a place where people of quality gather to have fun and make friends.*
> *Is a place of courtesy, good breeding and good manners.*
> *Is a place expressly for camaraderie, merriment, good cheer and good will.*
> *It humbles the mighty, draws out the tame, and casts out the sorehead,*
> *And is one of the noblest inventions of mankind!*

Oddly enough, the famous courses in St. Andrews (including the Old Course) are public [municipal!] facilities, owned by the St. Andrews Links Trust, and open to anyone and everyone. The private clubs in the village, including the Royal and Ancient Golf Club, are social clubs with their own clubhouses and get a certain number of preferred tee times on the links but have no role in the management or operation of the golf courses.

Of the various clubs, none is under more attack from the changes in our society than the low- and mid-tier private clubs. In a race to remain relevant, they are quickly diversifying from country clubs into family entertainment centers.

Forms of Municipal Golf Course Management

Municipalities operate golf courses with organizational structures that include the following:

- Employees—city or county workers run the place just like the water department or the police force. Often these employees are budgeted through the Parks and Recreation Department.

- Leases with concessionaires, dispersing responsibility to one or many of a golf course's revenue centers. Of the main revenue centers of a municipal golf course (green fees, carts, merchandise, food and beverage, lessons, range, etc.), the most "leased out" center is food and beverage. It is nearly impossible for most municipal snack shop operations to make money or even break even.

- Management companies such as American Golf, Billy Casper, Century Golf, Kemper Sports Management, OB Sports, Troon, etc., that contract to run all or part of a golf operation.

As illustrated below, municipalities have selected many different forms of operation.

In 2011, 57% of municipal golf courses are self-managed. Interestingly, 15% of municipalities have privatized during the past 12 months.

What is the best structure for the operation of a golf course? When using "employees," the swing of quality will hit both extremes, from outstanding dedicated employees to those merely "punching the clock."

Examples of the Diverse Options

- Self: Exclusively employees of Municipality – Milwaukee, Monmouth, and Morris County
- Self: Exclusively employees of the Municipality except for food and beverage – City of Los Angeles
- Self: Employees of Municipality for Administration and Pro Shop, with maintenance contracted – Anaheim, Modesto, Ocala
- Externally - Course managed by different concessionaires via a lease or management agreement – Indianapolis, Virginia Beach
- Externally - All courses are managed by a single concessionaire via a lease or management agreement – Chicago, Forest Preserve District of Cook Country, New York, Prince William County

Leasing to individual concessionaires often can also produce less than desirable results. Concessionaires are for-profit entities, which create a natural conflict of interest between scope of services and efficiency of operations.

Management companies provide a viable alternative in some circumstances. They can often provide the expertise and the economies of scale that may be afforded by operating multiple properties.

The National Golf Foundation directory lists nearly 180 management companies; the top 20 firms manage more than 1,300 golf courses, or about 8% of all courses in the United States.

The current economic climate has seen management companies significantly reduce their fees. While a $200,000 annually fee was the previous benchmark, management companies are now assuming operational responsibility for an annual fee of $75,000 plus recoupment of all expenses related to the golf course operation. Should a golf course privatize its operation? To the extent that professional management could increase the net income of the facility by an amount $75,000 greater than is likely to be earned by current management, the switch should be considered. These management fees, like stock market prices, change frequently. In 2011, some management companies are deferring their fees for equity in the facility.

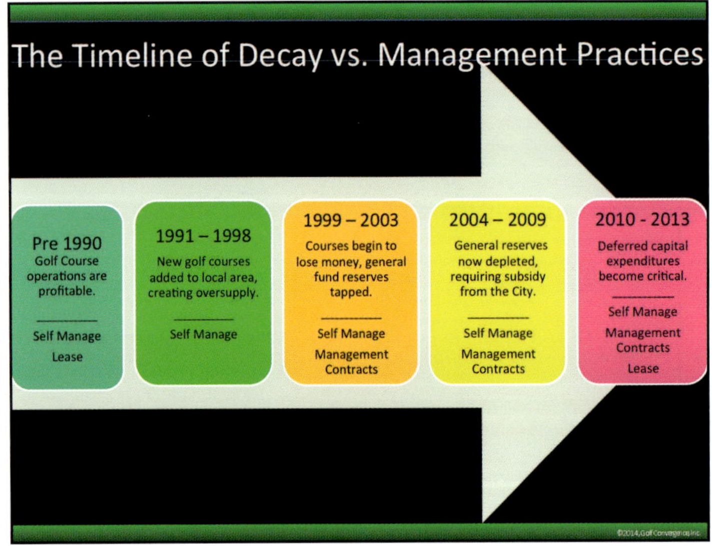

It should be noted that management companies are used not only at municipal golf courses, but also at daily fee courses, resorts, and private clubs. The evolution of self-management vs. the alternative forms of operation are highlighted in chart.

Who Has the Competitive Economic Advantage?

Most business owners appropriately seek a level playing field on which they can fairly compete.

When some private course owners perceive that unfairness exists because they are up against municipally subsidized operations that can offer a similar golf product for less money the disadvantaged can be become vocal and sometimes lose their perspective. Such dissension was on display in an Internet chat forum named Listserv, provided by the NGCOA.

When one course operator wrote:

> ". . . I'm not an attorney but this type of Public Sector competition versus the Private Sector is not only unfair, unethical or dishonest

with relationship to our Capitalistic System in this Country, it may be somewhat illegal."

Nevertheless, in reading the Listserv blog, one could conclude that a sizeable number of NGCOA members disapprove of municipal golf courses. Even if a municipal golf course joins the NGCOA, they are precluded from certain benefits, i.e., participation in state chapter meetings in some locations.

The operation of municipal golf courses can be via a "general fund" or an "enterprise fund." In a general fund, the golf course operation is merely a component of the City's total budget. In an enterprise fund, the golf course operation is accounted for as a separate economic unit. The enterprise fund, used by a (slight) majority of facilities in the United States, is structured as a separate, quasi-independent municipal economic entity in which profits and losses are separately measured and revenues not siphoned into the municipality's general operating budget.

Regardless of the form of business, municipal governments have a clear competitive advantage in the following ways:

1. Profit motivation is not as intense, since many Parks and Recreation activities, such as swimming pools, tennis courts, and soccer fields, are taxpayer supported without the expectation of profit. Many golf courses believe that if they are self-sustaining after depreciation, interest, municipal service charges, and amortization, everybody is happy.
2. They are better insulated from downturns in the business cycle, and they have the ability to reallocate funds, at least on an interim basis, which provides financial flexibility.
3. Many municipal golf courses are located near populated city centers, often because they were built decades ago.
4. Capital is usually easier to access, because the government guarantee ensures its availability. Borrowing is also more economical—underwriting a capital expansion project via a revenue bond nets the municipal golf courses 2% to 4% lower borrowing costs.
5. The land on which the course is situated can be free to the golf course operation.
6. Governments are not obligated to pay property, income, and often sales and alcohol taxes, and these courses benefit from the economies of scale when they purchase insurance coverage for fire, liability, and health.

Similarly, they can buy equipment under favorably negotiated municipal bid contracts. This advantage is minimized by those daily fee course owners who belong to the NGCOA, and its Smart Buy program, in which favorable pricing is negotiated for members.

7. Fees for water, sewer, electric, and gas are usually discounted.
8. Navigating zoning changes and the permitting process may be easier to achieve.
9. Employees are attracted and retained with lucrative fringe benefits such as health and life insurance, annual mandated merit increases, and retirement compensation packages.

Certainly, these advantages realized by a municipal golf course operation are impressive. Over the course of a year, they are worth as much as 15% of gross revenue (or $170,000) as the gross revenue for a municipal golf course averages $1,133,333, with an Earnings Before Interest, Depreciation, Taxes and Amortization of $206,000. Considering that the average daily fee course generates $1,300,000 in revenue with an EBIDTA of $200,000, the $172,667 difference in operating costs ($927,333 for a municipality versus $1,100,000 for a daily fee course) is almost solely attributable to the cost advantages accorded a municipality that are previously described.

That cost comparison might lead the casual observer to conclude that municipalities clearly have an advantage.

However, daily fee brethren have many incorrect perceptions about municipal courses, and operating a golf course in a municipal environment has many significant disadvantages.

First, the **incorrect** perceptions:

1. **Municipal courses intentionally underprice.** Because of their lower cost structure and because the underlying experience of most municipal golf courses is inferior to that of daily fee courses, lower pricing properly reflects the value of the product. For those municipal courses where greater value is accorded, such as Bethpage Black in N.Y., Torrey Pines South in Cal., and Brown Deer in Wisc., the rates are set at comparable levels to nearby daily fee courses for non-residents.

   The pricing of government golf products must be put in line with industry standards for similar facilities and must reflect the actual value created, regardless of the associated cost structure.

2. **Municipalities have the pleasure of responsibility without the accountability for showing a profit.** Many municipal managers may wish that were the case, but it is not.

   From the citizen-based golf advisory councils, to the Director of Parks and Recreation, to the City Manager, to the Mayor and City Council, to the taxpayers who have unlimited access to detailed data regarding the golf course under the Federal Freedom of Information Act, municipal golf courses operate under the full review and observation of everyone.

   Municipal employees are viewed by some as not as qualified as private operators. This perception is inaccurate. Their lives are clearly in the "fish bowl" and they work, on balance, very hard. The perception that a Municipal Golf Director works 40 hours per week could not be more incorrect. Many Directors of Golf and head PGA Professionals are required to attend City Council meetings, and working in excess of 50 hours is not uncommon.

3. **Most courses do not recognize the cost of depreciation.** This is simply not true. While the accounting systems of some municipalities are convoluted and use outdated technology, a detailed analysis will find nearly all golf courses being charged depreciation. In addition, entries for land, building, and developing property are also reflected on nearly all municipal golf course financial statements. While depreciation is booked, cash reserves are not segregated annually; hence, often there is a need to issue a revenue bond.

   Municipalities rarely calculate EBITDA and focus more on a "bottom-line" number.

4. **Municipalities are immune from the invisible hand of capitalism** that rewards those who manage well, and punishes those who underperform, by forcing them to close.

   With the downturn in golf, many municipal golf courses are evaluating their options, including privatization, sale, or transitioning to open park space. You can expect to see the transformation of many golf courses to open park space when the cost to maintain open space is less than the cost to operate the golf course.

   Since 9/11, the priorities of municipal governments are security, utilities, and fire protection. Recreational services have taken a diminished role, and many City Councils are now stating that unless the golf courses are self-supporting, alternatives will be considered.

More alarming than the incorrect perceptions are the many significant and costly disadvantages of operating a municipal course.

First, a municipal golf course has to overcome the brand image of being a "muni." The heyday of municipal golf construction was the Eisenhower years, and many of the buildings and courses look their age. The cost to repair the infrastructure (and the image) nearly equals the cost of building a new golf course.

Other significant disadvantages of municipalities include:

1. **The payroll cost structure is higher than incurred by daily-fee courses;** fringe benefits and retirement packages are mandated for all City employees consistently. With higher labor costs, municipalities are often forced to drastically reduce advertising and marketing.
2. **Labor issues are far stricter.** The process of hiring (job postings, interviews, testing, physical exams, etc.) is cumbersome. Just the negotiation of salary can be a long, tedious process. As for firing someone, it is nearly impossible. With the exception of drug, alcohol, or theft issues, it would take at least six months to terminate an employee for mere non-performance or tardiness.
3. **Where labor unions are present, the problems are exponentially more complex.** Salaries are fixed, overtime rates are double, and work schedules are firm. Maintenance crews, for example, are often limited as to what trees they can trim. Many times other departments of a municipal complex must be scheduled for such work and charge the golf course fully absorbed rates that far exceed what private-sector firms would charge. While daily fee owners may not see these as relevant issues, they truly are a huge challenge.
4. **Rate adjustments take at least 45 days.** Because they operate in a public forum ultimately accountability to the taxpayers, approval is required for all material decisions regarding fees and expenses that exceed a threshold ($15,000 in most cities).
5. **Because of the inflexibility on rates,** Directors of Golf are effectively precluded from engaging in proactively adjusting rates to keep up with changes in demand.
6. **Politics.** The influence of golfers on elected City officials, particularly Commission or Council members, should not be underestimated.
7. **Golfers are taxpayers who frequently demand low-priced season passes, improved conditions, and better service.** If councilmen or mayors balk,

they might find themselves on the wrong end of en election with a vocal and passionate constituency (golfers) campaigning against them.

8. **As a municipality, the course is constantly expected to provide a wide range of services that are not profitable.** Golf camps, youth education programs, and donation of the course for community-sponsored events are frequent distractions.
9. **Procurement is cumbersome, requiring a lengthy bidding process,** and there is no assurance that the best vendor will be selected. A municipal bid takes from 60 days to six months. One city golf course lost its water pump, and it took from September 2006 through July 2007 to replace it. The Superintendent was required to hand-deliver water in the interim because the cost of the item required a public bid.
10. **All of the financial information of a golf course is in the public domain.** One of the competitive advantages of a private business is the ability to mask your revenues and expenses from your customers. Municipalities don't have that luxury.

From the viewpoint of many daily fee owners, municipal golf makes valuable contributions as the entry point for new golfers. One owner wrote,

> "While those functions might compete with privately provided public access in some cases, it does not present the same conflicting threat to the privately owned/financed courses as new or extensively rebuilt municipal courses expressly aimed at the mid and upper levels of the public golf market."

What is clear is that to the extent municipal golf courses provide a basic golf operation at an affordable price, daily fee owners are comfortable. When the municipality expands and provides an extensive array of mid- to high-tier golf, food and beverage, and catering and meeting functions, then the daily fee owner believes the line of fair competition has been crossed. They daily fee owner fails to appreciate the daunting structural limitations of operating within the municipal environment, where the inability to make a decision without protracted review and approval is often crippling.

It is not the golfer's responsibility to ensure the profitability of a business operation. If there isn't a good value/financial balance, then the right business decision is to shut the facility down and have consumers find other places to play where their value point can be met.

Despite Apparent Advantages, Many Municipalities Are Losing Money

Google Alerts is a highly effective tool to monitor the golf course industry. By requesting that e-mails be automatically forwarded on a specific topic, the recipient is kept informed.

Creating a Google Alert for "Golf Courses Losing Money" results in 10 e-mails per day related to the struggle golf courses now face. Most focus on the plight of municipal golf courses because information about municipalities is in the public domain and the focus of the press.

In its October 16, 2012 presentation to the National Park and Recreation Association, the National Golf Foundation adroitly summarized the challenges currently faced by municipal golf courses, citing the following:[2]

- 70% cover operating expenses
- 39% have debt
- 40% cover debt service
- 73% deferring capital improvements

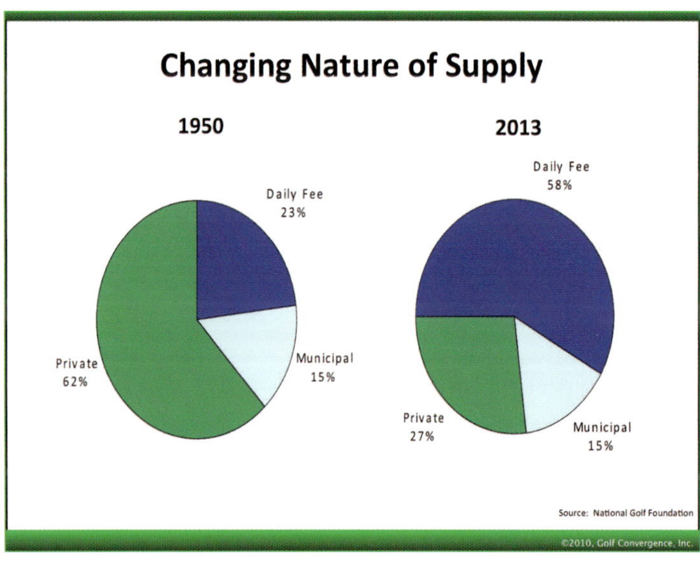

Perhaps the greatest challenge faced by municipal golf courses in 2014 is the accelerating labor costs and associated employment benefits. That begs the question, would you rather own a municipal or daily fee golf course? The answer, based on the reasons previously presented, is clearly daily fee. That preference is becoming increasingly ratified as municipal golf courses transfer management of their facilities to private companies.

2 National Golf Foundation, "Maximizing the Economic Potential Municipal Golf", October 16, 2012, Slide 25.

What About Private Clubs?

It is interesting to note that since 1950, the number of private clubs has shrunk from 62% to 27% of the golf courses in the United States.

It is a surprising statistic but there are fewer private golf clubs in 2014 than there were during the 1931 depression. There has been no growth in that area of the industry in nearly 80 years.

The change in these demographics makes one wonder, "Is the private club destined to become extinct with the changes in society's culture?" The answer is obviously no. Private clubs will always have their niche for social or practical reasons. The buzzwords surrounding a private club—exclusivity, culture, service, familiarity, tradition/history, quality, convenience, consistency—will always be applicable for a certain sector.

The Proper Governance

Historically, private clubs were run by committees. Structured like businesses, the clubs had boards consisting of members from diverse backgrounds and skill sets.

The typical organizational structure of a private club is reflected in the chart:[3]

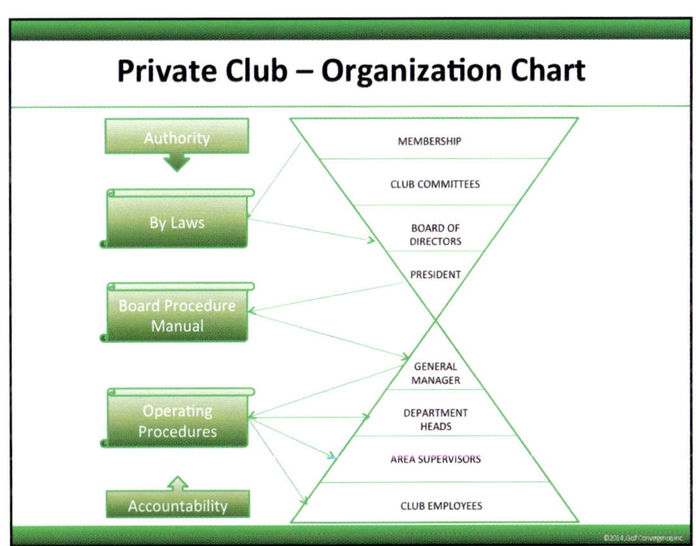

The Cacophony of Chaos

To operate a $4 million enterprise requires a lot of vision, talent, and patience.

Brad Klein, noted journalist and one of the leading professors of golf course architecture, wrote in *Golfweek*, "When it comes to running a private golf club

3 Club Managers Association, *Board Resource Manual*, "Club Organizational Information," Section 2, p. 1.

these days, most boards are overwhelmed. If the politics don't get them, the business demands will."[4]

While each person on a board may, individually, be a delight; collectively, the decision-making process in which they engage can be ineffective.

Klein echoed those sentiments by writing, "The folks who gravitate toward power at a private club tend, in my experience, to be the kind who like to set the agenda. Rarely does the self-selection process of club governance produce decision-makers of moderate temperance and firm wisdom."[5]

Why does this behavior occur? Most people seek consensus rather than discord. Most individuals will compromise their personal positions to achieve group harmony—especially in a country club board setting where they aren't being paid and the meetings often run late. Thus, the aggressive individual can wear down the group, resulting in consistently poor decisions.

For group decisions to be effective, the group must possess three characteristics: they must be diverse, they must be decentralized, and each member must be independent.

What is the perfect board? First, the president of the board should be required to go through the rotation of chairs from secretary (to learn the bylaws), treasurer (to understand the finances), and vice president (to learn the management and operational issues), before becoming president (having developed the vision to lead from years of serving). Second, the board should possess diverse educational background and have skills in the basic business disciplines: accounting, customer service, food and beverage, finance, human relations, and law.

The Delegation of Decision Making

Perfectly run clubs are "benign dictatorships." For a club to run properly, the general manager needs unilateral decision-making power, as long as it is consistent with the policies of the club.

4 Brad Klein, *Golfweek*, "Club politics in era of 'the deal'", January 13, 2007, p. 9.

5 Ibid. 9.

As Klein believes, "Governing boards should do little more than set basic policy, with the details of implementation, operations and rules enforcement in the hands of professionally trained management."[6]

The chart shows the ideal operational structure for a private club.

Private Club Management

Activity	Owner/Board	Management
Budget	Approves	Recommends & Provides Input
Capital Requests	Approves	Prepares Requests
Personnel Policy	Adopts	Recommends & Administers
Mission Statement	Adopts	Implements
Day-to-Day Operations	No Role	Makes All Management Decisions

Form Predicts Substance

For a municipal golf course, the ultimate ranking appears firmly rooted, based on City Council actions dictated by an annual budget. For a golf course that is cash-poor but asset-rich to balance the budget, it will ultimately be required to liquidate assets or privatize services. Since 9/11, the pecking order for the allocation of municipal funds has been entrenched, providing police and fire with the highest priority, with other municipal services competing for the remaining resources.

From a "business of golf" perspective, the daily fee ownership model seems most preferable. Owners make decisions that yield benefits to owners; this is the purest form of capitalism. Resorts are tied into large corporate decision-making models, and private clubs, with their ingrained committee system of member volunteers, can be ineffective.

Regardless of the type of golf course, understanding the market, the customer base and the facility's attributes are essential.

6 Brad Klein, *Golfweek*, "Club politics in era of 'the deal'", January 13, 2007, p. 9.

End Notes

The lessons in this chapter are:

1) Golf courses are considered either public or private. The forms of ownership include municipal, daily fee, semiprivate, resort, private-equity, private non-equity, and military.
2) The number of municipal golf courses and private clubs has remained static since 1931. The vast majority of the growth of the game has come from the growth of daily fee golf courses.
3) Municipal golf courses have four different and conflicting charters regarding the golf operation.
4) Municipal golf courses have three types of management systems: employees, independent leases, or management company contracts.
5) Private clubs offer a haven of refuge to have and make friends.
6) A municipality has, on average, a $172,667 cost advantage over their daily fee brethren.
7) Despite the cost advantage, many municipal golf courses are losing money.

Concluding Thought

You can only change your plan if you have one.

Randy Pausch, *The Last Lecture*

Chapter 5

The Golfer Local Market Analysis

Steps 1 and 2 of Golf Convergence WIN™ Formula

What gets us into trouble is not what we don't know; it's what we know for sure that just ain't so.

Mark Twain

Chapter Highlights

Global issues of the game are wonderful to know, but useless if they don't translate to your local market.

Supply and *demand* are more than buzzwords. Finding where those two graphs intersect in the local market requires looking at eight data points as well as undertaking a golfer local market analysis of age, income, and ethnicity, along with weather as a factor to a course's financial success.

The key rule in local planning is: Know Thy Market. The demographics of your local market are the most important piece of strategic information you can have.

Uncontrollable Factors

In creating a strategic plan, there are many uncontrollable factors. So far, we have ascertained the industry within which golf exists (entertainment and leisure), measured the impact of national supply versus demand, and considered the impact of other factors, including trade associations, equipment manufacturers, and service providers. We also examined which form of ownership provides the greatest competitive advantage.

Quantifying these uncontrollable factors is valuable because the data help us isolate and analyze the extent to which changes in rounds are attributable to uncontrollable influences versus controllable decisions made by boards of directors, owners, senior management and staff.

In this process we have progressed from those factors that have less direct impact on the golf course facility to those influences that more directly shape the strategic vision, the tactical plans, and the operation execution at a golf course.

Perhaps two of the most important uncontrollable factors are the local market supply versus demand and weather. These provide a first opportunity to calculate some benchmarks that will provide insights into the historical performance of the golf course and the likelihood of achieving future financial success.

Golfer Local Market Analysis

The ***first step in the Golf Convergence WIN™ process*** is getting a grip on your local market. While there are a lot of direct and indirect influences, none are more important than:

1. Number of courses in your market (supply)
2. Number of golfers (demand)
    - **a.** Age
    - **b.** Income
    - **c.** Ethnicity
    - **d.** Population density

Supply

To analyze supply, answers are ascertained for the following questions:

1. Competition: How many courses by type and price are in this market?
2. What is the potential for annual rounds?
3. How much are the courses being utilized?
4. What is your market share?

In understanding this analysis, golf courses located within 30 miles of a facility are considered, as 90% of all rounds originate within that radius.

Following is a chart that highlights these factors for five different cities as compiled by Golf Convergence licensing the Tactician and National Golf Foundation databases:

	Atlanta	Denver	Greenville	Pacific Grove	Sioux Falls
Number of Courses Within 30 Miles	102	90	16	29	20
Potential Annual Rounds per Course	84,510	83,560	88,765	100,360	66,670
Potential Rounds within 30 Miles	8,620,020	7,520,400	1,420,240	2,910,440	1,333,400
Actual Rounds Played Locally	3,851,513	4,264,862	432,849	1,100,318	839,365
Utilization	45%	57%	30%	38%	63%
Private Rounds *	18,600	21,000	18,000	28,500	18,850
Public Rounds Daily Fee *	19,228	31,500	22,500	32,500	20,976
Public Rounds Municipal *	**	35,601	28,759	48,000	26,400
Private/Public	51.00%	29.00%	56.00%	24.00%	15.00%
Public Premium: > $70	2	10	0	15	0
Public Value: $40 – $70	28	43	3	4	6
Public Price: <$40	20	11	4	3	11

* Source: PGA PerformanceTrak for Section course located
** Insufficient number of courses reporting.

With respect to supply, this chart confirms that there are many facilities within the competitive reach of each of the cities listed.

Course utilization, which blends components of supply and demand, at the time these figures were obtained, was as low as 30% up to 63%. The utilization numbers for golf are extremely low in comparison to businesses like airlines and hotels, which realize close to 80% utilization. That reflects the oversupply of golf courses in the United States. When considering price, quality, proximity, and accessibility, there are many viable alternatives for golfers. If other geographic areas were evaluated across the United States, the trends would likely be similar.

This chart also reflects the demand curves in these markets are normal. Demand curves should show most rounds played at public-price facilities, then, in descending order, public-value, public-premium, and private clubs as price is the dominant criterion by which value is measured. Markets where public-price rounds are lower than the rounds reported by public-value courses, indicate that the value being offered for the price is less.

Other valuable data points that should be obtained are the number of competitors, types of facilities, and price points within the local market.

Demand

To analyze demand, answers are ascertained for the following questions:

1. How many golfers are in your local market?
2. What is the household income, age, and ethnicity of the population?
3. How many rounds per year do they play?
4. What is the per capita "play rate"?

The chart at the top of the next page summarizes the key statistics for five markets within 10 miles of the client golf course as compiled from the Tactician Corporation database on behalf of Golf Convergence.

These statistics reveal which markets have the underlying demographics conducive for golf (e.g., Sioux Falls), and markets in which operating a golf course could be a challenge (e.g., San Antonio).

To illustrate further, Ann Arbor and Saint Paul have lots of players in an oversupplied market. Thus, price pressures exist. In Sioux Falls, ethnicity and income are strong factors but utilization is low as the population is quite young. In San Antonio, the market is dominated by the Hispanic-American population (who play little golf), and also by low income levels. Finally, in Ocala, price-sensitive senior citizens dominate in a market that is oversupplied with heavy play at the low end. Thus, season passes or constant discounting will create unfavorable economic consequences.

Age, Income, Ethnicity, Frequency

	Ann Arbor	Ocala	San Antonio	Sioux Falls	Saint Paul
Age	93	123	93	93	96
Ethnicity	103	112	69	121	109
Income	106	84	89	112	107
How many rounds per year – frequency	20	27	19	16	19
Per Capital Play Rate – participation rate	13%	9%	7%	16%	14%

Source: Tactician, Inc.

A golf course owner must grasp the local demographics of his or her market to understand the macroeconomic environment in which prices are to be established.

Age

Over 68% of all golf rounds are played by those older than 43 years of age. As has been demonstrated in economic surveys conducted throughout the world, golf thrives in cities where the population is aging.

What is concerning for golf are the statistics that show significant decreases in play among young and mid-range adults as noted in the following table.[1]

Age	Average Rounds/Yr.
18–29	18.6
30–39	18.2
40–49	20.3
50–59	25.9
60–69	40.2
70+	47.6

1 National Golf Foundation, "A Strategic Perspective on the Future of Golf, 2007," p. 7.

Young people play less (no surprise there), while young and mid-range adults ("Gen-Xers") are playing at 50% of the level of the general population. This is due to the emergence of soccer, lacrosse, and extreme sports. This fact doesn't bode well for the future of golf.

Income

Of the three factors of age, income, and ethnicity, income is the biggest predicator of a person's participation in golf.

The fact that golf is an elitist game is clearly demonstrated by a statistic indicating that those with incomes of less than $34,999 play only 3.45 rounds per year while those with incomes greater than $75,000 play 431% more, or 14.89 rounds per year. Golf is clearly lacking in middle-class appeal.

If we apply this lesson to the golfer market local analysis regarding income, in three of these five markets (Ocala and San Antonio being the exception), income is a positive predictor of demand. While the average age in Ocala is 18% older than the national average, that's offset by the fact that the community is 22% poorer than the national average. Thus, in a retirement area, the potential to profit from operating a golf course is a challenge. With respect to San Antonio, both income and ethnicity are factors that suggest that this market is challenging to operate a financial prosperous golf course.

Ethnicity

Golfer Ethnicity Demographics

Ethnic/ Nationality Group	Part. Rate (% of Pop.)	Freq. Rate (rounds/ golfer)	Play Rate (round/ capita)	'07-'12 Pop. Growth Rate
White	11%	21	2.3	4.1%
Black	5%	14	0.7	3.4%
Asian	9%	17	1.6	17.9%
Hispanic	4%	18	0.7	15.5%

Source: Tactician

Determining the ethnic composition within a 10-mile radius of the golf course is important for determining the demand potential for golf rounds. See chart of an ethnic analysis of golfers on the left.

Applying this concept of ethnicity will assist in ascertaining the rounds potential within a local market compared to the national average.

Of the U.S. population ages 6 through 70+ who play golf, only 9% play golf at the frequency of 1.95 rounds of golf per capita per year. In San Antonio, the participation rate is only 7% and the per capita round per year figure is only 1.3. Should the population or frequency rates among local golfers adjust downward, the impact on revenues would be dire. This underscores the importance of understanding your local market.

City of San Antonio Demographics

Ethnicity	Population	Percentage	National	Rounds Played
White	721,346	31.9%	2.2	1,586,961
Hispanic	1,221,701	53.9%	0.7	855,191
Black	118,617	5.2%	0.7	83,032
Asian	34,802	1.5%	1.6	55,683
Other	169,264	7.5%	0.4	67,705
Total Rounds			69	2,348,572
Rounds Potential				69

1) *Inbound tourist rounds* will have to drive any significant increase in golf demand.
2) San Antonio will have to uniquely *educate and introduce* diverse ethnicities to game.

Source: Tactician

Putting It All Together

In undertaking a geographic local market analysis, we need to study supply versus demand as well as facility performance. For example, consider the chart for a statistical profile for the Naperville (Ill.) Park District.

This chart reflects that the potential for golf in Naperville is very healthy as measured solely based on supply versus demand.

Local Supply Characteristics

Category	National Average	30 Minute Drive Time Naperville
Public Golfers per 18 holes	2,250	4,460
Market Over/Under Supply	10% oversupply	18% undersupplied
Private/Public supply	27%/73%	17%/83%
Premium/Value golf	45%/55%	50%/50%
Premium > $61 for green fees plus cart	18%	33%
Value = $45 to $61 for green fees plus cart	32%	39%
Price = < $45 for green fees plus cart	17%	3%

Source: National Golf Foundation

In analyzing the potential growth opportunities for golf within a market, a study of the age, income, and ethnicity of the population within a 30-minute drive time measured against the available supply of golf courses provides valuable. Provides valuable insights.

The chart below for Pacific Grove Golf Links indicates that the Monterey Peninsula and surrounding area is greatly oversupplied based on the demand demographics of golfers residing within the local market. Fortunately, with courses, such as, Pebble Beach, Cypress Point, Monterey Country Club, Spanish Bay and Poppy Hills nearby, the outstanding quality of these courses serves as an effective draw for tourists to more closely balance demand and supply.

Avid Intensity Index

Intensity Index - National	5 Miles	10 Miles	15 Miles	20 Miles	25 Miles	30 Miles	U.S.
Golf Intensity Index	29	34	47	69	101	96	100
Avid Golfers per 18 Holes	112	132	185	269	396	376	392
Private Golf Intensity Index	29	36	53	68	95	107	100
Avid Golfers per Private 18	393	490	722	922	1,286	1,457	1,360
Public Golf Intensity Index	29	33	45	69	104	92	100
Avid per Public 18	157	182	249	380	572	507	550

Note: "100" represents a baseline. The fact that the income, ethnicity, and number of golfers per 18 holes exceed 100 are positive factors that suggest the presence of demographic elements conducive to a successful golf operation.

Supply/Playable Days

The last uncontrollable to be examined is the dramatic impact of weather on a golf operation. The "playable days" statistic is crucial to the management of any course. Measuring this statistic is the ***second step in the Golf Convergence WIN™ process.***

Weather Trends International is one of the leaders in quantifying weather's impact on rounds from the total U.S. market down to the facility level.

Based in the Lehigh Valley (Bethlehem, PA) Weather Trends International's proprietary forecasting technology provides its clients a year-ahead weather forecast with business strategy recommendations by market, by day/week for 720,000 grid points across the globe. Manufacturing and agriculture rely on Weather Trends International for weather intelligence that helps them "manage the weather risk" and improve their strategic planning. Their Weather Impact Analysis (WIA) ties each of golf's 15,619 facilities to more than 1,600 local weather stations and provides key facility measures on weather variance, including season days; golf playable hours; equivalent golf playable days; and capacity rounds in total, by month, and by day of week. The analysis is segregated into 45 regions defined by latitude, elevation, and maritime influence.

A golf playable day measures daylight hours, temperature, precipitation, relative humidity, and wind speed. Among other things, we learn from these studies is that nearly 98% of all golf is played between a temperature range of 43 and 95 degrees.

Some anomalies about the weather have been labeled by industry pundits the "bear/squirrel syndrome." Golfers are more likely to play in adverse conditions in the spring, after their golf hibernation, than in the fall. Often, a day in the spring will generate 40% more rounds than a day with the same weather in the fall.

The first step in measuring the impact of weather is measuring the number of playable days during the past decade. An example is shown here.

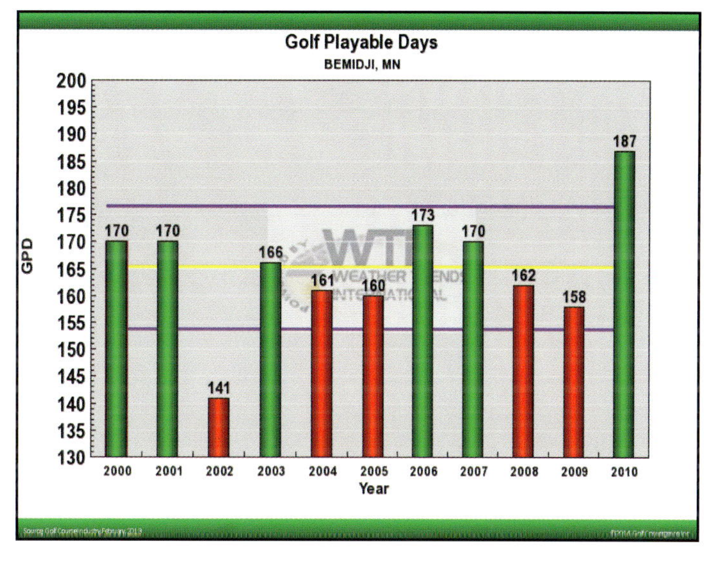

Analysis of the weather, which has not been embraced by industry management veterans, is a valuable index to measure the efficiency of management at a golf course. To illustrate, if a golf course normally has 162 playable days per year but in a given season has 178 playable days, rounds should be up 10%. If rounds are up more than 10%, management should be applauded. If rounds are not up by at least 5%, the quality of management rightly comes under scrutiny.

Following is a chart that measures the under vs. over performance of management eliminating weather as an uncontrollable. Without an examination of the underlying causes, one might attribute it all to weather. Or perhaps a owner manager might attribute the decline solely to poor management performance of the staff. Neither would be accurate.

	Base Averages	2010	Variance	2011	Variance	2012	Variance
Gross Revenue	$1,815,608	$1,975,110	$159,502	$1,730,385	$(85,223)	$1,741,329	$(74,279)
Playable Days (Weather Trends International)	214	219	5	205	(9)	234	20
Revenue Per Playable Day	$8,300	$9,019		$8,441		$7,442	
Revenue Change That Should Have Been Attributable to Weather			$41,502		$(74,704)		$166,008
Under Performance by Management			N/A		($10,519)		($240,287)
Over Performance by Management			$118,000		N/A		N/A

Weather is also an important statistic in calculating the annual potential capacity of rounds so that course utilization can be more accurately determined and benchmarked against industry statistics as illustrated in the chart presented in the section regarding golf course supply.

Presented below is a representative sample of playable days and course capacity in the United States.

Snapshot Across America

City	Days
Ann Arbor	183
Chicago	199
Denver	262
Flagstaff	258
Ocala	301
Sedona	313
St. Paul	184
Virginia Beach	236
Washington, D.C.	231
Winnipeg	167

Source: Golf Course Industry, February, 2013

For example, when the City of Ann Arbor accounted for the number of playable days, it was determined the actual capacity at the local golf courses was 55,392 rounds in 2005 and 54,010 rounds in 2006. When compared to actual rounds played, the course utilization rate at Huron Hills was only 33.3% and at Leslie Park was 43.7%. This compared unfavorably to a national utilization rate of 54.2% that year.

Weather's direct impact on a golf course is obvious. What is not fully understood is the direct correlation between changes in weather and the impact on rounds.

Based on a Weather Trends International scientific historical analysis of proprietary client sales data comparing historical weather trends for all markets, it has learned that if the temperature is 1° warmer on average, rounds will increase by 0.76%. If there is 1 inch of rain, rounds will decrease by 2.2%.

Weather and climate sensitive in industry's account for 1/3 of the US GDP or three trillion dollars. Statistically, year-over-year local weather conditions repeat less than 15% of the time.

For the astute golf operator, it is recommended that one subscribe to the weather reports that are illustrated in this chart.

REPORTS AVAILABLE

Rounds	Heat - Cold
Golf Playable Days - 10 years Average Playable Days by Month Weekend vs. Weekday Playable Days Yearly Playable Rounds (Capacity)	Days >90 Degrees Hot Days by Month Frost Frost Days by Months
Rain	**Statistics**
Days Rained past 10 years Heavy Days – 10 years Average per Month Yearly Total	Spring Last Frost Autumn First Frost First 80 Degree Day First 90 Degree Day First 100 Degree Day Sunrise/Sunset

A fourth example highlights a different challenge. Converting playable golf hours to the available capacity of rounds, weather-adjusted capacity in Saint Paul was 56,809 rounds in 2006 and 57,480 rounds in 2005. The utilization of the golf course was 61.8% [for both years].

The utilization realized at these golf courses lead to the creation of a strategic plan to address the vision, tactical plans, and the associated operational execution.

Positioning Your Golf Course for the Local Market

Understanding the supply and demand characteristics of your local market is the foundation to creating a strategic vision for your golf course.

To illustrate, would a high-end daily fee golf course with green fees in excess of $150 likely prosper in Ocala, Florida? No. The senior citizens, who are predominant, are seeking only a low-priced golf experience as their discretionary income is below national averages.

Is it likely that a golf course offering unlimited season play passes for $550 in a community of 10,000 in which Hispanics comprise 30% of the population would be financially prosperous? The answer is no.

Would a private golf club in the Dallas, Texas, suburbs that was oriented to exclusively serving the Jewish community prosper if within 10 miles of the golf club were there only 950 potential members? As the Columbian Country Club discovered, the answer is no. The club rebranded itself at the

Honors Club—Dallas and is seeking members with diverse religious affiliations successfully.

Therefore, each golf course facility in creating a strategic plan must understand thoroughly the local market in which it competes.

End Notes

The lessons of this chapter are:

1) A golfer local market analysis is part of the essential 1st step on the critical path of creating a dynamic strategic plan.
2) The essential variables that a golf course owner must understand within a 15-mile drive radius of his or her course is:
   a. The number of courses (supply)
   b. The number of golfers (demand)
      i. Age
      ii. Income
      iii. Ethnicity
      iv. Population Density
3) Currently 68% of all golf rounds are played by those over 43.
4) The "playable days" statistic is crucial to identifying the effectiveness of the management of any course. Measuring playable days is the 2nd step on the critical path of maximizing your financial return from a golf course.
5) There is great potential to position a golf course correctly based on proper brand image, as well as using pricing that is based on a local market analysis.
6) A golf course is a business; if it can't generate a profit, the highest and best use for the land should be found.

Concluding Thought

To become different from what we are, we must have some awareness of what we are.

Eric Hoffer

Chapter 6

The Strategic Planning Summary

A wise man recognizes the convenience of a general statement, but he bows to the authority of a particular fact.

Ralph Waldo Emerson

Chapter Overview

Section 1 of *The Business of Golf—What Are You Thinking?* concludes with some philosophical musings about the future opportunities and challenges in the golf business.

In this chapter, we apply the lessons learned from our overview of the business to provide golf course operators some insights on how to measure the potential of their business. Benchmarks are listed.

The final step is creating vision and mission statements. Examples are provided from both municipal and private golf clubs.

The Value Created

Value in golf derives from two basic components that all golf courses share: there's the physical infrastructure—property, plant, and equipment (the course, the clubhouse, and maintenance equipment); and there's the human element—the personnel. How these resources are applied determines the experience created. To the extent that the experience exceeds the price, value is created and customer loyalty developed. Conversely, to the extent that the price exceeds the experience created, value is squandered and customer attrition occurs.

A strategic plan offers a way to examine the gap between the facility's potential and its actual performance. There are several ways to calculate this gap.

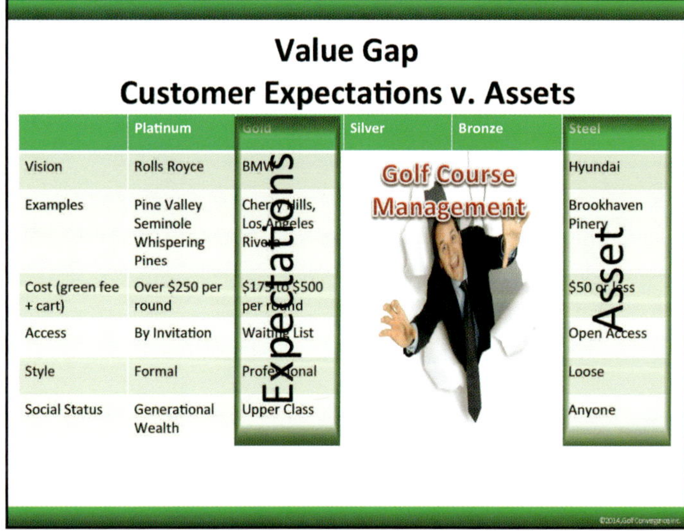

First, the expectation of the customer can be compared to the asset base. To the extent that they are divergent, challenges are raised, as the chart highlights.

To review, criteria that define customer expectations might include whether the course is ranked in national magazines, the architect, championships hosted, slope, conditioning, cart policies, amenities provided, customer touch points, cell phone usage, dress code, smoking, other activities, use of computers, tipping policies, gift policies, whether reciprocity is granted, gender/ethnicity barrier whether express or implied, whether members hold multiple memberships at other clubs, and whether the facility attract individuals who are first-time members or golfers.

As we will discuss in Chapter 8, The Key Financial Metrics, the investment made in the golf course serves as the asset base from which revenue is generated. Personnel costs, maintenance expenditures, and capital expenditures must be covered by the revenue generated from green fees, carts, merchandise, food and beverage, range, lessons, and other income.

The stratification of the investment return that golf courses generate from their assets is summarized in the following chart.

All Facility Types: What's Possible

	Platinum Top 10%	Gold Top 25%	Silver Median	Steel Bottom 25%
Rounds Played	42,000	32,000	23,000	16,192
Full Time Employees	54	28	12	6
Total Revenues	4,513,779	2,600,000	1,371,519	750,000
Green Fees	985,000	543,000	250,000	131,056
Cart Fees	389,000	258,616	170,000	100,000
Merchandise	365,000	225,000	125,000	66,847
Golf Shop Salaries	421,564	289,232	184,950	116,295
Maintenance Salaries	650,000	450,000	272,507	150,000
Maintenance Expenses	650,000	400,000	234,400	142,501
EBITDA	1,396,733	671,910	226,000	75,270`

Source: 2012 PGA Performance Trak Annual Operating Survey Conducted in 2013

We often forget that the ability of a golf course to create a customer experience is predicated on the assets available. While some personnel may be more creative or efficient, or better able to invest surplus time, on balance, the availability of capital to invest in assets or personnel largely influences the experience delivered.

Thus, to the extent the customers have the expectation of experiencing a "gold-level" course that only generates "steel-level" revenues, this gap will be problematic as operating losses are likely from providing superior value in excess of the price charged. The formula by which a course can be measured is simple: value = experience – price. To the extent that experience exceeds price, there is the possibility for success. To the extent that price exceeds the experience, customer attrition is very likely.

A second tool to assess the golf club's current state of affairs is through the examination of benchmarks.

Rounds are one of the basic benchmarks for the operation of a golf course. We have learned that local demand versus supply and the weather are uncontrollable factors that directly influence the success of a golf operation. By measuring these benchmarks, the overall value of a golf course can be determined. The formula is rounds + market supply + weather = value.

Presented in chart on the next page are additional examples of how a golf course can calculate the value provided to its customers relative to the competition.

To illustrate, rounds for the City of Ann Arbor were down 40% over five years. Twenty-five percent of that decline could be attributed to an oversupply of golf courses in its local market. Four percent of that decline could be attributed

The Summary Analysis

	Ann Arbor		Naperville		Sioux Falls		Saint Paul	
Category	Impact	Amount	Impact	Amount	Impact	Amount	Impact	Amount
Rounds	Decrease	40%	Decrease	12%	Decrease	33%	Decrease	19%
Market Supply	Adverse	25%	Positive	18%	Adverse	32%	Adverse	16%
Weather	Adverse	4%	Adverse	5%	Positive	8%	Positive	2%
Value	Adverse	11%	Adverse	25%	Adverse	9%	Adverse	5%

to adverse weather, reducing the number of playable days over that same period of time. Thus, 40% – 25% – 4% produces a value of 11. Thus, the fees charged and the overall experience provided were 11% higher than the value provided.

This guidepost is the foundation for the creation of a strategic plan. By providing a written document that defines the golf course's future direction, it becomes a beacon on which ownership, the golfers, and management and staff can align what the value proposition is for the facility.

Vision and Mission Statements

As a written document, a strategic plan provides a consensus for future direction, one that can be measured and evaluated.

Without a defined strategic vision effective tactical plans cannot be developed. Without tactical plans, efficient operational execution cannot occur. The result of this lack of strategic planning is highly predictable—policies, procedures, and practices become based on the ever-changing whims of the owner, management, staff, or upon the influences created by golfers. Management and staff, as best they might, will only respond to the latest self-imposed crisis or artificially defined priority. As the saying goes, "Vision without action is a daydream. Action without vision is a nightmare." Either way, chaos ensues.

The success of the storied golf clubs of the world all have one thing in common: a rigid discipline to adhere to the strategic vision for the club. This same discipline also can be applied to public golf courses. Thus, in crafting this strategic plan, a broad vision of the bold initiatives that must first be established is emphasized; this gains the upper hand over a more chaotic management style involving an intense, meticulous focus on details that overwhelm and become difficult to consistently execute.

The centerpieces of a strategic plan are the vision and mission statements that guide all decisions regarding the operation of the facility. A vision statement is a declarative statement as to why the facility exists and its goals for the future. A mission statement is a description of the guiding principles.

The vision statement is perhaps the most fundamental of all of elements in strategic planning. Dr. Ed. Merritt, an expert on strategic planning, states, "the Vision Statement is future-oriented and identifies what the facility is about—its purpose for being as well as where it is heading. Infusing the club with a definite sense of purpose, vision states a direction and describes the destination."[1]

The Park District's Vision Statement

We will provide, in a responsible fiscal manner, as a recreational component of our leisure programs, golf consistent with the standards of the leading municipalities with respect to green fees, maintenance, and administrative operations in order that we maximize revenue, increase operational efficiency, and ensure optimum customer service as prudent stewards of a government-owned asset.

An example of a vision statement for a municipal golf course is depicted here.

The strength of the vision statement, which is about ideals and not the current environment, is that the golf course knows what it represents and, just as importantly, what it does not. By defining its vision, the club has the ability to align its infrastructure, facilities, and labor resources to match the service ideals envisioned.

The Private Club Vision Statement

(Name Withheld) Golf Club will offer an innovative and exclusive international private club experience that will represent the finest quality, service and reputation in Asia. Continuously on the progressive edge, the club will be proactive in developing member loyalty and enhancing their lifestyle furthering worldwide prestige while preserving the tradition and history of the game.

Shown here is the vision statement for a private club in Asia whose owner sought to create a club with an international membership

1 Dr. Edward A. Merritt, "Leading the Strategic Planning Process," *Premier Club Services*, p. 8.

that serves as an example of the finest that this developing country could provide on the world stage.

From this statement, the vision of the facility clearly focuses on:

- Exclusive
- Finest array of recreation and leisure centered on golf
- Respectful, unparalleled service
- Focused differentiation

The vision statements can be very short. For example, "the finest public links course on the Monterey Peninsula" would suffice for the Pacific Grove Golf Links. For the City of Grand Rapids' Indian Trails Golf Course, "The entry door to the game where family and friends enjoy value-based recreation" is appropriate.

The connection between vision and operation is captured with the facility's mission statement, which defines "the highest level goals and objectives. A written mission statement includes not only the facility's vision and purpose, but also the basic services that the club provides."[2]

The Private Club Mission Statement

Blending the rich history of Chinese culture, (Name Withheld) Golf Club will embrace international operating philosophies and provide members and their guests an exclusive haven to participate in an experience comparable to the most prestigious clubs in the world. Members are responsible to support the club and respect the staff, while five-star diamond service will be the cornerstone of the club operation.

Thus, an appropriate mission statement for this Asian private club is shown here.

Once created, the club's "mission statement should be used everywhere to communicate and reinforce the vision and to remind the golf course community—owners, management, staff, members or golfers, and vendors—why the facility exists

2 Ibid, p. 16.

3 Ibid, p. 16.

and what basic services it provides."[3] It clarifies who is the likely customer, at what level they are to be served, and what facilities and services are to be provided.

The communication of the mission statement and management's expectations should be summarized on a small card that is carried within the wallet of each employee. Such is done at The BRO^ADMOOR Hotel in Colorado Springs, Colorado, which has the very clear mission statement, "Above and Beyond Guest Expectations." The card that each employee carries includes its 16 guidelines for interaction with guests:[4]

1. Make eye contact, smile, and greet the guest or employee immediately.
2. Use the guest's or employee's name.
3. Escort guests or employees to their requested location when possible.
4. Immediately approach a guest or employee who seems to be lost and offer assistance.
5. Learn what is expected from your department so you can anticipate the needs of the guests and employees you service.
6. Follow up on requests, even when it is not a duty of your department.
7. Never say: "I don't know." Say: "I'll find out."
8. Never appear hurried, even if you are very busy.
9. If unable to comply with a guest's wishes, offer an alternative. Avoid negative expressions like: "That's against hotel policy," or "This is not my table."
10. Keep The BRO^ADMOOR spotless! If you see something that's out of place, pick it up! Remember, we are all part of The BRO^ADMOOR Beautification Committee.
11. Act professional in public areas at all times. Stand erect and avoid leaning against walls or furniture.
12. Always recommend The BRO^ADMOOR restaurants and shops to our guests before suggesting other alternatives.
13. Take "ownership" of a guest's problem. Ensure the matter is resolved and that the guest is satisfied with your solution.

4 The BRO^ADMOOR Management, "Exceptional Services Begins with Exceptional People."

14. Respond to a guest's request within 10 minutes.
15. Know the services the Hotel offers and the location of the banquet facilities and meeting rooms.
16. Go the extra mile!

Goals and Objectives

"Goals focus on a future that a club strives to achieve. The strategic vision of the club translates into performance targets through goal-creation."[5] As objectives, goals are evidence of the commitment by management to achieve specific outcomes or particular results within defined periods of time: short-term (1 year), mid-term (5 years) and long term (10 years).

History, tradition, and culture are difficult to create. None of them can be created through capital investment alone. They all must evolve over time through a meticulous set of standards that remain consistently implemented and often are very elusive to all except for the very discerning.

Thus, the importance of strategic planning.

5 Dr. Edward A. Merritt, "Leading the Strategic Planning Process," *Premier Club Services*, p. 16.

End Notes

The lessons of this chapter are:

1) Expectations of the customer must be measured against the assets available to create the experience desired.
2) The formula by which a golf course can be measured is simple: value = experience – price. To the extent that experience exceeds price, there is the possibility for success. To the extent that price exceeds the experience, customer attrition is very likely.
3) To maximize the investment potential of a golf course, vision and mission statements provide the clarity of focus that the ownership, management, staff, and golfers can understand, appreciate, and collectively achieve.
4) A vision statemcnt is the ability to foresee what is going to happen and to create a mental image of what we want to happen in the future. A mission statement simply describes why the golf course exists.

Many facilities exist with the vision and mission statements implied but not expressed. As a written document, a strategic plan provides a consensus future direction, which can be measured and evaluated. Without one, the results will be unpredictable.

Concluding Thought

It seemed rather incongruous that in a society of super sophisticated communication, we often suffer from a shortage of listeners.

Erma Bombeck

SECTION 2

Tactical Planning
Chapters 7 through 11

Tactical planning is considered the process of creating actionable goals that will be accomplished from today up to three years into the future that are aligned with the strategic vision. Thus, in Section 2, we are going to cover the following:

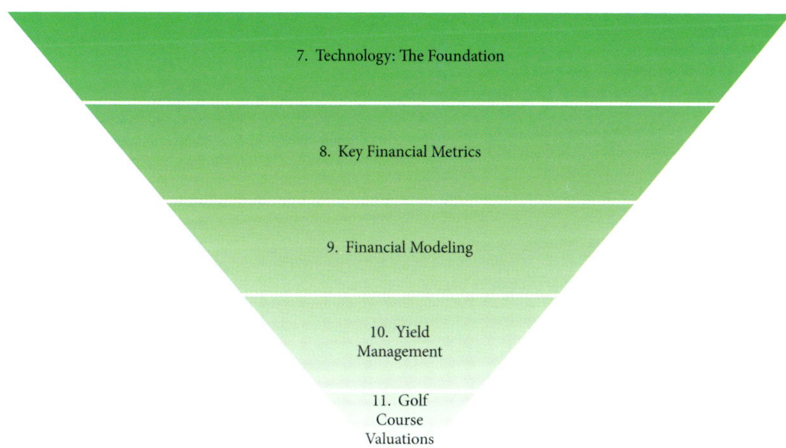

This entails an understanding of the components beyond daily golf operations that determine success in the golf market: technology, key metrics, financial modeling, yield management principles, and proper golf course valuation. Embracing these concepts is essential for the investment return of a golf course to be realized.

Perfect markets do not exist in the world. Capitalism is simply the smart understanding of dislocations and taking advantage of the lazy who are unable or unwilling to search for the competitive advantages.

Unknown

Chapter 7

Technology—The Foundation

Step 3 of Golf Convergence WIN™ Formula

Look, there's always going to be somebody to complain about something.

Robert De Niro[1]

Chapter Highlights

Technology is the foundation for meaningful proactive management, and it is the first chapter on tactical planning.

The foundation of every successful golf course is a technology platform that seamlessly integrates the elements of all profit centers into a streamlined information and reporting system that managers can proactively manage based on current financial data.

This chapter presents a model of how to select technology and provides templates of Requests for Proposals. Interestingly, vendors, though they serve clients, often lack the willingness to foster the best business interests of their clients and have adversely impacted the ability of their clients to transact business smoothly by refusing to integrate with other software applications. These dilemmas with possible solutions are explored.

Understanding the role of technology is important because software systems produce the numbers in which an adept manager can increase revenue and control expenses.

Core Fundamentals

How would a football, hockey, soccer, or basketball game be played if there were no goalposts or nets? Without goals, there is no game. The same applies for business; without a goal there is no way to measure how effectively you are managing the business.

The financial statements of a business are the instruments by which a business is managed. As a plane is not flown without instruments, a business shall not be operated without precise guidelines as to financial goals. The technology implemented serves as the foundation for the creation of accurate financial statements and is the ***third step in the Golf Convergence WIN™ process.***

The easiest way to create meaningful financial information is through the acquisition, implementation, annual training, and constant upgrade of a fully integrated golf management system.

Golf course owners can generate value from a computer in many ways, including:

Objective	Result
Better Control	Uniform policies consistently applied. If the choice is to improve decision making at a staff level, a computer is a good answer.
Security	Monitor theft and control price changes.
Better Data Collection	From information comes the power to manage.
Accessibility	Access to data when you need it and wherever you are.
Customer Demographics	Increase customer share in relation to market share.
Open to Buy	Optimize inventory turnover while minimizing cash investment.
Yield Management	Optimize revenue per tee time.

It is important to understand that technology is merely a tool whose investment return should be measured.

Many outstanding golf management software solutions are available today. They are vastly different, yet nearly all meet the requirements of courses to provide an attractive rate of return on investment. Active Network, Club Prophet, EZ Links, Fore Reservations, IBS, and Jonas products all provide a superior product for their defined niches within the marketplace.

1 Robert De Niro, Travel and Lesure.com, June 2008, p. 101.

While other firms in the golf software market will come and go given that the barriers for entry into this niche are low, selecting a leading vendor is warranted.

The Challenges Are Many

Surprisingly, golf course owners believe that having the tools to establish an effective technology strategy requires a five-figure investment per facility. In fact, a low four-figure investment is often sufficient: in the golf technology field, more expensive isn't always better.

Geoffrey Moore, in his book *Crossing the Chasm*, classifies buyers and the pace at which they adopt new technology into five distinct groups:[2]

Innovators, representing 2.5% of the population, are the first people to adopt any new technology, and they are the first to appreciate the technology for its own sake. Being technology enthusiasts, they want access to the most technically knowledgeable person; they want to get the new stuff first, in spite of the known inconveniences they are likely to suffer.

Early Adopters, representing 13.5% of the population, are the rare breed of people who have the insight to match an emerging technology to a strategic opportunity. The core of their dream is a business goal, not a technology goal. Visionaries are not just looking for improvement; they are looking for a fundamental breakthrough.

The Early Majority, representing 34% of the population, are the pragmatists seeking productivity improvements for their existing operations. They are change agents seeking to get a jump on the competition, whether from lower product costs, faster time to market, more complete customer service, or some other comparable business advantage.

The Late Majority, representing 34% of the population, are conservatives who are against discontinuous innovation. They seek tradition more than progress. Having a slight fear of high tech, the late majority tends to invest only at the end of a technology life cycle, when products are extremely mature, market-share competition has driven prices low, and the products themselves can be treated as commodities.

Laggards, representing 16% of the population, find committing to a new system is a much greater act of faith than they imagined. For a vendor, selling to this segment is a shaky venture at best.

2 Geoffrey A. Moore, "*Crossing the Chasm*," (New York, Harper Business, 1999), p. 17.

Golf course owners are slow to accept and adapt to change and are considered to be lagging consumers of technology. For a software firm, the sales cycle is very long, averaging six to nine months. Course managers, overwhelmed with many choices, typically elect to do nothing.

The complexity of business rules compounds this confusion. No two golf course facilities operate with the same set of procedures. Rate structures, access policies, and operating formats vary at each facility. Therefore, they each desire the software vendor to tailor the solution to conform to their existing business rules. Trying to develop and support all of the required software changes often proves too complex and expensive.

It is always amazing to me how a single golf course manager can dictate to a software vendor the necessity for extensive customization of a software package to conform to the business practices at that course, even though the vendor's software product has been successfully installed on more than 400 golf courses. Rather than using the best practices of their peers, managers in many cases refuse to change their habits, policies, and procedures when adopting an integrated system.

The implementation of an integrated golf management system is essential, however, if a facility seeks even a remote chance of optimizing net income. As Bill Gates said more than five years ago:

> "Continuous improvement is the essential nature of technology, especially in a capitalist society, and paying for it is a necessary part of evolution. Complaining about the ongoing cost of technology is like disliking water because it's wet. Technology can't sit still or stay static any more than science or business can. And, like it or not, the technological advances that will ultimately transform the way we live and work are just beginning, so people should get used to paying for them."[3]

However, despite the benefits, which far outweigh the cost of an integrated system, the installation of the integrated system is always met with understandable resistance from the staff:

1. Individuals are already "at capacity" in a zero-sum game.
2. The volume of information available is paralyzing.

3 Bill Gates, http://www.brainyquote.com/quotes/authors/b/bill_gates_2.html.

3. Humans value routine.
4. Despite the merit of an innovation, most people will not readily adopt it if they have to change habits.
5. Staff who are intimidated by their lack of technical knowledge become aggressive and claim the software is flawed or lacks support.

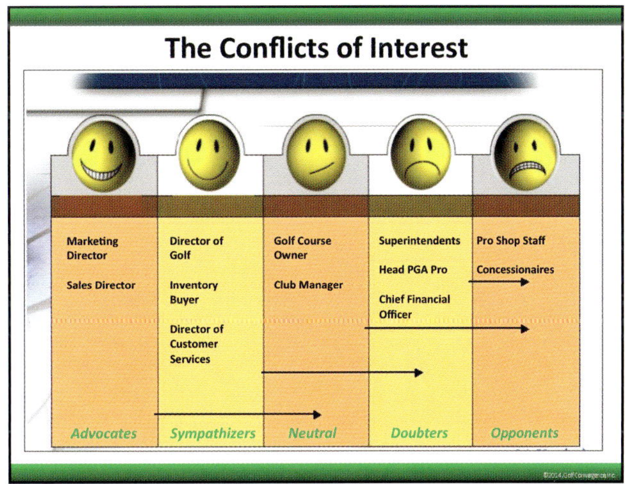

Within a golf course hierarchy, the advocates and opponents for implementing a system can usually be categorized according to their level of responsibility, as depicted on this page.

As a result of this internal dissension as to what functionality is required and what vendor should be selected, many purchase decisions are made on the basis of the recommendations of friends, the brand image of the vendor, proximity of the vendor to the golf course, technical support, or price.

Rarely is the actual functionality of the software the real deciding factor. Often the decision makers can't accurately differentiate one software product from another. The look and feel seem to have a far greater weight in the decision than the actual capability of the product.

Why? Having multiple proposals by multiple presenters to multiple decision makers creates a process that often leads to wrong choices when golf courses choose software vendors.

When a customer can't differentiate between products, price or friendship unfortunately become the criterion on which a decision usually is made.

Impeding Yourself While Being Impaled

Golf courses succumb to many faulty practices that preclude effective marketing. Because of their previous investment in legacy hardware and software, many golf course operators try to make the existing system work when the optimal solution is to start over.

Other challenges frequently seen include:

1. A golf course has disparate technology from different vendors that isn't integrated.
2. Some management companies use multiple vendors for a diverse array of their courses.
3. A golf course uses only certain components of a comprehensive solution in an attempt to save money.
4. A golf course selects an integrated golf management system that does not uniquely and automatically create a customer access unique number. This is a fundamental requirement to tie a tee time reservation to a point of sale transaction for a specific customer. Lacking this integration, all transactions are dumped into a single omnibus account.
5. Golf course staff are not required to or don't capture salient customer information.

Some of the challenges facing golf courses are increased by their software vendor. Many vendors lack the ability, and in some cases are outright unwilling, to work with other service providers to create the integration tools necessary to serve their common client. The territorial nature of software firms seems to be prevalent for a couple of understandable but unsustainable reasons:

1. Many of the providers sell competitive products and want to encourage end-to-end solutions of their own products.
2. Integration to a third-party vendor requires work for which direct compensation is rare.
3. An inherent belief that their own software creates the information required for meaningful analysis prevents firms from being flexible enough.

Software vendors are small businesses. They are very protective of their client bases and often loathe integrating with third-party vendors, especially if the third-party vendor has comparable software modules.

When golf course personnel are technologically phobic, the introduction of a golf management system creates inherent resistance. Those who reject change cite costs, the inability to train staff, and objections to abandoning the human touch of customer service. But the adoption of a comprehensive golf management system, when properly implemented, will increase the net income of a golf course by approximately $25,000 annually.

The Ideal Data Flow

The contents of five modules are needed to create an effective customer relationship program. For golf, the ideal system will have the following components: 1) web site, 2) electronic tee sheet, 3) customer database, 4) a customer relationship management system, and 5) a broadcast e-mail system linked together as depicted here.

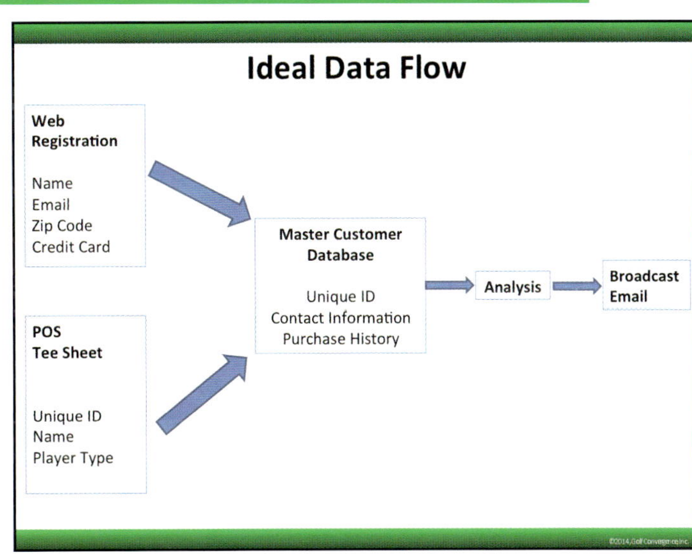

A truly useful software system will provide golfers with the ability to either self-register on the Web, or to be registered by staff personnel.

Because there are many customers who may be one-time visitors at a municipal, daily fee, or resort golf course, many golf course managers don't have a compelling desire to register all customers. However, it can and should be done. We have observed that the best golf courses may capture up to 95% of customer names and e-mail addresses but capture only 60% of the transactions but not beginning the POS process by linking the customer's name to the transaction. Merely gathering the e-mail address allows you to know who your customers are. Tracking the transaction data provides insight as to how much revenue each customer generates.

The electronic tee sheet is the basic building block of a well-designed customer relationship management system. Each golfer should be registered by the day of play and time of day. When the golfer or the employee clicks to process the transaction, the POS system automatically calculates the correct green fee for that golfer by category, day of week, and time of day. Most people don't realize that a golf course may have more than 75 different rates. The POS system that processes the cart, merchandise, and other items creates a unified customer record.

Without the integration of these systems, a repository of meaningful customer information (i.e., customer spending, inventory turns, accurate round statistics by golfer type, or the ability to ascertain statistical course utilization as measured by revenue per round or revenue per available tee time) is not created. In which case, it's also lost as a potential resource for future management.

By amassing a customer database of meaningful information, customer loyalty can be created. The by-product is that the golf course derives the following benefits:

- Maximized Revenue
  - Web-based marketing presence for national exposure
  - Reservation cards sold for premium access
  - Dynamic yield management
- Increased Operational Efficiency
  - Better internal control
  - Improved reporting
  - Elimination of repetitive tasks by staff
- Enhanced Customer Service
  - 24-hour access to tee-time reservations
  - E-mail communication of promotions, tournaments, updates
  - Sell prepaid gift cards online

The vision of integrated technology in the golf industry is not a question of "if"; it's a matter of "when." The benefits of leveraging the fundamental power of technology are too great for the golf industry to ignore. This movement will be accelerated when golf courses demand that software vendors make it happen and require, as part of their software license agreements, that vendors integrate the course owners' required solutions. This provision is now silent in all software licensing agreements between vendors and golf courses. It may even require a few facilities switching POS providers from the inflexible to the more flexible. Without full integration of the essential components, golf course management is at a disadvantage in engaging in meaningful customer relationship management. The ultimate ability of an integrated solution to drive higher revenue and provide competitive advantage is too great to be constrained by the efforts of the service providers to "protect their turf."

When integration occurs, the sophistication and affordability of the tools will erase one of the historical advantages that large management companies had possessed over daily fee operators in having superior financial and customer information by which to effectively manage.

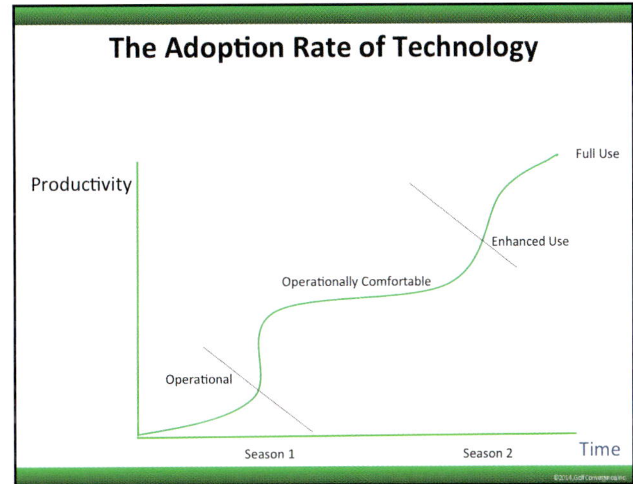

There is a caution: The expectation to achieve the benefits of a fully integrated golf management system will take longer than you hope. The chart seen here highlights the normal rate of adoption and acceptance of a new system.

Golf course personnel tend to go through four phases as they learn new software:

1. Unconsciously incompetent—don't know what they don't know. (35%)
2. Consciously incompetent—frustration, anger, and finger pointing during which the individual blames others for their failure to accept accountability or responsibility for their plight. (40%)
3. Consciously competent—basic skills are learned and used. (20%)
4. Unconsciously competent—use of the product is second nature, and all features are used. (5%)

These percentages reflect the competency of staff at any point in time in using a golf management system.

Selecting the Right System

For a golf course to select the proper vendor, it is vital to understand that the acquisition process involves three steps:

1. Issuing a Request for Proposal
2. Web-based online demonstration
3. On-site demonstration

Request for Proposal

This step is easy to skip, but would you construct a building without blueprints? A software system will be an integral part of your operation for at least five years, and the purchase should be carefully contemplated.

In 2014, the watchword is "simplicity." In today's society, we are overwhelmed by e-mail, voice mail, media, sales hype, and the diminished lines of delineation between home and work.

The fundamental question a golf course owner or manager should ask is, "How does my investment in their product increase the net income of a golf course?" The golf course manager must be able to answer that question in fewer than 50 words before selecting the vendor.

Requests for Proposals that are brief, focused, and clearly presented will differentiate your course from most others and will help the vendor ascertain how the unique features of its software can be leveraged by your course.

An RFP, to attract the interest of a vendor, should be less than 12 pages.

Look for a software firm that, in responding to the RFP, clearly differentiates its strengths, identifies how its software best matches the unique operational requirements of your facility, and provides examples of how its solution will generate a positive return on investment. Examples that the vendor is focused on your operation include:

- Training

  "With turnover at your golf course nearing 40% annually with seasonal hiring, keeping the staff trained in the full use of the software is difficult. While our software is intuitive, we provide a Web-based training course at the beginning of each golf season for your staff.

  Also, we are empathetic that the daily pressures of operation limit the time available to yourself as the general manager and your staff to effectively manage the tee sheet and implement timely and creative proactive marketing programs.

  Our solution provides an answer for this dilemma. Our forecasting tools, which integrate with the NGCOA benchmark program and PGA PerformanceTrak, facilitate adjusting your policies dynamically. Our consulting services will guide you to ensure that your revenue is maximized."

- Unique Requirements

  "Your proposal identifies three specific requirements as your most important criteria in selecting a new firm:

  1. Ability to host a private label Web site,
  2. Integration to an accounting system, and
  3. The ability engage in customer relationship marketing.

  Of our X,XXX customers, we fulfilled this exact requirement for XXX of our clients. You can witness the benefits of this solution at XX golf courses that use our software within 30 miles of your course."

- Dynamic Return on Investment

  "Today's leading golf course operators are leveraging the benefits of current software solutions to maximize revenue by ensuring a heightened customer experience. Online reservations, e-mail marketing, social networking, wireless services in the clubhouse, and according recognition to loyal customers are just a few of software services being adopted today by our clients.

  We look forward to implementing these tools on your behalf, which will reduce labor expenses in handling reservations and provide instant identification of your best customers. We believe that an investment in our software will produce a demonstrable return of $25,000 next year in incremental income."

Favor vendors that limit their proposal to a one-page summary of the "exact" investment required by the course and a few appendices that list the modules available, provide pictures of key screens, and provide references from golf courses in the immediate geographic area.

On-Line Web-Based Demonstrations

Requesting on-line Web-based demonstrations will quickly filter the number of responses to a short list of qualified vendors.

While on-line Web-based demonstrations are a great tool, their use comes with some risk. While these tools herald the ability of remote users to get quickly connected, the average time expended by the golf course staff to link four remote computers with the vendor can approach 10 minutes. Additionally, some course staff personnel are "intimidated" by this process, and walking them through connecting, logging in, and joining the session can create tension.

A second risk is that the software screen being presented by the vendor is out of sync with the viewer's monitor. Golf course personnel will rarely comment when the presenter is describing features that are not displayed on their screen. The predictable reaction of the staff usually is, "Their software is confusing. I could never find what the presenter was discussing; the product must be hard to learn." Amazing how a wrong conclusion is quickly reached.

The expression that "a picture is worth a thousand words" is exemplified by these demonstrations. A Web-based demo is like window shopping. The course personnel can quickly identify their likes and dislikes without getting involved in many details.

On-Site Presentations

Creating a long circus-like parade of vendors is a disservice to your staff and disrespectful to the vendors who are investing their time and financial resources in the hope of making a net profit of no more than several thousand dollars over the first couple of years. On-site demonstrations are a bad deal for software vendors.

The key determinant usually measured by the staff during an on-site presentation is the depth, breadth, and ease of perceived use of the software. Scoring of the on-site presentation is similar to that of ice skating. The evaluation of a presentation is almost always measured by how few mistakes the presenters make. This is sad but true. Corporate PowerPoint presentations, reports, and marketing literature are rarely a factor as to the golf course staff. Such information all looks comparable.

Before the presentation, the vendor should distribute the following material to the audience:

1. Agenda as to what will be presented in sequence by functional area.
2. Key reports printed in advance. The operative word is "key." Having a binder with about 10 reports (tee sheet, daily close, yield forecast, etc.) is very effective.
3. A list of clients within 30 miles of the course, if possible, including contact name, phone number, and e-mail address.
4. Having a clear description of how the software is "priced" is important. Vendors use many different pricing models: (a) licensing simply based on the number of courses; (b) number of workstations installed; (c) number of employees accessing the workstations; (d) fixed monthly fee; and (e) number of reservations booked. With so many different pricing modules, course personnel can become confused.
5. "Scoring sheet" for the staff.
6. Form for people to write questions without interrupting the flow of the presenter.

The RFP process is debilitating to vendors; they are customarily treated like cattle and grouped in a herd. Showing concern and compassion for vendors is important if a solid professional relationship is to be built.

The Future of Technology Holds Change

Golf courses, once having selected a vendor, rarely change software providers. Thus, the initial decision is important.

Software is constantly evolving. Golf courses are advised to plan for annual upgrades of their software, usually embedded for free during the off-season with an annual support contract from most vendors.

What new features are likely to be seen in the next five years?

1. The adoption of Twitter/Facebook by golf courses.
2. Text message confirmation of tee time reservations, i-Phone and other mobile applications.
3. Number of "access points" to the tee sheets will be increased via kiosks and Internet—both course-operated and public Web sites.
4. Tee time auctions led by independent third parties such as Golfnow.com will become commonplace.
5. The NGCOA and PGA PerformanceTrak database repositories will grow.
6. Simplified yield management systems will automatically adjust course green fee pricing based on demand.
7. Customer survey tools will be integrated into golf management software.
8. Seamless integration of e-mail marketing with golf management system.

Technology provides a fabulous competitive edge to the golf course that uses it properly and extensively.

End Notes

The lessons of this chapter are:

1) Many outstanding golf management software solutions are available today that should represent a low four-figure investment.
2) Golf course personnel are laggards with respect to the adoption of technology.
3) There is much fear, uncertainty, and doubt when selecting a software vendor. Once selected, golf course staff are loathe to change systems.
4) The attitude and aptitude challenges of the staff are compounded by the reticence of software vendors to cooperate in creating effective integrated solutions.
5) The process of selecting a golf management system comprises issuing a brief RFP and conducting Web-based demonstrations and on-site presentations.

Having fully integrated golf management systems is a prerequisite for maximizing the investment return of a golf course. These systems facilitate the creation of a customer database with meaningful demographic data in which the relationship can be cost effectively managed.

Concluding Thought

Truth is like the sun. You can shut it out for a time, but it ain't going away.

Elvis Presley

Chapter 8

The Key Financial Metrics

Step 4 of Golf Convergence WIN™ Formula

If I have the belief that I can do it,
I shall surely acquire the capacity to do it.

Mahatma Gandhi

Chapter Highlights

Some numbers are more worthy than others. Make sure you get the right data.

Operating margins in golf are getting squeezed. With water and fertilizer costs increasing and labor extracting a high financial and emotional cost, the owner-operator faces daunting challenges.

There is a tremendous value to participating in Golf Datatech and PGA's PerformanceTrak. They are a "must" for every golf course that is serious about maximizing the investment potential of its facility.

If you can read the financial statements (balance sheet, income statement, and cash flow statement) you have already gleaned 75% of the information needed to effectively manage a golf course.

The Generally Accepted Goalposts

Financial statements are the goalposts of business. For a golf course, the financial information that each course requires comprises:

1. Historical Financial Statements
2. Budget
3. Revenue Plan
4. Capital Expense Plan
5. Utilization Profiles
6. Key Performance Indicators

Examining the financial statements against related industry benchmarks is the ***fourth step in the Golf Convergence WIN™ process.***

Historical financial statements include the balance sheet, the income statement, and the cash flow statement. The balance sheet reflects the financial strength of the golf course. The income statement mirrors the health of operations. The cash flow statement provides analysis of the operating, investing, and financing activities and is a useful tool in determining the short-term viability of a company.

As a former CPA, I have long thought that a review of a golf course's financial statements is comparable to a doctor reviewing a patient's x-rays. A tumor or broken bone is easy to spot. Is the business properly capitalized? Is liquidity sufficient? Are the receivables at risk? Are the payables tardy, or the deferred liabilities extensive? The most valuable, insightful tools regarding the efficiency of an operation are the financial statements. More information can be learned about an operation from reviewing financial statements than from any other source.

Because of the myriad numbers available, being able to rely on a few financial statistics is beneficial.

Financial ratios can be used to easily quantify the many indices of a business, providing an indication of financial health. For example, profitability ratios measure the firm's use of its assets and the control of expenses necessary to generate an acceptable rate of return. Liquidity ratios measure the availability of cash to pay debt. Activity ratios measure how quickly a firm converts non-cash assets to cash assets. Debt ratios measure the firm's ability to repay long-term debt. Market ratios measure investor response to owning a company's stock and also the cost of issuing stock.

While there seems to be a limitless number of financial ratios, the key ones include:

- Profitability Ratios
  - Profit margin = Net Income/Revenue
  - Operating profit margin or Return on sales = Earnings before interest and taxes/Sales
  - Return on equity = Net profits after taxes/Stockholders' equity or tangible net worth
  - Return on investment = Net income/Total assets
  - Asset turnover = Sales/Assets
  - Return on assets (ROA) = Net income/Total assets
- Liquidity ratios
  - Current ratio = Current assets/Current liabilities
  - Acid-test ratio (quick ratio) = [Current assets—(Inventories + Prepayments)]/Current liabilities
  - Receivables turnover ratio = Net credit sales/Average net receivables
  - Inventory turnover ratio = Cost of goods sold/Average inventory
- Activity ratios
  - Average collection period = Accounts receivable/(Annual credit sales/365 days)
  - Average payment period = Accounts payable/(Annual credit purchases/365 days)
  - Inventory turnover ratio = Cost of goods sold/Average inventory
- Debt ratios
  - Debt ratio = Total liabilities/Total assets
  - Debt to equity ratio = (Long-term debt + Value of leases)/Stockholders' equity

- Long-term debt/Total asset (LD/TA) ratio = Long-term debt/Total assets
- Times interest-earned ratio = Earnings before interest and taxes EBIT/ Annual interest expense
- Debt service coverage ratio = Net operating income/Total debt service

Debt ratios are not applicable for municipal and military golf complexes, but with this list of ratios you should be able to determine the financial stability of a golf course.

There is a catch. Financial statements and their various derivatives present a dilemma to the golf course owner. So many numbers are available—from general ledger accounts, to budgets, to labor man-hour reporting, to daily operations, to monthly and annual financial statements—that it is easy to become overwhelmed. There is also a certain resignation that the numbers viewed are historical and not accurate predictors of the future. Thus, many within the industry give their financial statements a cursory glance after Sports Center signs off the air.

In a world full of data, it's comforting to know that owners and managers can view a precise set of numbers to determine the financial solidity of the operation from Golf Datatech and PGA PerformanceTrak. Gaining a grasp of these key performance indicators begins with understanding the unique terms applicable to the golf industry.

Definitions

While "assets," "liabilities," and "equity" are common financial terms, there have been, in the golf business, varying opinions as to the definition of certain terms. In March 2002, the NGCOA, the NGF, and other associations adopted a set of standards to ensure that growth indicators are measured consistently from year to year.

The more important definitions included in this industry list follow:[1]

1 NGCOA, "Golf Industry Definitions," http://www.ngcoa.org/pageview.asp?doc-511.

Rounds

Regulation Round: A *regulation round* of golf is defined by one person who tees off in an authorized "start" on a regulation golf course. The round is not defined by the number of holes played or the fees paid.

Participation

Participant: A *participant* is a person five years of age or older who played at least one regulation round of golf, or utilized an alternative facility or golf range at least once in the past 12 months. The total number of participants is determined by adding the number of golfers, alternative golfers, junior participants, and range users.

Golfer: A *golfer* is a person age 18 or older who has played at least one regulation round of golf in the past 12 months.

Occasional Golfer: An *occasional golfer* is a golfer who plays less than eight regulation rounds in a year.

Core Golfer: A *core golfer* is one who plays 8 to 24 regulation rounds in a year.

Avid Golfer: An *avid golfer* is one who plays 25 regulation rounds or more in a year.

Types of Facilities and Courses

Regulation Golf Facility: A *regulation golf facility* is defined as a golf complex where there is at least one regulation golf course.

Regulation Golf Course: A *regulation golf course* is defined as any 9- or 18-hole golf course that includes a variety of par 3, par 4, and par 5 holes, and is of traditional length and par; a 9-hole facility must be at least 2,600 yards in length and at least par 33; an 18-hole facility must be at least 5,200 yards in length and at least par 66.

Alternative Golf Course: *Alternative golf courses* include the following:

Par 3 Courses: *Par 3 courses* are courses consisting exclusively of par 3 holes that average at least 100 yards in length.

Executive Courses: *Executive courses* are short courses with a variety of par 3, par 4, and/or par 5 holes. Eighteen-hole executive courses are 5,200 yards in length or less, with a par of 65 or less.

Pitch & Putt Courses: *Pitch & putt courses* are short par 3 courses where the holes average less than 100 yards in length.

Courses: Structure

Public Access Golf Course: A *public access golf course* is a facility that provides the least limited access and which may or may not offer memberships.

Public access courses include:

Municipal Golf Course: A *municipal golf course* is one that is owned by a tax-supported entity such as a city, county, or state and which is open to the general public at all times.

Daily Fee Golf Course: A *daily fee golf course* is a privately owned course that is open to the public without restriction.

Semiprivate Golf Course: A *semiprivate golf course* is a public course that also offers memberships.

Military Golf Course: A *military golf course* is one affiliated with a military base where members of the military and their families receive preferred rates.

Private Golf Course: A *private golf course* is a facility where play is restricted to members and their guests. A private golf course can be either equity (owned by the membership) or non-equity (corporately-owned).

Resort Golf Course: A *resort golf course* is a golf facility usually affiliated with a lodging component.

Benchmarking and Data Repositories

These definitions are important because they serve as the foundation for the generally accepted accounting principles for the golf industry. By ensuring that the financial statements are consistent with industry definitions, meaningful comparisons can be made.

To the industry's credit, several data repositories are in place and serve as an invaluable resource.

Golf Datatech, with the sponsorship of the National Golf Course Owners Association and The Professional Golfers' Association of America (through its PerformanceTrak service), has taken an important leadership role in compiling vital information for course owners.

Golf Datatech creates a monthly national rounds report and provides specialized market research covering retail sales, inventory, pricing and distribution. This report highlights changes in rounds from prior periods, temperature and precipitation.

Prior to 2010, Golf Datatech produced a Revenue Per Available Tee Time (RevPatt) and Revenue Per Utilized Round (RevPUR) index for competing facilities. These reports allowed course owners to see how competitive their facility was and to learn their course's ranking with their local golf marketplace.

PerformanceTrak At-a-Glance - December 2012

December 2012 Highlights	December 2012[1,2]	December 2011[1,2]	Change	% Change	Sample Size[3]
Mean (Average) Rounds Played - December	829	860	↓	-3.6%	3,339
Mean (Average) Days Open - December	15.9	15.9	↑	0.0%	3,339
YTD December 2012 Highlights					
Mean (Average) Rounds Played - YTD	24,884	23,383	↑	6.4%	2,964
Mean (Average) Days Open - YTD	290.5	272.8	↑	6.5%	2,964
December 2012 Median Gross Revenue Per Facility[4]					
Median Golf Fee Revenue - December	$27,506	$28,387	↓	-3.1%	1,154
Median Merchandise Revenue - December	$8,905	$8,755	↑	1.7%	1,023
Median Food & Beverage Revenue - December	$30,614	$29,973	↑	2.1%	742
Median Total Revenue - December	$111,063	$110,655	↑	0.4%	889
YTD December 2012 Median Gross Revenue Per Facility					
Median Golf Fee Revenue - YTD	$788,839	$739,654	↑	6.6%	1,168
Median Merchandise Revenue - YTD	$149,147	$137,025	↑	8.8%	1,018
Median Food & Beverage Revenue - YTD	$462,724	$437,296	↑	5.8%	735
Median Total Revenue - YTD	$1,948,471	$1,870,619	↑	4.2%	880

In 2010, the PGA of America assimilated Golf Datatech's revenue reporting into PGA PerformanceTrak, another valuable benchmarking tool. The PGA PerformanceTrak provides the opportunity to compare the facility performance of a golf course to the local area, by PGA section, or nationally.

The PGA of America also undertakes an annual operations survey that provides upwards of 50 invaluable reports, including:

- Total Rounds Played
- Peak-Season Combined Golf and Cart Fee
- Number of Full-Time Employees Facility-Wide
- Total Facility Revenues
- Total Green Fees and Guest Fees
- Total Cart Fees
- Golf Merchandise Revenue
- Range Revenue
- Food and Beverage Revenue
- Cost of Goods Sold
- Combined Food and Beverage Cost of Sales
- Golf Operations Payroll, Employee Benefits

- Golf Course Maintenance Payroll, Employee Benefits, Contractor and Temporary Staffing Costs
- Total Facility-Wide Net Operation Income

It is disappointing, but not surprising, how few golf courses participate in this service. Fewer than 25% of golf courses submit their confidential financial information to these repositories. The golf course owner or manager who doesn't contribute information into this repository or access its data operates in the dark, in spite of the fact that light and insight are available for free.

However, the NGCOA and the PGA are seriously committed to this "benchmarking" initiative as reflected in the following press release:

> "'Recruiting, training and supporting PGA Professionals as the front-line manager of the golf industry is at the core of the mission for PGA PerformanceTrak,' said Brian Whitcomb, President of The PGA of America. 'Our most important goal is to assemble quality data on golf facility operations to guide our members in planning and managing their facilities for their employers.'
>
> The service is specifically designed to deliver 'data and tools' to support PGA Professionals, owners and the industry in managing and evaluating the performance of golf facilities. Monthly rounds played data collection and key performance indicators, such as golf fee revenue per round, are some of the primary features of PGA PerformanceTrak. Through this service, participants can access reports for 41 PGA Sections, 50 States and in excess of 50 local markets. Participation is available through either www.PGAPerformanceTrak.com or www.NGCOA.org/benchmark."[2]

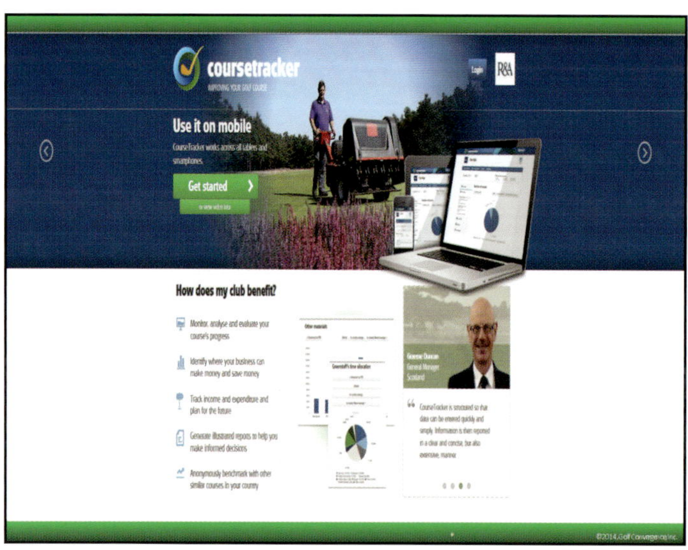

2 PGA of America, http://www.pga.com/2008/news/pga/01/18/trak011808/index.html?eref=sitesearch.

Items being tracked include total rounds, revenue, expenses, total days of course closure, course budget, annual member subscriptions, visitors green fees, number of dominant grass types, green construction type, average annual rainfall, and high and low temperatures.

It should be noted that the Royal and Ancient also provides a benchmarking repository which is shown in the chart on prior page.

The Key Numbers

It is essential that a golf course owner grasp a few fundamental financial relationships in order to guide the operation. Financial analysis does not have to be exhaustive or all-consuming. As in any business, a lot of numbers are generated. In golf, there are only several that really matter:

1. Who are your best customers?
2. Which customers did you acquire this year and who defected?
3. Where do your customers come from?
4. Is the inventory properly stocked with the right vendors and the right price points?
5. Are the green fees properly set?

These reports answer those questions by providing multiple data points that can be examined to adjust current practices to maximize the investment return from the golf course.

We believe that there are fifteen key reports from which golf course operators can realize the potential of their facility as summarized here:

Customer Analysis

1. Customer Distribution
2. Customer Demographics
3. Customer Retention
4. Customer Spending by Class
5. Customer Spending by Individual
6. Zip Code Analysis

Facility Analysis

1. Merchandise Sales by Vendor
2. Reservations by Booking Method
3. Reservations by Day of Week
4. Revenue Benchmarks
5. Revenue per Available Tee Time
6. Revenue per Department
7. Revenue per Hour
8. Rounds per Revenue Margins
9. Course Utilization

The following sections include an explanation of each report and its vital role in golf course management. Note that the vast majority of these reports are available within the programming of leading golf management software firms.

Customer Analysis

Report 1: Customer Distribution

Customer relationship management is focused on identifying a facility's best customers to ensure that they are accorded service commensurate with their loyalty to that facility. At a golf course, 12% of the customers typically generate about 60% of the revenue. The chart at the top of the next page highlights the importance of identifying customers, and further segmenting them as acquired, core, or defectors to ensure their continued loyalty. Look at the revenue per player per round generated from just 21 customers: $1,794.02. Do you think this course can afford to lose one of these customers? Not likely. Without undertaking this analysis of a golf course's database, a typical general manager might report revenue was up slightly over the prior year and fail to realize that the course had a 33% customer turnover. In analytical work performed for clients, the amount of revenue from acquired customers, approximating 20% of gross revenue, approximates the revenue lost from defectors.

Here are some additional statistics regarding customer distribution. A golf course has on average 8,000 golfers visit it per year. Of those, 50% of the golfers will play the facility just once, 13% will play six or more times, and the average customer will play four times, which represents 20% of his or her "wallet share" allocated to golf.

This report is designed to provide an index by which you can compare customer usage at your facility to industry standards and provides, in 10% incremental brackets, the number of golfers it took to generate the 10% of the course's gross revenue.

Customer Revenue Distribution Report

Distribution	# of Player	% of Players	Total Rounds	Rounds /Player	% of Total Rounds	Revenue /Player	Total Rev/Round
1	7	0.14 %	166	23.71	3.68 %	$1,900.61	$80.15
2	60	1.20 %	222	3.70	4.92 %	$214.56	$57.99
3	131	2.62 %	276	2.11	6.12 %	$98.18	$46.60
4	191	3.81 %	289	1.51	6.41 %	$67.38	$44.53
5	247	4.93 %	405	1.64	8.98 %	$52.11	$31.78
6	332	6.63 %	426	1.28	9.44 %	$38.71	$30.17
7	374	7.47 %	400	1.07	8.87 %	$34.39	$32.15
8	499	9.96 %	598	1.20	13.25 %	$25.77	$21.51
9	706	14.10 %	862	1.22	19.10 %	$18.21	$14.91
10	2,461	49.14 %	868	0.35	19.24 %	$5.00	$14.18
Total	5,008	100.00 %	4,512	0.90	100.00 %	$25.66	$28.48

Report 2: Customer Demographics

Who is your customer? The ability to effectively market your facility is highly dependent on knowing the detailed demographics of your customers—their name, zip code, e-mail address, etc. From direct mail to targeted e-mails, to zip code analysis for print or other media ads, it is critical for your club to collect this data. This report will give you a quick look at statistics that are vital for effective marketing.

Report 3: Customer Retention

The purpose of this report is to identify the core customers, those customers who played the course for the first time during the defined interval, and those defectors who previously played your golf course but have not frequented it recently. When unique marketing messages are created for each of these targeted segments, the response rate contributes materially to building revenue.

Fifty percent of the customers that play a golf course in a specific year will not return in the following year. Those "defectors" are often offset by newly acquired customers. This turnover velocity within a customer database is often not realized because of the time horizon, 12 months, in which the changes occur. If a golfer has not played a golf course within 90 days, there is a high probability that the customer has been lost.

The Customer Retention report is designed to compare two time periods. It can compare days, weeks, months, years, etc. The report will show you the names of

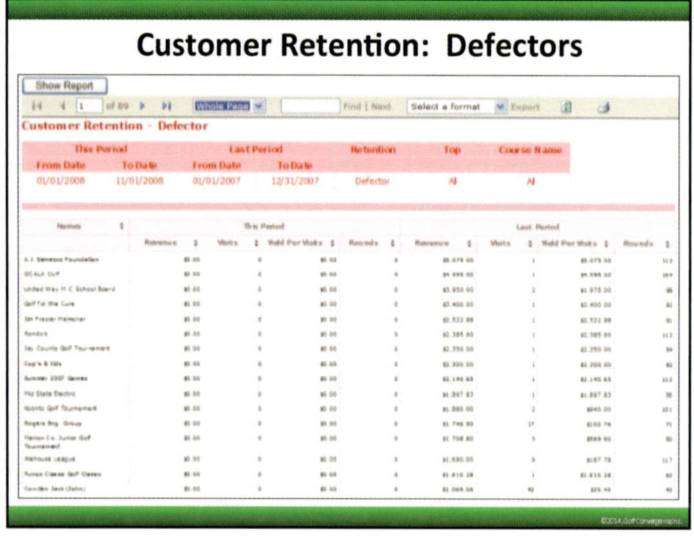

the players and compare "This Period" vs. "Last Period" for revenue, visits, yield, and rounds.

An example of this report is depicted on the left.

This report shows numerous golfers who were frequent customers in the prior year but didn't return. Surveying these customers would be a source of insightful information and help course managers reconsider a facility's operational practices to enhance retention.

Tournaments are one of the largest revenue sources. Filtering this report to highlight tournaments indicates that there were 18 groups generating more than $40,000 in one year that did not return to the course the next year. With the average earnings before taxes, interest, depreciation, and amortization at $200,000, these lost customers represent 20% of the course's annual earnings. In another exercise, we saw a four-course daily fee complex lose $1,522,871.06 in revenue representing 14,549 total visits and 30,945 rounds from customers who did not return the next year.

Report 4: Customer Spending by Class

By customer class, we mean which group generates the highest gross revenue and the most revenue per round?

This report allows you to identify which group is actually producing the most revenue. It also helps you affirm the importance of that group by enabling you to create a targeted e-mail message to the segment you identify.

Report 5: Customer Spending by Individual

This report measures gross revenue by individual customer so that you can identify which customer generates the most revenue for the facility.

It also reveals the importance of tournament and outing playing to gross revenue. Often, 20 tournaments on 20 days will contribute 20% of the gross revenue of that facility for the entire year.

This report highlights a facility's best customers and allows you to understand when customer recognition is appropriate.

Report 6: Zip Code Analysis

How, when, and where should a golf course advertise? Are national, regional, or local publications appropriate? This report helps answers that question by displaying the residential location of your customers.

Data analysis shows that 90% of a facility's customers generally come from within 10 miles of a golf course or a 30-minute drive time. For most courses, the vast majority of revenue is generated within as few as four zip codes. Knowing those zip codes determines which publications are best selected for optimum utilization of advertising expenditures.

Facility Analysis

Report 7: Merchandise Sales by Vendor

This report analyzes the merchandise inventory and rank orders vendors by revenue and by net income. The report will display which vendors generated the most revenue at the highest gross margin. Conversely, this report will identify vendors that are underperforming and should be deleted from the inventory.

The typical golf course should have about 15 to 20 vendors. If this report extends to several pages, there is a great opportunity to reduce the number of lines carried, which will simplify purchasing and reduce inventory on hand that has low margin and/or low likelihood of selling.

Report 8: Reservations by Booking Method

The first contact a golfer often has with the facility is in booking tee time reservations. There are many ways to make tee time reservations: by an individual in the golf shop, via touch-tone telephone, via a kiosk, or via Internet booking.

This report shows you how golfers are reserving tee times at your facility. It is important that each booking method be quick and easy. As the most cost-effective method for booking a tee time for a golf course, the on-line reservation system merits special attention. This report will measure the effectiveness of the on-line reservation system and the efficacy of efforts by the course to encourage that method of booking.

Report 9: Reservations by Day of Week

The goal of any golf course is to maximize its revenue. It is assumed that weekends, when most customers are not working, are the busiest days of the week and therefore prices are set higher, often as much as 25% higher, than on weekdays. This assumption often proves incorrect, however.

This report will display which days of the week are busiest and will facilitate your determining should Friday be set at weekend rates or should the same rate apply to every day of the week. Ultimately, the decision on setting rates is a subjective science, but having quantitative information available reduces the error rate significantly. The purpose of this report is to guide you in setting the correct green fee.

Report 10: Revenue Benchmarks

The purpose of this report is to provide key benchmarks on a revenue per round basis for the five departments according to generally accepted financial reporting for golf courses: green fees, carts, merchandise, food and beverage, and other.

These benchmarks can be compared to industry averages created by Golf Datatech and PGA PerformanceTrak that are developed by the PGA sections, states, and throughout the U.S.

This report also shows the interrelationship between the departments. Green fees drive the volume of revenue for each of the segment categories.

Report 11: Revenue per Available Tee Time

Optimizing gross revenue is finding the proper balance between the number of rounds and the price per round. A key statistic is net rate per round.

Each golf course, depending on the market niche it serves (Platinum, Gold, Silver, Bronze, or Steel), has a revenue target. At a minimum, that target represents total expenses divided by projected rounds. That number represents the break-even point of the golf course.

This report is designed to help a golf course manager ascertain to what extent his facility is achieving its revenue per round goal and whether the prices per hour are appropriately balanced. Best practices suggest that well-run golf facilities will attain a net rate per round of 70% to 75% of the average posted green fees rate.

Many operators will wait until the end of each month to assess rounds played each day. That is too late. Tee times are a perishable commodity that can be sold only once. Therefore, daily tracking of rounds and anticipation of slack time within each day is key to administering yield management.

In what I like to call "The Good, The Bad, and The Ugly," the purpose of this report is to quickly identify timeslots where you are hemorrhaging money versus those that are performing well. Use of marketing tools and pricing strategies can help you improve your bottom line.

Report 12: Revenue by Department

This report represents gross revenue in the aggregate by the five key departments at the golf course. This report allows a golf course manager to easily ascertain whether the departments will meet their budget for the month and, if not, which of the revenue centers underperformed. When contrasted to the revenue benchmark reports that reflect revenue on a per-round basis, this report aggregates total dollars generated by each department.

Report 13: Revenue per Hour

The goal of a golf course is to generate revenue. It is widely felt that "prime time" is from 8 a.m. to 10 a.m. This report reflects in which hour most of the revenue is actually generated. Surprisingly, it is often not during prime time but rather, in the early afternoon, when revenue per hour is maximized. That fact is contrary to the popular wisdom that Monday–Thursday noon to 3 p.m. are the slowest times at the golf course. This report is designed to facilitate identification of which hours of the day generate the most revenue.

Gross Revenue By Department

Gross Revenue by Month Detailing Five Profit Centers

Months	Rounds	AVG Rounds /Day	Total Revenue	AVG Revenue/ Day	AVG Revenue/Round	Green Fees	Green Fees/Round	Merchandise	Merchandise/ Round	F&B	F&B/Round	Other	Other/Round
Jan	2,829	91.26	84,568.89	2,728.03	29.89	42,447.62	15.00	5,936.88	2.10	4,694.09	1.66	31,490.30	11.13
Feb	5,696	203.43	167,747.30	5,990.98	29.45	92,947.96	16.32	12,176.30	2.14	10,587.27	1.86	52,035.77	9.14
March	6,882	222.00	195,868.47	6,318.34	28.46	109,374.74	15.89	15,463.28	2.25	13,832.23	2.01	57,198.22	8.31
April	5,984	199.47	182,708.77	6,090.29	30.53	84,103.35	14.05	24,494.60	4.09	16,880.57	2.82	57,230.25	9.56
May	6,309	203.52	180,960.02	5,837.42	28.68	84,150.79	13.34	17,792.40	2.82	19,349.11	3.07	59,667.72	9.46
June	6,111	203.70	179,759.79	5,991.99	29.42	80,349.09	13.15	19,785.27	3.24	21,441.96	3.51	58,183.47	9.52
July	5,826	187.94	159,813.97	5,155.29	27.43	75,612.75	12.98	15,542.36	2.67	18,977.05	3.26	49,681.81	8.53
Aug	5,664	182.71	172,134.28	5,552.72	30.39	68,875.58	12.16	21,188.72	3.74	19,519.87	3.45	62,550.11	11.04
Sep	4,665	155.50	146,266.09	4,875.54	31.35	53,270.06	11.42	11,750.27	2.52	12,799.85	2.74	68,445.91	14.67
Oct	5,348	172.50	173,906.58	5,609.89	32.52	57,578.85	10.77	20,298.35	3.80	13,018.06	2.43	83,011.32	15.52
Nov	6,168	205.61	177,213.81	5,907.13	28.73	67,025.55	10.87	13,944.58	2.26	13,018.08	2.11	83,225.61	13.49
Dec	6,966	224.71	208,277.00	6,718.61	29.90	80,519.07	11.56	25,265.81	3.63	18,070.34	2.59	84,421.78	12.12
Total	68,448	187.53	2,029,224.97	5,559.52		896,255.41		203,638.82		182,188.48		747,142.27	
Course Average				100.00%	29.65	44.17%	13.09	10.04%	2.98	8.98%	2.66	36.82%	10.92
Industry Benchmarks				100.00%	38.12	61.62%	21.67	8.28%	2.56	19.28%	4.17	10.82%	9.72
Variances					(8.47)	-17.45%	(8.58)	1.76%	0.42	-10.30%	(1.51)	26.00%	1.20

Though the largest revenue per hour may be in the early afternoon, that doesn't necessarily mean that rates should be raised to the highest level during that time interval. Again, it is a question of balancing rounds versus the rate per round to achieve the desired goal.

Report 14: Rounds per Revenue Margin

Each golf course sets rates based on customer type, day of week, and time of day. This report focuses on the differential between the resources consumed (the number of tee time used by a customer type) versus the revenue generated by that customer type. For example, volunteers and season passes often use the golf course to a far greater extent than they generate comparable revenue. On the reverse side, a classification such as non-resident at a municipal golf course often contributes far more to the gross revenue than the percentage of rounds they play.

This report provides managers insight on which groups are generating the greatest "margin" to their facility. Are you seeking to raise revenue? The answer is often simple—provide the group that yields the highest revenue per round the greater access to the tee times and the course. Following is an extract of such a report for a public golf course:

Green Fees	Yield Margin
Golf Course Employee	–5.13%
Season: Staff/Faculty	–3.67%
Season: Alumni	–1.94%
University: Twilight	–1.86%
University and Public: Evening	–1.85%
Season: Retired Staff	–1.53%
League Rate	–1.35%
Public: Twilight	–1.32%
PGA Card: Monday–Thursday	0.26%
PGA Card: Friday–Sunday	0.40%
University: Tuesday–Thursday	0.50%
Senior Special	1.31%
Public: Weekday	2.78%
Special	2.85%
University: Friday–Sunday	3.36%
Public: Friday–Sunday	11.45%

In this case, all those with negative numbers are using the facility to a greater extent than they are paying for. It would suggest the rates in these categories could be increased.

Here Is Why Annual Passes Are a Bad Deal

Year	Revenue Contribution	Rounds Consumed	Unfavorable Variance
2005	16.02%	42.35%	-26.33%
2006	16.90%	38.33%	-21.43%
2007	14.37%	35.74%	-21.37%
2008	7.91%	30.32%	-22.41%
2009	6.61%	24.36%	-17.75%
2010	16.57%	24.02%	-7.45%
2011	19.88%	29.32%	-9.43%

This report will also illustrate why season passes, offered by 71% of municipal and many daily fee golf courses, are usually a very bad deal. Presented is a chart highlighting a California golf course that eliminated its unlimited play annual pass program in 2009.

Note the significant improvement in the revenue contribution margin starting in 2010 when the modified rate structure was implemented.

Report 15: Course Utilization

In 2011, the average golf utilization—the number of rounds divided by the capacity—was slightly higher than 50%. This report provides a benchmark against that national average.

This report also shows which hours within a month are near capacity, suggesting that an increase in green fees within those time slots might be appropriate, and alternatively, showing the slack periods in which, if dynamic pricing were in place, the green fee rates might be lowered.

Another purpose of this report is that it will often reflect whether the tee time prices within the day are properly set. For example, if the afternoon rates are discounted too significantly, one might notice a significant drop off in play the hour before the afternoon rates become effective. Such a scenario would suggest that three- or four-tier pricing might be more appropriate than a dual-pricing schedule.

A tee time is a perishable commodity. There exists a theory that if the green fees were accurately priced by day, hour, and month the course would operate at 100% of capacity. In comparison to the 50% utilization of a golf course, in early 2009 hotels were operating at 80% utilization, while the airline industry was operating at near 60% capacity.

Utilization Report

From Date	To Date	Start Time	End Time
01/01/2008	12/31/2008	07:00:00	16:59:59

Tee Time	Jan	Feb	March	April	May	June	July	Aug	Sep	Oct	Nov	Dec	Avg
WEEKDAYS													
7	0.31%	0.00%	0.10%	4.11%	27.32%	44.08%	49.69%	40.41%	39.07%	12.82%	1.49%	0.17%	18.30%
8	0.12%	0.00%	0.25%	14.21%	39.88%	44.54%	46.11%	47.43%	34.74%	21.85%	7.54%	0.00%	21.39%
9	1.42%	0.00%	5.19%	16.67%	31.49%	48.32%	52.92%	50.00%	45.22%	28.95%	8.20%	0.24%	24.05%
10	3.19%	0.11%	9.06%	16.18%	37.94%	44.39%	57.52%	55.13%	48.70%	27.75%	15.72%	1.54%	26.44%
11	4.02%	0.00%	10.24%	12.28%	33.15%	44.60%	48.52%	44.64%	47.13%	18.07%	10.86%	1.42%	22.91%
12	1.65%	0.11%	9.90%	11.40%	25.92%	43.56%	49.78%	46.71%	48.14%	21.30%	9.53%	1.22%	22.44%
13	0.65%	0.00%	8.04%	12.56%	21.61%	38.99%	42.19%	45.50%	38.75%	20.21%	4.39%	0.53%	19.45%
14	1.24%	0.11%	8.77%	9.51%	17.84%	28.28%	33.42%	39.27%	40.28%	25.02%	4.28%	0.43%	17.37%
15	0.41%	0.00%	7.54%	32.10%	57.12%	60.29%	62.14%	60.82%	40.87%	9.38%	1.01%	0.08%	27.65%
16	0.00%	0.11%	3.40%	21.49%	37.63%	49.17%	52.13%	48.43%	28.77%	5.27%	0.13%	0.04%	20.55%
WEEKENDS													
7	6.11%	0.00%	3.50%	42.11%	67.35%	78.46%	65.46%	78.86%	55.15%	51.38%	5.36%	0.00%	37.81%
8	10.39%	1.16%	3.14%	53.68%	70.24%	75.42%	68.22%	75.51%	57.42%	55.00%	13.17%	0.68%	40.34%
9	13.82%	1.74%	9.47%	57.46%	73.39%	79.53%	72.37%	79.12%	57.24%	57.37%	21.48%	0.93%	43.66%
10	13.61%	2.18%	17.51%	39.98%	58.19%	67.98%	65.89%	62.20%	35.81%	49.59%	13.35%	0.68%	35.58%
11	11.78%	1.02%	10.49%	43.20%	46.88%	66.60%	64.69%	70.26%	42.11%	37.13%	14.50%	1.75%	34.20%
12	5.38%	1.45%	9.62%	39.09%	54.90%	57.91%	58.16%	66.53%	51.48%	36.99%	9.50%	1.02%	32.67%
13	0.96%	0.73%	7.41%	28.07%	33.04%	41.52%	45.39%	51.93%	52.19%	26.74%	2.42%	0.00%	24.20%
14	2.37%	0.15%	5.77%	11.33%	14.69%	25.42%	35.70%	43.64%	42.80%	36.92%	8.96%	0.45%	19.02%
15	0.64%	0.00%	2.78%	33.11%	47.78%	60.54%	63.27%	65.65%	38.05%	11.96%	1.02%	0.00%	27.07%
16	0.16%	0.00%	1.11%	9.00%	28.99%	42.68%	49.26%	37.88%	11.33%	5.51%	0.00%	0.00%	15.49%
Average	3.91%	0.44%	6.66%	25.38%	41.27%	52.12%	54.14%	55.50%	42.76%	27.96%	7.65%	0.56%	26.53%
Average	3.91%	0.44%	6.66%	25.38%	41.27%	52.12%	54.14%	55.50%	42.76%	27.96%	7.65%	0.56%	26.53%

Key: Blocks in red indicate that the course has less than 40% utilization for the month. Yellow indicates utilization between 40% and 60% and green reflects utilization of over 60%.

These reports, while important, provide little benefit if the insights created are not implemented. With this information, however, course operators find it easier to make informed decisions that will lead to an increase in the investment return of the facility.

The opportunity to enhance the investment income at a golf course dramatically increases when detailed information is gathered and used. Pricing can be adjusted, marketing altered, and expenses reviewed proactively, not reactively.

The Bottom Line

In an editorial, Jim Dunlap reported on the resistance he has noticed in attempting to compile golf facility data. Regrettably, he quoted one owner as saying, “The first time my head pro releases my financial information is the last day he works for me.”[3] This type of thinking, preferring isolation to inclusion, adversely impacts the ability of all golf courses to effectively maximize the net income of their facility as independent benchmarks provide valuable data. This narrow-minded thinking still exists in 2014 among many golf course owners.

Successful operators must understand, manage, and anticipate certain key operating statistics and industry benchmarks in order to maximize the bottom line.

Though lessening demand in many markets has caused hardship for some, information, used properly, can be an invaluable source and a tremendous competitive advantage.

3 Jim Dunlap, “Shared Numbers Benefit Everyone,” *Golf Inc.*, August 2008, p. 38.

End Notes

The lessons of this chapter are:

1) Financial statements are the goalposts of business.
2) There are four kinds of key ratios that measure the strength of a business: profitability, liquidity, activity, and debt. A fifth standard ratio, market activity, is not applicable for golf courses.
3) A golfer has played a regulation round if he or she teed off in an authorized start on a regulation golf course, regardless of the number of holes played or the fees paid.
4) A golfer is a person age 18 or older who has played at least one regulation round of golf in the past 12 months. Occasional golfers are defined as those who play less than 8 regulation rounds, core golfers play between 8 and 24 regulation rounds, and avid golfers play 25 or more regulation rounds per year.
5) Golf Datatech, PGA PerformanceTrak, and the National Golf Foundation provide incredible valuable data repositories in which the financial performance for golf courses can be compared.
6) There are fifteen key performance metrics for the golf industry. Among the most important are gross revenue by department per round, course utilization, revenue per available tee time, revenue by golf type, customer quintiles, acquire/core/defectors, zip code analysis, and net income break-even analysis.

By understanding the financial statements of a golf course, facility managers can undertake tactical planning designed to enhance the strengths, address the weaknesses, exploit the opportunities and deal with the threats that the facility faces.

Concluding Thought

Most people see what is and never see what can be.

Albert Einstein

Chapter 9

Financial Modeling
Step 4 of Golf Convergence WIN™ Formula (continued)

The degree of one's emotions varies inversely with one's knowledge of the facts.

Bertrand Russell

Chapter Highlights

There are many uncontrollable factors that influence the net income of a golf course. With industry benchmarks available through PGA PerformanceTrak that reveal the operating performance of many golf courses, golf course owners are afforded the opportunity to highlight strengths and weakness against their competitors.

This analysis, when integrated into financial models, facilitates to an extreme degree the financial accounts that need to be monitored, the probable revenue product mix, and how to best minimize controllable expenses, including what constitutes reliable labor standards.

The result of financial modeling is a comprehensive financial projection that also offers key benchmarks. These metrics can be monitored through a daily flash report to ensure revenue is maximized and that the operations are efficiently managed.

Lost in the Details

It often seems that hundreds of everyday events influence the net income of a golf course. However, in focusing on those details, most golf course managers lose the perspective necessary to bolster the net income and investment return from their golf course. Management and staff become so preoccupied with individual moments that the implementation of strategy is compromised.

Simply stated, an income statement has three components: revenue, expenses, and the resultant net income. A manager should focus on a few key items.

As highlighted in the following chart, golf course owners have influence over only the following areas of their operations:

Revenue:

Green Fees and Guest Fees

Member Dues and/or Season Passes

Expenses:

Maintenance

General and Administration

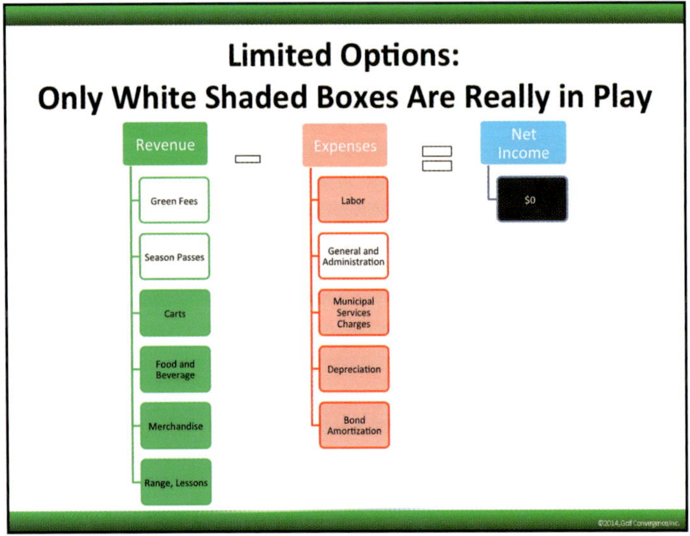

Rounds as measured by green fees, member dues, and season passes account for about 60% of gross revenue and materially impact all other revenue departments. The revenue derived from carts, food and beverage, merchandise, and lessons is directly correlated to the number of rounds. It takes a lot of additional work to increase incrementally the revenue in those departments.

But the amount of money golfers spend for carts, merchandise, and food and beverage is fairly predictable based on total rounds played.

With the average golf course operating at near 50% of capacity, in theory, a course should be able to double its revenue and increase its net income at least tenfold with little more than a marginal increase in operating expenses.

For a golf course operator today, revenues are challenged by market oversupply. This leads one to think that increased profits are available from the effective control of expenses. If it were only that easy.

Expenses are a continuing and nettlesome concern for the golf industry, especially as operating margins get squeezed. As Jim Dunlap accurately summarized, "It would be hard to identify an aspect of course development and operations that has not been negatively impacted by inflated costs, from construction materials to fuel to food and beverage supplies to maintenance products and equipment to labor."[1]

Water, fuel, fertilizer, and labor costs all are extremely volatile and seem to increase exponentially in price.

As reported in *Golf Business*, "obtaining enough water to grow the grass for the nation's 16,000 courses—yes, even yours—may soon become the most important issue impacting the golf industry."[2] Add to that the lack of natural water, with drought conditions in many parts of the United States, and the availability and cost of water is likely to adversely influence golf course operations in the United States, where golfers have become accustomed to manicured golf courses that are expensive to maintain.

While there is the temptation to cut costs, or, as the expression goes, "suck the paint off of the walls," such a strategy is a short-term accommodation and a long-term strategic mistake. It is difficult to shrink your way to greatness.

The economic challenges within the golf business will remain in the short run. Mark Frost, author of *The Greatest Game Ever Played: Harry Varden, Francis*

1 Jim Dunlap, "Cost," *Golf Inc.*, October 2008, p. 18.

2 Golfbusiness.com, "Troubled Waters," October 2008, p. 17.

Ouimet, and the Birth of Modern Golf, wrote the following in a *Wall Street Journal* article titled, "Golf's Crash Course in Humility":

> "Then came . . . the next avatar. He swept away most of the last vestiges of restriction. Golf was big business now, and money streamed in from flush and eager corporate partners. High-end day courses cropped up like weeds, offering amenities that had remained out of most players' reach . . .
>
> Most of the money for those courses and their membership fees flowed from superheated Wall Street spigots, then greed, hubris and the stubborn human inability to see danger coming from a distance led to September 2008. Amid the economic wreckage of all this steroidal excess, the future of golf's high-flying recent past seems at best uncertain. The grand old clubs, built on sustaining cultures rooted deeply in their communities, will weather any storm, but many of those daily-fee courses had already gone under, and the survivors face hard times."[3]

During these hard times, comprehensive financial analysis is one of the few medicines available to manage the current ills.

Financial Analysis—Where Have You Been?

With the preparation of historical financial statements, we can examine variances within industry data to determine abnormal operating patterns at the facility.

Financial analysis studies of 18-hole golf facilities in the United States are available from Golf Datatech, PGA PerformanceTrak and Club Benchmarking. The key indices for each facility type from PGA PerformanceTrak[4] are at the top of the next page.

The range in net income, as a percentage of gross income, from one type of golf course to another is amazing.

3 Mark Frost, "Golf's Crash Course in Humility," *The Wall Street Journal,* October 18–19, 2008, p. w6.

4 PGA PerformanceTrak, http:apps.pgalinks.com/professionals/apps/memberinfor/AOSurvey/index.cfm.

Key PGA PerformanceTrak Indices

2012 Median Statistics	All Facility Types	Municipal	Daily Fee Semi-Private	Private	Resort
Total Rounds Played	23,000	32,000	25,000	18,000	22,416
Total Facility Revenues	1,371,519	1,000,000	997,500	4,500,000	1,773,000
Golf Operations Payroll	184,950	190,000	140,000	210,000	232,285
Maintenance Payroll	272,619	247,507	200,000	433,000	207,751
Number of Full Time Employees	12	6	9	28	20
Number of Part Time Employees	25	20	20	37	30
Net Income (EBITDA)	226,000	200,000	200,000	270,000	305,000
Net Income as a % of Gross Revenue	16.48%	20.00%	20.05%	6.00%	17.21%

Source: PGA PerformanceTrak, Annual Operating Survey, 2012 (conducted in 2013

In its annual operating and financial performance study, the NGF also creates some valuable insights. The NGF, taking into consideration regional variations in weather and prices, divides its survey sample into public mid-range frost belt, public mid-range sun belt, public premium frost belt, and public premium sunbelt. A composite of those regional statistics created by the NGF results in the following insightful perspectives as shown on the next page:[5]

Club Benchmarking focuses on private detailed financial analysis for private clubs as shown in the chart below. Their extensive analysis has provided some remarkable insights regarding the "available cash model and maintenance expenses." Private clubs maintain available cash as a percentage of total operating revenue from 56% to 62% throughout the

5 National Golf Foundation, Operating and Financial Performance Profiles of 18-hole Golf Facilities in the United States, 2010, 2–25.

Category	Public Sunbelt & Frostbelt All Revenue Ranges	Public Sunbelt Revenues < $1 million	Public Sunbelt Revenues: $1 to $2 million	Public Sunbelt Revenues > $2 million
Green fee and golf cart revenue	$878,433	$476,000	$957,000	$1,741,700
Other golf revenue	$100,600	$58,300	$69,100	$249,500
Food and beverage revenue	$298,217	$92,300	$226,800	$810,000
Merchandise revenue	$105,800	$50,400	$104,100	$227,500
All other revenue	$124,983	$68,800	$126,000	$303,000
Total operating revenue	$1,508,033	$745,800	$1,483,000	$3,331,700
Total maintenance expenses	$650,117	$442,600	$641,700	$1,274,800
All other operations expenses	$702,333	$295,100	$734,100	$1,641,800
Capital expenditures	$106,017	$85,270	$66,080	$170,500
Total revenue per round	$49.85	$30.81	$42.86	$88.18
Golf revenue per round	$34.98	$24.11	$31.81	$54.83
Food and beverage revenue per round	$10.76	$4.32	$7.7	$23.83
Merchandise revenue per round	$4.13	$2.32	$3.36	$7.03
Play days	296	320	342	349

Category	Public Frostbelt Revenues < $800,000	Public Frostbelt Revenues: $800,000 to $1.3 million	Public Frostbelt Revenues > $1.3 million
Green fee and golf cart revenue	$357,500	$651,200	$1,087,200
Other golf revenue	$44,700	$71,100	$110,900
Food and beverage revenue	$83,000	$162,200	$415,000
Merchandise revenue	$44,000	$85,600	$123,200
All other revenue	$38,900	$68,900	$144,300
Total operating revenue	$568,100	$1,039,000	$1,880,600
Total maintenance expenses	$308,700	$486,600	$746,300
All other operations expenses	$227,200	$442,800	$873,000
Capital expenditures	$82	$87,300	$226,870
Total revenue per round	$29.30	$41.26	$66.67
Golf revenue per round	$22.60	$32.80	$43.73
Food and beverage revenue per round	$4.88	$8.31	$15.52
Merchandise revenue per round	$2.98	$3.92	$5.14
Play days	249	244	269

United States. Maintenance costs at private clubs are also within a very tight bandwidth of 31% to 33% of gross revenue, regardless of the geographic location of the club.

A comparison of a golf course's financial numbers to these industry benchmarks serves as a good reference point to measure both strengths and weaknesses in a golf operation.

Financial Modeling—Where Are You Going?

With a firm understanding of a golf course's historical performance in comparison to industry standards, there exists a great opportunity to create financial projections that emphasize a golf course's existing strengths and to correct its weaknesses.

Creating a proper financial model has two benefits: (1) Historical data can be compared to industry benchmarks to detect and evaluate operational efficiencies; and (2) financial projections can be created in which the rates and expenses can be dynamically or experimentally adjusted to calculate the likely impact on the golf course's financial statements.

The PGA of America also provides on their Web site a vast array of templates to assist golf course managers with their fiscal responsibilities. For example, the PGA provides a golf course financial model designed to evaluate golf course acquisitions, development, renovations, and investment opportunities.

Components of the model address the following categories:[6]

- Input parameters regarding the project/model assumptions
- Facility revenues, including detailed supporting schedules addressing:
  - Golf rounds utilization by customer type
  - Golf green fees and cart fees
  - Membership fees and dues
  - Other golf and operating department revenues

6 PGA of America, "PGA Golf Course Financial Model," http://www.pgalinks.com/professionals/content/index.cfm?ctc=1524 and http://apps.pgalinks.com/professionals/apps/memberinfo/AOSurvey/index.cfm?.

- Facility expenses, including detailed supporting schedules addressing:
  - Cost of goods sold
  - Staffing levels and payroll
  - Maintenance department expenses
  - Other operating departments and undistributed expenses
- Vertical and horizontal construction costs, including:
  - Golf course constructions costs
  - Physical facility/vertical structure development costs
  - Development and acquisition soft costs
- Construction loan and permanent financing assumptions

Comparable templates are also available for the PGA annual budget model, which covers user components, input parameters, revenue, operational costs, development costs, debt service, and a five-year financial performance model.

This systematic process for collecting financial and operational data, along with the construction of a predictive financial planning template, will allow a golf course to effectively monitor the cost of programs, services, and facilities and to realistically determine user fees and charges.

The process we use, which is comparable to the PGA model, involves the following steps:

1. The income statement for the past three years is reviewed for anomalies.
2. The general ledger trial balance by account is examined.
3. The data by general ledger category is exported into Excel worksheets.
4. The general ledger accounts are aggregated into appropriate golf course industry standard financial reporting models.
5. Three-year historical income statements are created consistent with generally accepted accounting principles for golf courses.
6. The historical financial statements are analyzed for trends and compared to industry benchmarks for reporting variances and operational deficiencies.

7. The variances with industry data are examined closely to determine abnormal operating patterns at the facility.
8. Five-year financial projections are developed using different estimates for rates, labor, and other expenses.

The process of undertaking this financial modeling is reflected in the index, which includes the necessary worksheets from which cells are linked to facilitate a thorough examination of the operating performance of a golf course.

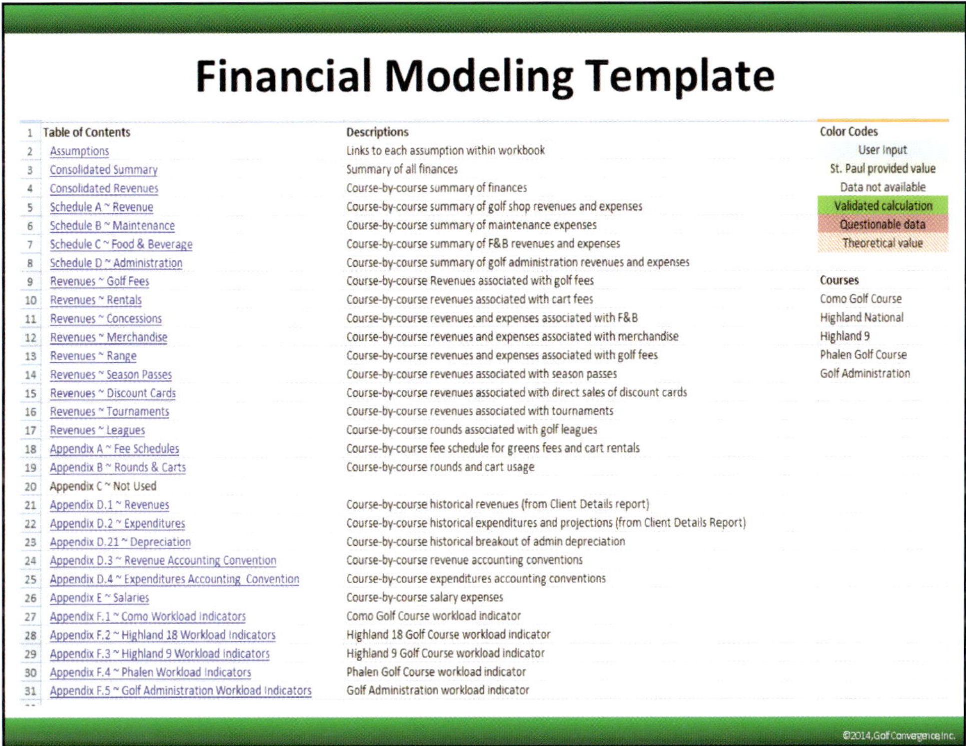

Financial Modeling Template

	Table of Contents	Descriptions	Color Codes
1	Table of Contents	Descriptions	Color Codes
2	Assumptions	Links to each assumption within workbook	User Input
3	Consolidated Summary	Summary of all finances	St. Paul provided value
4	Consolidated Revenues	Course-by-course summary of finances	Data not available
5	Schedule A ~ Revenue	Course-by-course summary of golf shop revenues and expenses	Validated calculation
6	Schedule B ~ Maintenance	Course-by-course summary of maintenance expenses	Questionable data
7	Schedule C ~ Food & Beverage	Course-by-course summary of F&B revenues and expenses	Theoretical value
8	Schedule D ~ Administration	Course-by-course summary of golf administration revenues and expenses	
9	Revenues ~ Golf Fees	Course-by-course Revenues associated with golf fees	Courses
10	Revenues ~ Rentals	Course-by-course revenues associated with cart fees	Como Golf Course
11	Revenues ~ Concessions	Course-by-course revenues and expenses associated with F&B	Highland National
12	Revenues ~ Merchandise	Course-by-course revenues and expenses associated with merchandise	Highland 9
13	Revenues ~ Range	Course-by-course revenues and expenses associated with golf fees	Phalen Golf Course
14	Revenues ~ Season Passes	Course-by-course revenues associated with season passes	Golf Administration
15	Revenues ~ Discount Cards	Course-by-course revenues associated with direct sales of discount cards	
16	Revenues ~ Tournaments	Course-by-course revenues associated with tournaments	
17	Revenues ~ Leagues	Course-by-course rounds associated with golf leagues	
18	Appendix A ~ Fee Schedules	Course-by-course fee schedule for greens fees and cart rentals	
19	Appendix B ~ Rounds & Carts	Course-by-course rounds and cart usage	
20	Appendix C ~ Not Used		
21	Appendix D.1 ~ Revenues	Course-by-course historical revenues (from Client Details report)	
22	Appendix D.2 ~ Expenditures	Course-by-course historical expenditures and projections (from Client Details Report)	
23	Appendix D.21 ~ Depreciation	Course-by-course historical breakout of admin depreciation	
24	Appendix D.3 ~ Revenue Accounting Convention	Course-by-course revenue accounting conventions	
25	Appendix D.4 ~ Expenditures Accounting Convention	Course-by-course expenditures accounting conventions	
26	Appendix E ~ Salaries	Course-by-course salary expenses	
27	Appendix F.1 ~ Como Workload Indicators	Como Golf Course workload indicator	
28	Appendix F.2 ~ Highland 18 Workload Indicators	Highland 18 Golf Course workload indicator	
29	Appendix F.3 ~ Highland 9 Workload Indicators	Highland 9 Golf Course workload indicator	
30	Appendix F.4 ~ Phalen Workload Indicators	Phalen Golf Course workload indicator	
31	Appendix F.5 ~ Golf Administration Workload Indicators	Golf Administration workload indicator	

©2014, Golf Convergence Inc.

In undertaking financial modeling, the forecast of revenues is a simple process of estimating the number of rounds and revenue mix by golfer type, time of day, day of week, and season of the year. As indicated previously, revenue from carts, merchandise, food and beverage, and other is estimated based on a derivative of the green fee per round. Thus, changing the rounds assumption drives the entire revenue model, with the only exceptions being tournament play and catering.

Expenses—The Burden of Labor Lifted

Examining expenses in detail can be exhausting, but it can definitely be rewarding. Labor costs are one of the major operational expenses. Closely evaluating these expenses is a must. The second step in such an examination is to prepare an accurate labor forecast using a worksheet similar to the following:

Labor Expense Forecast

	Avg. Hourly Pay	Start of Season	End of Season	Weekday Hours	Weekend Hours	Annual Hours	Payroll					
								Day	1	2	3	4
								Day2	Tue	Wed	Thu	Fri
								Begin Civil Twilight	717	717	717	717
								End Civil Dusk	1715	1716	1717	1718
								Hours of Sunlight	9.97	9.98	10.00	10.02
GOLF SHOP												
GOLF PRO	30.44	1/1/2008	12/31/2008	8	0	2,080	63,315.20		0.00	8.00	8.00	8.00
FACILITY SUPERVISOR	26.73	1/1/2008	12/31/2008	8	0	0	0.00		0.00	8.00	8.00	8.00
GOLF FULL TIME 3		1/1/2008	12/31/2008	0	0	0	0.00		0.00	0.00	0.00	0.00
PARKS & RECREATION WKR I/II	8.76	4/1/2008	10/31/2008	A	A	3,161	27,691.24		0.00	0.00	0.00	0.00
PARKS & RECREATION WKR I/II	8.76	4/1/2008	10/31/2008	A	A	3,161	27,691.24		0.00	0.00	0.00	0.00
PARKS & RECREATION WKR I/II	8.76	4/1/2008	10/31/2008	2	8	0	0.00		0.00	0.00	0.00	0.00
PARKS & RECREATION WKR III-V	18.04	4/1/2008	10/31/2008	0	A	896	16,166.85		0.00	0.00	0.00	0.00
REFECTORY ATTENDENT	10.54	4/1/2008	10/31/2008	20	24	4,160	43,846.40		0.00	0.00	0.00	0.00
Total Golf Shop						***13,458***	***178,711***					
GOLF ADMINISTRATION												
GOLF FULL TIME 1		1/1/2008	12/31/2008	0	0	0	0.00		0.00	0.00	0.00	0.00
GOLF FULL TIME 2		1/1/2008	12/31/2008	0	0	0	0.00		0.00	0.00	0.00	0.00
GOLF PART TIME1		4/1/2008	10/31/2008	0	0	0	0.00		0.00	0.00	0.00	0.00
GOLF PART TIME2		4/1/2008	10/31/2008	0	0	0	0.00		0.00	0.00	0.00	0.00
GOLF PART TIME3		4/1/2008	10/31/2008	0	0	0	0.00		0.00	0.00	0.00	0.00
Total Golf Adminstration						***0***	***0***					
MAINTENANCE												
GOLF COURSE SUPERINTENDENT	26.73	1/1/2008	12/31/2008	8	0	1,040	27,799.20		0.00	8.00	8.00	8.00
ASSISTANT SUPERINDENT	22.12	1/1/2008	12/31/2008	8	0	1,040	23,004.80		0.00	8.00	8.00	8.00
ASSISTANT SUPERINDENT	22.12	1/1/2008	12/31/2008	8	0	1,040	23,004.80		0.00	8.00	8.00	8.00
PARKS WORKER III	20.15	1/1/2008	12/31/2008	8	0	2,080	41,912.00		0.00	8.00	8.00	8.00
PARKS WORKER I/II	9.17	4/1/2008	10/31/2008	24	12	5,200	47,684.00		0.00	0.00	0.00	0.00
PARKS WORKER GOLF	16.22	4/1/2008	10/31/2008	40	16	5,200	84,344.00		0.00	0.00	0.00	0.00
GOLF PART TIME3		4/1/2008	10/31/2008	0	0	0	0.00		0.00	0.00	0.00	0.00
GOLF PART TIME4		4/1/2008	10/31/2008	0	0	0	0.00		0.00	0.00	0.00	0.00
GOLF PART TIME5		4/1/2008	10/31/2008	0	0	0	0.00		0.00	0.00	0.00	0.00
Total Maintenance						***15,600***	***247,745***					
				226								
FOOD & BEVERAGE												
GOLF FULL TIME 1		1/1/2008	12/31/2008	0	0	0	0.00		0.00	0.00	0.00	0.00
GOLF FULL TIME 2		1/1/2008	12/31/2008	0	0	0	0.00		0.00	0.00	0.00	0.00
GOLF FULL TIME 3		1/1/2008	12/31/2008	0	0	0	0.00		0.00	0.00	0.00	0.00
GOLF FULL TIME 4		1/1/2008	12/31/2008	0	0	0	0.00		0.00	0.00	0.00	0.00
PARKS & RECREATION WKR I/II	9.54	4/1/2008	10/31/2008	7	0	1,040	9,921.60		0.00	0.00	0.00	0.00
REFECTORY ATTENDENT	10.54	5/1/2008	9/30/2008	7	A	1,040	10,961.60		0.00	0.00	0.00	0.00
ZOO ATTENDENT	10.65	4/1/2008	10/31/2008	4	2	0	0.00		0.00	0.00	0.00	0.00
		4/1/2008	10/31/2008	0	0	0	0.00		0.00	0.00	0.00	0.00
GOLF PART TIME5		4/1/2008	10/31/2008	0	0	0	0.00		0.00	0.00	0.00	0.00
Total Food & Beverage						***2,080***	***20,883***					

This template points out how much labor is required by position for every day within the year and is a viable benchmarking, budgeting, and financial modeling tool. The information gathered should simplify the need to juggle employees who work full-time or part-time, by day or by week or by season, based on rounds and daylight hours.

The key to efficient utilization of labor, according to Stuart Hayden, a leading industry expert, is to ensure that work flow is properly designed and that clear task management is supported by effective labor scheduling, monitoring, and scheduling adjustments.

Effective labor management, Mr. Hayden believes, includes the following:

- Assessment of golf operation in the aggregate
- Workflow analysis of each position
- Daily schedule development
- Consolidation of schedules to reconcile to budget
- Development of administrative reports to monitor and manage.
- Training specific to the duties of each staff person.[7]

The detailed labor schedules created in the work-flow design process are required to compensate for the loss of institutional knowledge when there is management turnover.

With the work-flow process created and labor schedules prepared, a course manager needs next to consider the following:

1. Each department head should prepare the labor schedule seven days in advance. Adjustments should be made to reflect the demand from the previous week, any special events in the coming week, and the number of rounds on the tee sheet.
2. Employees should be assigned specific jobs for the day (from each employee's specific job task list) and allocated enough time to complete the tasks. Opening duties for the outside services staff, such as washing golf carts, and picking up the driving range, are examples of timed tasks. Jobs where specific timed service tasks are not as structured, such as answering phones in the shop, should be staffed based upon the current day's demand.

On the next page is an example of a labor schedule for a week.

This schedule is made with the help of a software program that takes into account opening times, sunrise and sunset, facility utilization, and minimum service requirements. It is prepared weekly for the major departments at a golf course: outside services, pro shop, restaurant/snack bar, and catering. This program is so dynamic that the schedules for the entire year can be printed in advance to develop annual labor budgets.

7 Hayden, "Labor Proposal," e-mail message dated November 11, 2008, p. 1.

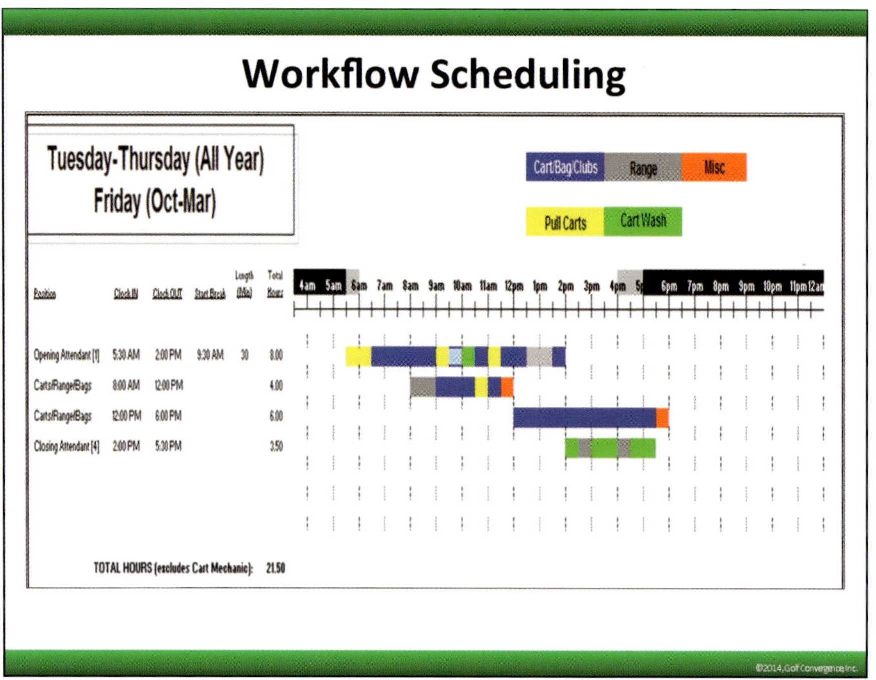

When interviewed for this book, Stuart Hayden stated,

> "Hourly staff is usually not in alignment with the objectives of the management team when it comes to minimizing their own labor hours. Therefore they have to be managed closely. It is not uncommon for staff to clock in early, although they are not needed, or to clock out late, even though they are not busy. Self-interest isn't the only horse in the race, but it is always the one to bet on. The hourly staff, many of whom are seasonal, want to make money and therefore is incentivized to stay on the clock. They do not share the owner's or the GM's concern for the bottom line."[8]

3. It is important to minimize the number of people on salary or guaranteed full-time 40-hour employment because the fixed costs of these employees makes it impossible to cut labor costs when the business is slow.
4. In seasonal markets demand is predictably slower in the off-season, and this is when staffing should be at a minimum.
5. The challenge is managing labor as a variable cost when there are periods of low demand or when weather (rain, snow, heat, cold) reduces play. Fewer staff members are required for fewer rounds.

8 Stuart Hayden, e-mail to author, June 15, 2009.

The most important thing department heads and general managers can do is compare each department's schedule (which was built based upon historical and forecasted demand, projected weather, and planned events) against the actual hours worked on a daily basis. Monitoring labor hours worked compared to those scheduled on a daily basis gives the manager the information needed to coach staff on the need to work according to the schedule.

Impressive Results Emerge from Inspired Analysis

The results of managing all of this detail can be impressive. The following is an excerpt from the strategic plan created for the city of Saint. Paul, Minnesota:

> "The foundation of a business is the financial statement. For management and staff to be able to plan, execute and forecast, having timely, accurate and meaningful financial information is imperative.
>
> We believe the largest weakness observed in the city's golf operation was their accounting and information reporting system called FMS. It is so antiquated that producing meaningful reports is a challenge. During the process of preparing the business plan, financial reports were provided by very well-meaning and dedicated professionals.
>
> Because of the staff changes in the accounting department during the past two years, historical documentation is insufficient, and a complete understanding of the various fund transfers is very difficult to reconstruct. In the information provided, some transfers from the golf courses were classified as administrative expenses, transfers from the general fund were allocated to reduce interest expenses, bond principal payments were classified as operational expenses, capital expenditures and capital lease principal payments were allocated as operational charges, and depreciation was aggregated versus being separately identified in the calculation of E.B.I.T.D.A: earnings before interest, taxes, depreciation and amortization—a key benchmark of a golf course's financial performance.
>
> It took a tedious amount of work to obtain financial statements that reflected the golf operation as a separate, independent economic

entity. The net income reported differs from the audited reports published as follows:

	Year 1	Year 2	Year 3
Net income per the Audited Financial Statements	$633,910	$850,247	$677,514
Actual Net Income determined by Recasting Financial Statements to Reflect Golf Operations Properly	633,910	562,428	467,469
Variance	$0	$287,819	$210,045

Finally, monthly financial statements are not prepared with the proper accruals reflecting ending inventory in food and beverage, merchandise, depreciation or interest expense. Thus, interim financial statements are not meaningful as to expenses incurred.

We recommend that the following enhanced accounting and budgeting policies and procedures are implemented:

- Adopting generally accepted accounting principles with respect to the treatment of capitalized versus operational expenses.
- Creation of monthly reports for the operational staff highlighting course utilization revenue per available tee time (RevPATT) by five profit centers (green fees—tournament, carts, merchandise, food and beverage—catering and other—range).
- Identification of core customer spending, customer retention, composition of golfers, and season pass rate analysis.
- Presentation of monthly financial statements (budget versus actual) consistent with golf industry standards, for both the pro shop operation and maintenance.
- The allocation of administrative expenses from an omnibus account to the respective courses for which the expenses were incurred. While St. Paul's current practice is adopted by other municipalities, we believe that the actual net operating income of each course is masked by the use of a consolidated account for administrative expenses.
- Comparison of monthly operational information to national benchmarks prepared by Golf Datatech and PGA PerformanceTrak."[9]

9 Golf Convergence, "City of St. Paul Business Plan, Golf Operations," March 27, 2008, pp. 29–30.

What is the implication of the previous statements? Only by benchmarking these general ledger accounts against industry models was it made apparent that administrative expenses were way off industry standards. The variance was caused by the amortization of bond principal, a balance sheet item, being charged to the income statement. If net income is incorrectly stated, that fact has both political and financial implications. If accurate financial information cannot be created, how can management effectively operate the facility?

The City and County of Denver maintains a vibrant golf franchise. Benchmarking their financial performance reveals that their revenue per round is below industry norms. As a result, net income is low and deferred capital expenses are increasing. This is a classic example of, though the financial results are adequate, the potential investment return with appropriate pricing and consistent reinvestment to ensure customer value is really good.

City and County of Denver Comparison
to 2010 PGA PerformanceTrak Benchmarks

Description	Denver (7 Course Average)	Municipal	Daily Fee/Semi-Private	Private
Total Rounds Played	42,585	37,087	30,985	23,000
Total Facility Revenues	$1,085,720	$1,133,333	$1,300,000	$2,800,000
Revenue Per Round Utilized	$25.49	$30.56	$41.96	$121.73
Course Maintenance Payroll	$285,554	$270,000	$227,819	$409,043
Pro Shop Operations	$204,539	$273,468	$230,000	$289,000
Net Income (EBITDA)	$153,538	$206,000	$200,000	$250,000
Net Income as a % of Gross	14.14%	18.17%	15.38%	8.92%

©2014, Golf Convergence Inc.

The potential of Denver's golf courses is further evidenced by an analysis of salary expenses which reflects that though fringe benefits are reasonable, salary expense, particularly in administration, has the opportunity for cost reductions generating additional capital for reinvestment.

				2010				
Department	Course	Seasonal Hours	Seasonal Labor - Financials	2010 Hourly	2010 Full Time Labor	Benefits	Total Salary Cost	Fringe Benefits
Administration	Total Admin	0	$0	0.00	$315,637	$122,516	$438,153	27.96%
	Junior Golf	1,250	$19,955	15.97	$92,319	$30,149	$142,423	21.17%
	Total Admnistration	1,250	$19,955	15.97	$407,956	$152,665	$580,576	26.30%
Maintenance	City Park	11,037	$129,685	11.75	$181,512	$113,305	$424,502	26.69%
	Harvard Gulch	6,997	$78,430	11.21	$30,681	$15,875	$175,008	17.70%
	J. F. Kennedy	19,919	$234,806	11.79	$223,531	$160,863	$619,200	25.98%
	Overland Park	11,731	$132,408	11.29	$163,258	$118,048	$413,714	28.53%
	Wellshire	10,081	$119,892	11.89	$157,821	$126,237	$403,950	31.25%
	Willis Case	8,707	$103,172	11.85	$116,868	$78,015	$298,055	26.17%
	Total Maintenance	68,472	$798,413	11.66	$873,673	$612,343	$2,284,430	26.81%
Pro Shop	Aqua Golf	3,652	$36,959	10.12	$58,360	$38,382	$133,701	28.71%
	City Park	13,464	$129,777	9.64	$83,125	$23,397	$236,300	9.90%
	Harvard Gulch	0	$0	0.00	$0	$0	$0	N/A
	J. F. Kennedy	17,555	$161,284	0.00	$116,943	$50,383	$328,610	15.33%
	Overland Park	0	$0	0.00	$0	$0	$0	N/A
	Wellshire	10,674	$114,965	10.77	$110,619	$57,897	$283,481	20.42%
	Willis Case	8,773	$84,943	9.68	$84,753	$42,255	$211,951	19.94%
	Total Pro Shop	54,117	$527,928	9.76	$453,799	$212,314	$1,194,042	17.78%
Total		123,838	$1,346,296	10.87	$1,735,429	$977,323	$4,059,048	23.63%
Gross Revenue							$8,874,230	
Salary/Gross Revenue							45.74%	

©2014, Golf Convergence Inc.

Another illustration of the value of benchmarking can be seen in the chart

Comparison to the National Municipal Golf Course

Maintenance Department	California Course	National: Bottom 25	Median	Top 25%	Top 10%
Full Time	9	3	4	7	11
Part Time	0	4	7	10	16
Payroll	$821,084	$167,000	$251,085	$400,000	$587,000
Other Expenses (Supplies/Repairs)	$206,000	$110,000	$179,262	$285,000	$401,800
Maintenance Expenses (Fertilizer, Seeds, Gasoline)	$86,000	$100,000	$160,000	$293,820	$443,066
Other Expenses (Building Repairs, Cleaning Supplies)	$411,733	$10,000	$35,000	$84,500	$163,015
Total Maintenance Expenses	$1,524,000	$387,000	$625,347	$1,063,320	$1,594,881

on this page. The labor expense of this California municipal golf course has an unfavorable labor variance of $233,499. This is not uncommon where a staff becomes tenured but is the Achilles heel for the government operation of municipal golf courses.

From the examples presented, the financial and operational opportunities and challenges of these golf courses becomes evident. A strategic plan that incorporates these findings offers the opportunity to implement positive changes.

The Future of Financial Management—Data Streaming

The evolution of technology during the past two decades has fundamentally changed how employees perform their jobs. While we are certainly working harder, working smarter remains elusive. As technology evolves, I believe that working smarter will also occur.

Streaming Alert Template

Financial Data Streaming

POS	Notice Interval	Event	Trigger	Variance
1 Green Fee	I, D, W, M	Green Fee Sold	Transaction Discounted	Less than: Percentage to be specified - could be 50% of rack rate
2 Food and Beverage	I, D, W, M	Food and Beverage Sold	Markdown	Less than: Quantity to be specified - could be 25%
3 Merchandise	I, D, W, M	Inventory Sold	On Hand Count	Less than: Quantity to be specified - could be 0
4 Merchandise	I, D, W, M	Inventory Sold	Markdown	Less than: Quantity to be specified - could be 25%
5 Total Revenue	D, W, M	Daily Close Out	Gross Revenue Benchmark	Less than: Quantity to be specified - could be $5,000
6 Cash Variance	I, D, W	Daily Close Out	Variance	Greater than: Quantity to be specified - could be $100
7 REVPATT	D, W, M	Daily Close Out	Variance	Less than: Quantity to be specified for Green Fee, Cart, Merchandise, Food and Beverage per player

Reservation	Notice Interval	Event	Trigger	Variance
8 Core Customer	I, D	Tee Time Reservation	Booking by Customer	Booking by Top 10 customer measured by total spending, or yield per visit
9 Tee Sheet Utilization	I, D	Tee Sheet Bookings	Reservations	Less than: Percentage to be specified - could be 30% of capacity
10 Tee Sheet Utilization	I, D	Tee Sheet Bookings	Reservations	Cancellation of Number of Tee Times on Specified Day - Could be Greater than 20
11 Weather	I, D	Weather Forecast	Temperature Range	Forecasts calls for temperature less, greater than, or precipation exceeding

The next enhancement in golf management software will be "financial data streamlining alerts." These will be similar to Google alerts, and golf course owners and managers will have management systems that automatically monitor changing economic conditions and provide them with cell phone, text, or e-mail alerts so they can adjust prices or labor or customer service when appropriate.

Managers will be able to create a template of important alerts, as depicted on this page.

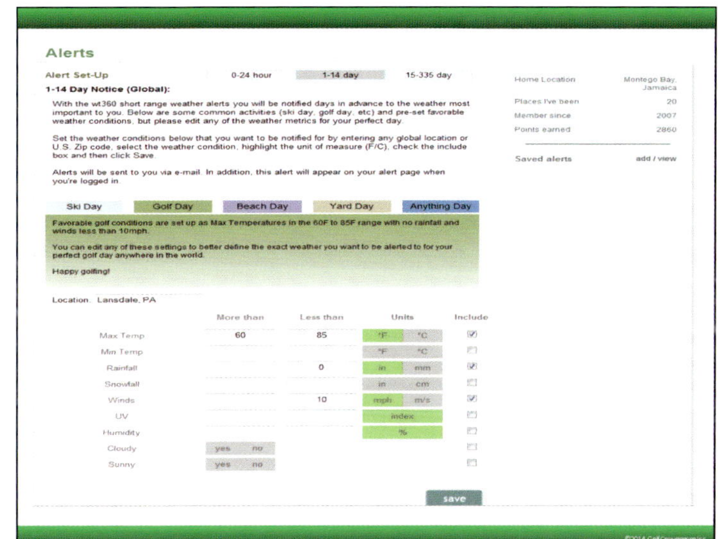

One example that offers great possibility is weather alerts provided in a 1- to 14-day time window by Weather Trends International.

These alerts can be issued to adjust decisions pertaining to

- Employee scheduling,
- Revenue predictions/goals,
- Course watering maintenance/timing
- Favorable/unfavorable promotional/marketing periods.

The astute manager will be able to develop a "flash" report that will allow course managers and owners to focus on those items that directly influence income.

The opportunities for enhanced management and reduced labor hours are very promising. Key alerts for each course would be unique. But the concept is fundamental. The manager of a business should anticipate changing events.

End Notes

The lessons of this chapter are:

1) Simply stated, an income statement has three components: revenue, expenses, and the resultant net income.
2) Rounds as measured by green fees, member dues, and season passes account for about 60% of gross revenue and materially affect all the other revenue departments. The revenue derived from carts, food and beverage, merchandise, and lessons is directly correlated to the number of rounds.
3) With the preparation of historical financial statements, variances with industry data can be examined closely to determine abnormal operating patterns at the facility.
4) With a firm understanding of a golf course's historical performance in comparison to industry standards, there exists a great opportunity to create financial projections that emphasize a golf course's existing strengths and to correct its weaknesses.
5) The key to efficient utilization of labor is to ensure that work flow is properly designed and that clear task management is supported by effective labor scheduling, monitoring, and scheduling adjustments so that each member of the staff is operating efficiently.
6) The most important thing department heads and general managers can do is compare each department's schedules (which were built upon historical and forecasted demand, projected weather, and planned events) against the actual hours worked on a daily basis.
7) Future technology will provide for data streaming in which golf course managers will receive text/e-mail alerts when certain thresholds that they establish are met, prompting the need for management review and action.

Concluding Thought

Leahy's Law—If a thing is done wrong often enough, it becomes right.

Chapter 10

Pricing and Yield Management

Step 4 of Golf Convergence WIN™ Formula (continued)

No man was ever wise by chance.

Seneca

Chapter Highlights

Yield management is squeezing the most money you can out of every customer who walks through your door, and making him happy while he gives it to you.

This chapter discusses what tools are available and how to apply the formulas to increase the revenue per available round.

While it is an oversimplification to say that there is no number in the golf business more meaningless than the rack rate, with the proliferation of coupon books, third-party Web sites, on-line specials, and advertising, the effective yield of a golf course is under siege.

What Is Fair?

Fair market value is defined as "the price for which property can be sold in an 'arm's length' transaction; that is, between informed, unrelated, and willing parties, each of whom is acting rationally and in its own best interest."[1]

Realizing that most golf courses have more than 75 different rates that vary by day of the week, time of day, day of the year, and age of the golfer, there is no more subjective area than green fees.

How then is the green fee determined? In theory, if the green fee were properly set for each individual tee time, it is logical to assume that 100% of the available times would be sold.

Some golf course owners, particularly those at newer facilities, establish the green fees based on cost plus desired return on investment. The expenses are estimated, the required debt service coverage calculated, and the desired investment return projected; then the green fees are set based on the aggregate total divided by the projected rounds. Of course if that green fee number is out of whack with the market, nobody will be satisfied. This sort of pricing might pacify the banker, but it does nothing to assure that value was provided to the golfer.

Others set the green fees based on market value. This is the "feels right" method. Either the fees from the prior year are adjusted for inflation, or perhaps a sampling is taken of comparable facilities and a rate is chosen that feels competitive.

Still others base their fees on some subjective perception of the value of the golf experience. How else could one justify the difference between a golf course charging over $475 per round and one that costs less than $30? Both courses are between 6,000 and 7,400 yards, have 18 holes, and take roughly 4½ hours to play.

That substantial difference would have to be justified based on the location of the course, conditioning, strategic shot values, time of the year, surrounding scenery, the architect, or championships held at the facility. Pebble Beach does a good job of filling the golf course at a premium rate. But there is only one Monterey Peninsula.

1 Cisco Systems Capital, "Financial Glossary," http://www.cisco.com/warp/public/csc/about_financing/glossary.html.

There is a formula, often invisible to the owner, for what golfers are willing to pay, and it is based on the value of a golfer's experience. The key to a successful golf operation is for the course manager to see if the gap between the actual rate charged and the value provided can be determined.

The Value Gap

By examining all of the components of a golf experience, a golf course manager can calculate the value of the experience, compare that to the rate charged, build a marketing campaign based on its unique value, and stimulate revenue. Recall that value = experience – price.

For purposes of stimulating creative thought on alternative methods, a potential model for establishing green fees would comprise six variables: slope rating (difficulty and shot values), strategy, conditioning, playing texture variety, ambience, and customer amenities. Each of these components and their effect on the proper price for the green fee is discussed next.

1. **Slope Rating:** The greater the slope rating, the greater the challenge, and the greater the diversity of golf shots provided, the higher the green fees should be. To play a flat municipal golf course short in length with nominal hazards is a completely different experience than a championship bunker-strewn, lake-filled, tree-lined golf course.

   While a debate on shot values is subjective, a quantitative way to measure shot values might be on the course's slope. Hence the premium charged by difficult courses like the Stadium Course at TPC would be justified.

   The green fees could be set based on the following:

Slope from Middle Tee	Base Green Fee
Under 113	$20
114–120	35
121–130	50
131–140	75
Over 140	$100

2. **Strategy:** What is better—the 120-yard par 3 strewn with bunkers, the island green, the dual fairway hole that provides both a safe and a hazardous route, or the well-designed dogleg left that places the hazards on the left? The answer is all of the above. Hit the precise shot, and you are rewarded.

Take the first safe route, and the second shot becomes more of a challenge. Risk for reward—the essence of the game. You might consider adjusting your green fees for the following:

Strategy	Adjustment to Green Fee
Vast majority of holes are straight; course is flat; few trees, bunkers, dunes, and water hazards; and options to play hole are well-defined, providing few options. No requirement to position shots. No risk/reward options.	–10
A few doglegs with modest bunkering and trees, some rolling terrain, green complexes are uniform throughout the course. One or two risk/reward options.	–5
Terrain, bunkers, water hazards, trees, and green complexes provide typical golf experience.	0
One-third of golf holes provide a unique golf experience requiring thought to successfully navigate risk/reward.	+5
Up to two-thirds of golf holes provide a challenging experience where placement of the drive and the second shot has a significant impact on the ability to score well.	+10
The par 3, 4, and 5 holes have varying length, i.e., par 3s of 120, 150, 180, and 210 yards. Course may have dual fairways, bunkering that pinches the fairway, streams crossing the fairway and/or the green, narrow green openings, green side bunkers of varying depth, and heavily contoured putting surfaces.	+20

3. **Conditioning:** Well-manicured golf courses should charge a premium. The investment made in maintaining a course ranges from $200,000 to over $2 million, and the conditioning is rated by golfers as one of the two most important criteria.

   The following chart suggests adjustments that could be made to the green fees based on the current course condition:

Condition	Adjustment to Green Fee
Poor, requiring winter rules to be played	–10
Greens aerated during past two weeks	–10
Standard, greens stimped at 8 to 9	0
Good, one cut of rough, single mowing pairing on fairway and greens	+10
Excellent, two cuts of rough, cross cut fairway, green stimped at 9 to 10	+20
Tour quality, greens stimped at over 11	+30

4. **Playing Texture Variety:** For the golf devotee, nothing is prettier than a golf course that has well-manicured bentgrass tees, fairways and greens that have been cross cut, Kentucky blue grass rough with two cuts, and bunkers lined with rye for stability and fescue and Scottish broom for appearance. Conversely, a course that is poa annua or Bermudagrass looks less defined.

Grasses	Adjustment to Green Fee
One strain	−10
Two strains	0
Three to four strains	+10
Four or more strains in which bent, blue, fescue, and Scottish broom are used	+20

5. **Ambience:** In the mountains, along a river, by an ocean, spectacular vistas, a well-known architect, a fabulous clubhouse, an extensive practice facility—all would command a premium that should be added to the green fee.

Ambience	Adjustment to Green Fee
Unique tee markers	+5
Flower garden at entrance	+5
Flower garden at three or multiple locations on course	+10
Extensive practice facility with unlimited practice privileges for registered golfer	+20
Top 10 architect	+25
11th–50th ranked architect	+10
River or ocean comes into play. For each such hole...	+10
Theme to course: Tour 18, Cowboy's Club, etc	+10
Conducted LPGA or Senior PGA event	+10
Conducted PGA Tour event	+20
Conducted USGA national championship	+20

6. **Customer Service Amenities:** While every golfer is looking for "something free," amenities provided could be packaged into the basic green fees.

   We have observed over 100 different amenities disbursed at golf courses starting at the bag drop area, locker room, first tee, the cart, pro shop, on the course, and in the cart return area. These range from engraved bag tags, bottled water and suntan lotion, to certificates of accomplishment for besting par on a signature hole. The creativity of golf course managers in making the customer's experience special has been noteworthy. We have even witnessed free food on the course, for example, fish tacos at Cabo del Sol or chocolate chip cookies at Hualai.

The green fee could be increased based on the number of amenities provided the golfer based on the following chart:

Amenities Provided	Adjustment to Green Fee
0–2	+0
3–5	+2
6–10	+5
11–20	+10
21–40	+20
Over 40	+50
Note: 0–2 would likely represent tees and ball markers in the pro shop.	

If you take this model and apply it, it provides an approximate estimate of the correct price. Following are two examples:

Category	City Park—Denver, Colorado	Cowboys Club—Dallas, Texas
Slope	$35	$75
Strategy	0	10
Conditioning	–5	10
Playing Texture	–10	10
Ambience	0	30
Customer Service	0	20
Estimate Value Based Green Fee	$20	$155

Looking for another alternative pricing model? Consider charging by the hour, which might be based on the following chart:

Type of Course	Hourly Rate
Steel, i.e., entry-level municipal	$ 6.00
Bronze, i.e., average daily fee	12.00
Silver, i.e., above-average daily fee or mid-tier private club or resort	25.00
Gold, i.e., top end daily fee, above average private club or resort	50.00
Platinum, i.e., top-end golf facility.	75.00
Note: The average green fee of a *Golf Magazine* Top 100 the Public Can Play is $172.30.	

For those seeking to use a cart, one could add $4 per hour for the cart per golfer at the steel level and slightly tier the pricing as the quality of the facility improves. The permutations are limitless, but the concept of a single hourly rate is simple.

Yes, there are many logistical hurdles to implementing such a concept (collecting at the end of the round for golf secured in advance by credit card; a fast group gets stuck behind a slow group and demands the lower rate; individuals wanting to play only for one or two hours and returning to the clubhouse via fairways being used by other golfers). Notwithstanding the challenges, this novel approach could create a marketing buzz that might attract golfers.

The alternatives to merely setting green fees based on competitive rates focus on the concept that, all things being equal, golfers pay for the value of the product received, just as they pay for any other commodity.

Thus, each facility should ask—

> "What would be the perfect round at our facility?"
>
> "How do we consistently deliver that experience?"
>
> "How can we exceed expectations?"

The Potential to Grow Utilization

Why the need to examine alternatives? While golf has seen many challenges in the last five years, the perception still exists that golf courses are busy and that getting a tee time, particularly on the weekend, is a challenge.

The fact is that getting a time tee between 6:00 a.m. and 10:00 a.m. is a challenge on the weekends. What the golf industry has done a poor job communicating is the fact that courses are wide open on Sunday through Thursday after 1 p.m. As a matter of fact, during those times, you can get on most courses in the United States within one hour, except for when the course is having a shotgun tournament or charity event.

The chart at the top of the next page is an illustration that can be applied anywhere in the United States where there is a tremendous available supply of tee times that far exceeds demand.

Description		Amount
Number of Playable Days	Courses north of I-80 (a line from New York to Chicago to Salt Lake to San Francisco)	192
Available Daylight Hours	To complete 9 holes	11
Tee Time Interval		7½
Players per Tee Time		4
Rounds Potential		67,584
Average Rounds Played		33,000
Average Utilization of Course		48.83%

Considering that the leisure industry is at 80% utilization and transportation is at 70%, the fact that golf courses are at 50% utilization speaks to the financial woes of the industry.

Yield Management Theory

Tee times are like airline seats. Once the plane takes off, the empty seat is worthless, and once the 1:15 tee time comes and goes, it's gone forever. The goal is revenue optimization.

Revenue management has been described as "the application of information systems and pricing strategies to allocate the right capacity to the right customer at the right place at the right time."[2]

In practice, revenue management has meant setting prices according to predicted demand levels.[3] An alternative is building value by creating new products by combining green fees, carts, food and beverage, and range access at a set price.

While some feel that yield management can result in price discrimination (charging customers consuming otherwise identical goods or services different prices), demand pricing is used by many industries. From Expedia to Orbitz to eBay, customers have accepted that very rarely do different customers pay the same price. Sophisticated software systems and staff provide airlines, car rental agencies, and hotels the ability to manage price based upon availability, time, and demand.

---

2 Barry C. Smith, John F. Leimkuhler, and Ross M. Darrow, "Yield Management at American Airlines," *Interfaces*, Vol. 22, pp. 8–31.

3 Sheryl E. Kimes, "Revenue Management on the Links: Applying Yield Management to the Golf Course Industry," *Cornell Hotel and Restaurant Management Administration Quarterly*, February, 2000, p. 120.

Demand pricing has gotten very little attention in the golf industry. Some golf courses use pricing schemes such as early bird back 9, twilight, super twilight, night owl, beat the heat, pay the temperature in cold markets—all of which are examples of demand pricing in golf. Yet most golf course managers use a traditional approach to setting green fees. They set weekday and weekend prices based on a minimal amount of data. Then, to stimulate rounds, they use newspaper advertising, participation in coupon books, and providing inventory to third parties.

A Revenue Management Primer

Because a golf course has a perishable inventory of tee times, fixed capacity, predictable time-related demand, and high fixed and low variable costs, it is an ideal industry for revenue management.

While it sounds precise, it is very subjective, and requires a lot of guesswork—at least initially. Understanding sales history and improving demand forecasts require time. It must be monitored and adjusted frequently, as fickle customers will always remain unpredictable.

The laws of retail pricing control. As the "rack rate," or "published rate," is adjusted upwards, rounds fall. Conversely, lowering rates boosts play. If golf were free, in theory, the course would be at capacity. If the fee was $10,000 per round, no one would play. The essential question is: What is the appropriate mix between price and rounds, the mix that will maximize gross revenue?

A single price point model is flawed, as shown in the Walt Disney World example.[4]

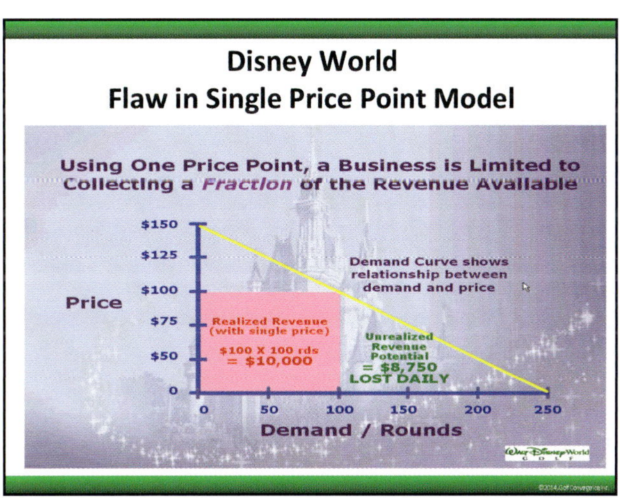

Finding the balance between the price and demand is essential. What is better off—the course that plays 24,000 rounds at $40 per tee time or a facility that plays 40,000 rounds at $24 per tee time? From a gross revenue perspective, both facilities generate

4 Steve Harker, "Maximizing Profit Using Yield/Revenue Management—A Walt Disney World Case Study," October 29, 2009, Slide 21.

the same gross revenue. While the wear and tear on the course was higher on the course that played 40,000 rounds, that cost is often negligible. The objective is simple: maximize revenue. It is the only benchmark that truly matters, as noted in the chart on the left.

Many golf course managers are lulled into the economic trap of believing higher rounds, albeit at slight discount, is a best practice. Discounting is a slippery slope. The following chart highlights the perils:

Price Decrease	Number of Additional Rounds Required to Offer Discount
5%	5.26%
10%	11.11%
15%	17.65%
20%	25.00%
25%	33.33%
30%	42.86%
35%	53.85%
40%	66.67%
45%	81.82%
50%	100.00%

The following is a key point that will determine the financial success of a golf course:

It is critical to match a golf course's perceived value to the posted rate; the accuracy of this match will likely determine the financial success of a golf course. This process of matching perceived value to the posted rate is achieved by undertaking a customer survey, which includes not only the course's core customers but also a statistically valid sampling of golfers within the local market. A slight exception to this pricing paradigm is for tournaments, which are less price sensitive. For these groups, starting with the rack rate and adjusting the rate charged based on actual demand is a safer approach.

Without undertaking a survey and examining closely historical demand, setting rates is pure guesswork. To illustrate, the following is an example of guesswork. It was reported that Little River Golf Course, owned by the town of Windsor, Canada, elected to reduce green fees to encourage more play and stem financial losses.[5] The press release stated,

> "As of the end of June, revenue at the nine-hole golf course had dropped $20,400 over the same period last year. 'We can't figure that out,' Coun. Percy Hatfield, who sits on the city committee that oversees the golf course, said Tuesday.
>
> For the rest of this month, green fees at Little River will be $12 for adults any day of the week. The fees had been $17 on weekends and $16 on weekdays. For seniors aged 55 and older and juniors aged 18 and younger, the new green fee will be $10.
>
> Hatfield said the fees are tentatively set to go up again in August, but may stay at the lower level if the course continues to lose money. 'We'll gauge the response to see if we should continue it for the rest of the season.'
>
> Fellow board member Coun. Drew Dilkens said the tracking should have happened before the green fees were reduced. 'I think we should have had more data,' Dilkens said. 'Once you lower a price, it's harder to raise it again.'"

Yield management is as much guesswork as it is a science, and attention to detail is needed to ensure that the competitive price pressures within the industry are properly assessed.

Yield Management Applied to Golf

The options available by the course owner have been limited due to:

1. **Technology—the golf industry software is behind other industries.**

   A sophisticated yield management approach requires a large investment. The golf market is not big enough to justify such an investment by small

5 Sarah Sacheli, "City Owned Little River Golf Course Losing Money," *Windsor Star*, July 22, 2008.

entrepreneurs who head the leading golf software management companies. Development costs to build a yield management software system for golf would exceed $2 million, which is prohibitive for almost all golf operations.

2. **The average aptitude and attitude of golf course personnel at public golf courses.**

   Course personnel are historically technology-phobic. Those who reject change cite costs and the inability to train staff.

What are owners to do?

The Keys to Revenue Management

The key is understanding predictable demand. Price-sensitive customers should be able to purchase off-peak times at favorable rates, while price-insensitive customers who want to purchase at peak times will be able to do so as well.

If this is done perfectly, revenue per available tee time sold should be 80% of the rack rate. Currently, the average golf course is only realizing around 50%.

Thus, the key element to any successful rate strategy is gaining insights on customer activity and customer demand. Your posted rate (green fee) should be set at a price that most people will pay, without discounting, tournament pricing aside.

How to Implement

How many people are paying my highest posted rate? Most golf course managers are pretty proud of this rate, even if only 2 to 10 people are paying it, and they are using three different third-party vendors to sell tee times. The goal should be selling the maximum number of rounds at the posted rack rate daily. For a public premium course (green fees in excess of $70), 50 rack rate tee times is an ideal target. For public value courses (green fees between $40 and $70), 70 rack rate tee should be the goal. For public price courses (green fees less than $40), 90 is the target.

With rack rate goal established, an owner should set a benchmark: "What is the average yield achieved during the past year?"

To determine that number:

1. Calculate total rounds.
2. Divide total rounds by revenue.
3. The answer is the effective yield-per-round required to break even.

With the benchmark established (current revenue per tee time), the goal becomes to implement a revenue program in which the average yield exceeds that of the prior year.

Ask yourself if that number is achievable. If not, the guesswork starts. To achieve break-even, should the rack rate be increased, decreased, or left unchanged? Opting to increase the rate or leave the rate unchanged suggests marketing will be required. Decreasing the rate presumes a close look at utilization.

This exercise is best demonstrated by the revenue management techniques used by Walt Disney World Golf World, which creates up to six buckets for its various rate categories. Note that 50 rack rate tee times per day is its goal. Following is an example of how Disney attempts to maximize its revenue.[6]

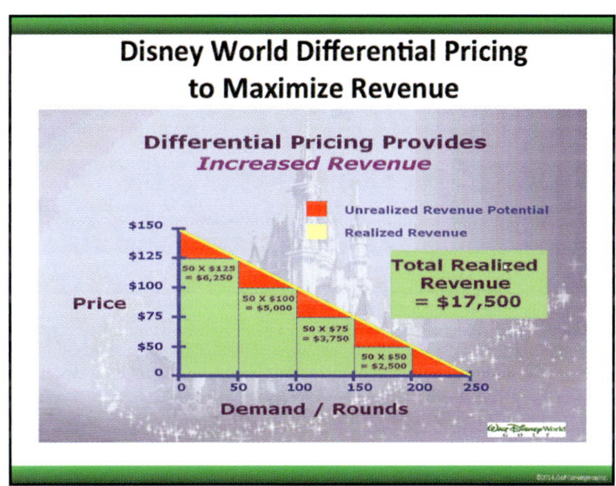

Walt Disney World Golf provides no discounts for rack rate rounds, full paid package and groups. A 5% to 10% discount might be provided to local community and corporations, AAA members, and other affinities. A 10% to 20% discount would be provided to Annual pass holders, Florida resident golfers, and vacation club members. Deeper discounts would be allocated to commissioned business while the deepest discounts would be allocated to local hospitality and junior golf. The key is that discounts are only provided when rack rate demand doesn't first fill the times available. Disney uses a "wizard," a feature within the software, to ensure everyone reserves their tee times through the same booking engine where the yield management rates have been pre-established.

6 Steve Harker, "Maximizing Profit Using Yield/Revenue Management—A Walt Disney World Case Study," October 29, 2009, Slide 22.

The Barriers to Liquid Commerce

One of the golf industry's most sophisticated and seasoned veterans in yield management is Jeff Levine of Century Golf Group. Levine believes that most golf course managers use a traditional approach to setting green fees, which creates inefficiency. He feels:

> "Incorrect pricing fuels these businesses because an ineffective posted rate results in the inability to sell inventory. Operators then fall into panic strategies to fill in an empty tee sheet. The end result is usually a pretty good round count, but with few paying the posted rate and many paying the e-mail or other 3rd party discount rate.
>
> The 3rd party companies gain market strength because they are in control of your inventory and you rely on them to produce rounds. This is caused by establishing an ineffective posted rate. If you take the daily average of this revenue per tee time purchased, it's usually pretty close to what your posted rate should be."[7]

Maximizing green fee revenue boils down to these simple facts:

1. Customer activity drives revenue.
2. There are many types of players with different demographics who will play at different times of the day, week, and year.
3. Tournament and catering are important ancillary components to a course.

All a golf manager needs to do is determine the various customer types and what rate they will pay for what times. All this must be based on empirical data.

The key element to any successful rate strategy is to understand customer activity and customer demand and then anticipate the level of demand in an upcoming period of time. Weather, time of year, and course conditions are the driving factors in this determination.

The ultimate goal is a strategy espoused by Peter Hill, chief executive officer of Billy Casper Golf, who believes that the mystery number for maximizing

7 Jeff Levine, "Selling the Fringe Times Is Key to Financial Success," *Divergent Views*, June 2007.

revenue is as follows: "How many golfers tried for a reservation and were turned away from that time slot? If you have detailed information on that, well, that's where the business gets kind of fun. You're learning about pricing power." Hill envisions a yield management scenario in which the tee sheet computers know the average dollars per visit spent by each golfer and assigns the tee time to the golfer who generates the highest yield. Hills concluded, "Things like that aren't here yet, but they're on the radar screen."[8]

It will be an exciting time when that arrives.

Guidelines for Other Revenue-Generating Ideas

Golf course operators in today's market should hope to achieve at least 66% utilization during prime season. This is defined from sunup to two hours before sundown. Given that a golf course's most profitable customer is often the repeat customer, consider the following:

1. All green fees and tournaments should be prepaid at the time of reservation with credit card guarantees.
2. No "complimentary" rounds during prime time.
3. Golfers on Friday should be charged the weekend rate.
4. Tournaments should be booked for the "shoulder periods," if possible.
5. Tournaments should pay a premium of 25% over the standard green fees for prime time.
6. Carts should be mandatory for all tournament play.
7. Audit the starter sheet daily to avoid "situational morality." The cashier's ring number should be written next to the each player's name.
8. Properly price and restrict season passes to low utilization periods.
9. Introduce value pricing only during slack periods of time.
10. Use a "wave" or "crisscross" during prime times to increase revenue.
11. Put a winter enclosure on carts to encourage play during the shoulder seasons.

8 David Gould, NGCOA Golf Business, "Standing Out from the Herd," July 2006, p. 33.

12. Don't participate in charity cards that give away free golf. Package your own card with other local golf course owners, focusing solely on non-peak periods.
13. Put your course brochures in the off-course golf shops.
14. Have the staff write a weekly golf tip for the local newspaper.
15. Food and beverage at most golf courses is merely a break-even endeavor. To minimize the downside, provide quality service, which drives profit. The food must be affordable, and a beverage cart and halfway house will increase revenue. By adding a phone to the ninth tee, phone orders will increase. A best practice is to have a barbecue at the turns. It creates a great smell and enhances the experience.
16. The clubhouse food and beverage operation should be modest.
17. Selling bottled water rather than providing on-course water coolers is a profitable revenue source.

The opportunities for the creative mind are great. Merely note how effectively Bay Creek Resort and Club in Cape Charles, VA up sells a customer when they are leaving the 18th green.

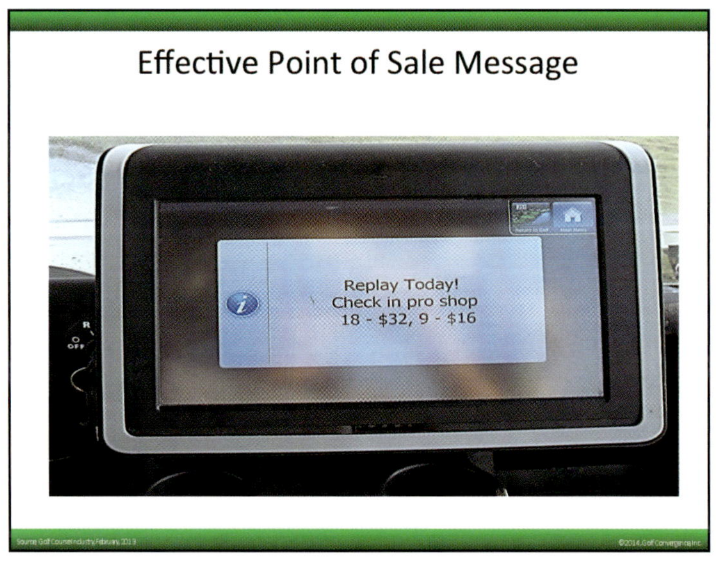

End Notes

The lessons of this chapter are:

1) There is perhaps no more subjective area in the business of golf than determining green fees.
2) A golf course can precisely calculate the value of the experience delivered, compare that to the rate charged, build a marketing campaign based on its unique value, and thereby stimulate revenue.
3) Green fees could be set based on the slope, strategic options, conditioning, grass texture, ambience, and customer amenities. Green fees could also be set, similar to other entertainment venues, based on an hourly fee.
4) Golf courses are currently slightly above 50% utilization.
5) "Yield Management." While it sounds precise, it is very subjective. It requires a lot of guesswork initially under the sales history before demand forecasts models can be constructed.
6) The daily fee golf business boils down to the simple fact that customer activity drives revenue. The goal should be selling 90 rounds daily at the posted rack rate.
7) Prices for greens fees are often set based on the ego of the management team and not based on the factors of supply and demand.

Concluding Thought

There can be no progress unless people have faith in tomorrow.

John F. Kennedy

Chapter 11

Golf Course Valuation

Step 4 of Golf Convergence WIN™ Formula (continued)

Work expands to fill the time available for its completion, the thing to be done swells in perceived importance and complexity in direct ratio with the time to be spent in its completion.

Parkinson's First Law

Chapter Highlights

In entering into the golf business, the operative word is "business." In seeking a return from the investment in a golf course, understanding how golf courses are valued can ensure the acquisition is made wisely and that the sale optimizes the investment return.

There is a formula for what a golf course is worth. Whether buying or selling, you can ascertain a fair price.

An Axiom

There is an axiom, "You make money when you buy, not when you sell." The focus of this book has been to demonstrate how golf course owners can maximize their return in the short term. Only by properly managing the business in the short term is its long-term value maximized, and that value is determined only when the golf course is sold.

A golf course owner should always have an exit strategy, even if he or she never plans on using it. This will insure that the owner's investment return will be maximized. Knowing the value of your golf course provides a useful snapshot of where the course currently stands, what options it has, and how it can improve long term. The valuation of your golf course is, in essence, a reality check.

Unfortunately, most golf course owners have a tough time determining value. Most golf courses will only pay for a valuation when it is required to obtain financing or because of some other kind of transaction, such as a divorce, a death, or for estate planning purposes. These mandatory responses to outside circumstances often result in mistakes, which lead to flawed valuations. The value of a golf course can be determined much more accurately if the owner keeps a frequent tally of the market.

A frequent, perhaps annual, valuation also gives the owner a better sense of how to use the resources available; most businesses use leverage by utilizing the value of their equity to borrow.

The process of selling a golf course involves the following steps:

1. Obtain an appraisal, which includes an opinion of the competitive market value.
2. Develop a strategy to sell, one that includes preparing a cohesive business plan that strategically positions the property. Such a business plan should include a realistic financial forecast, a list of potential buyers, and an investment analysis that reinforces the course's potential opportunity.
3. Find a real estate agent/broker who can represent the golf course.
4. Create a marketing program to contact identified prospects and to promote the opportunity.

5. Negotiate and complete the transaction, including reviewing offers, managing the due diligence, and ensuring a timely close through coordination with counsel.

While this five-step process seems simple, the sale of a golf course is a complex commercial transaction. The legal issues alone are daunting. Van Tengberg, partner of the law firm of Foley and Lardner, offers a list of the 10 most important things that have to be addressed:

1. Title Survey
   - **a.** Review and assess the impact of all exceptions to the title—covenant condition restrictions, (CC&Rs), covenants, deed restrictions, and cost-sharing agreements.
   - **b.** Determine the impact of all encroachments of golf course improvements onto adjoining properties.
2. Phase 1 and Phase 2
   - **a.** Inspect the maintenance facility and confirm the existence, use, or discontinuance of underground or above-ground storage tanks, pesticides, fertilizers, fuel tanks, or oil drums.
   - **b.** Determine the existence of any organized dumps on the property.
3. Memberships
   - **a.** Review the seller's waiting list and determine the number of memberships on the list.
   - **b.** Review all membership agreements regarding refund obligations.
4. Permits and Licenses
   - **a.** Verify the existence of all required permits and licenses (health, resale, liquor, petroleum, storage tanks, pesticides, etc.).
   - **b.** Confirm that all permits and licenses are transferable.
5. Leases—Purchase Contracts—Furniture, Fixtures, and Equipment
   - **a.** Confirm that all contracts, agreements, and leases are transferable.
   - **b.** Confirm the right to purchase leased furniture, fixtures, and equipment upon expiration of the lease (fair market value or fixed dollar amount).
6. Sensitive Habitat, Wetlands, Biological
   - **a.** Determine what exists and its status.
   - **b.** Analyze short-term and long-term maintenance, upkeep, and enhancement obligations.

7. Structural Issues, HVAC, Utility Accessibility, Irrigation Systems
   a. Itemize required repairs, replacements, or improvements.
   b. Determine what repairs, replacements, or improvements are mandatory for transfer or issuance of a certificate of occupancy.
8. Employees and Independent Contractors
   a. Review salary and benefits packages.
   b. Review all employment and independent contract agreements.
9. Irrigation Water
   a. Conduct a hydrology study and ascertain ownership of water rights.
   b. Confirm any alternative sources of irrigation water.
10. Surrounding Community Issues
   a. Review all golf course CC&Rs.
   b. Consider hours of operation and enforcement issues.[1]

Just from reading that list, buying and selling can seem to be overwhelming tasks.

But for those still inclined to sell, the first step is to learn the true value of the golf course. Seventy percent of all golf courses sold each year are transacted without being formally listed. This is often because the owners fear that nobody will want to play a course that's up for sale—all the more reason to have a thorough understanding of valuation.

Valuing the Golf Course

The value of a golf course is determined by an appraisal, a complex process no matter what form it takes. Golf courses are a mix of real estate and business, and before you can come up with a proper valuation, you have to understand the mix of the two.

Components that influence the value of a golf course include location, site configuration, population, topography, scenic appeal, course features, and amenities such as access to major highways and expressways. A comprehensive appraisal also looks at things like irrigation and pumping systems, cost and availability of irrigation water, drainage, ADA compliance, food and beverage operation, safety issues resulting from poor golf hole design, maintenance

1 Vang Tenberg, "Buy-Sell Checklist," *Golf Inc.*, March 2008, p. 33.

equipment, chemical and fuel storage, bridges, cart paths, utility of the clubhouse, maintenance barn and pro shop buildings.[2]

At a minimum, the value of a golf course is worth the value of the land. This can be a big deal, especially at older clubs where the town has grown around the property and the "highest and best use" of the real estate is a high-rise and not a golf course. For example, the raw land value of the Los Angeles Country Club, located within the heart of Beverley Hills, is estimated to be worth $20 billion. Would the course ever be sold? No. But for the vast majority of course owners, that sort of number gets your attention. When asked what he sees as his economic security, the owner of 36 holes at Stow Acres, the very astute Walt Lankau, said, "I see townhomes."

Highest and best use, a term common in the real estate industry, is a wild card that can have a significant impact on value. Steve R. Hughes, a real estate appraiser specializing in golf courses, wrote, "The highest and best use of the site involves determining whether a golf course is the use that supports the highest present value on the land. This analysis comes into play when the course is a core design with a good location, and it would provide a higher return to redevelop the site with a more dense use. I recently appraised a golf course that was worth about $2.5 million, but with the commercial zoning already in place, the redeveloped land put to its 'highest and best use' would be worth more than $8 million."[3]

Having a golf course valued, with all the variables and legal issues analyzed, can take 90 days or more and can cost anywhere from $5,000 to $50,000. A table of contents for a valuation would look similar to this:

Description	Page Number
Summary of Salient Facts	4
Client/Intended User(s)	5
Intended Use	5
Report Format	5
Analysis	5
Purpose of Report	5
Interest Appraised	5
Property Identification	5
Previous Sales	5

2 Gorman Group, "Golf Course Appraisals," www.gormangrp.com/golf_course_appraisals.html.

3 Stephen R. Hughes, "Golf Course Management—The Price Is Right," www.gcsaa.org/gcm/1999/jul99/07price.html.

Description	Page Number
FIRREA Compliant	5
Scope of Appraisal	5
Tax Comments	6
Brief Property Description	6
Highest and Best Use	10
Valuation as a Country Club	13
Market Approach	13
Income Approach	20
Conclusion as a Country Club	27
Valuation as Vacant Land	28
Conclusion as Vacant Land	31
Highest and Best Use Conclusion and Final Value Conclusions	32
Definition of Market Value	33
Underlying Assumptions and Limiting Conditions	33
Certificate of Appraisal	37

While there are plenty of appraisers who will come up with whatever number you want, the talented business appraiser acts like a consultant, stripping down the numbers to determine real value. If really good, the appraiser will also provide suggestions to make the value higher.

Valuation Methods

The range of values is determined by one of seven valuation methods:

Book Value: Assets (including cash, receivables, and property, plant, and equipment) less liabilities and debt. This asset-based method could result in a number that seems too low because the intangible personal property is not valued.

Liquidation Value: This value is determined by asking, "How much money could be raised by selling all assets (receivables, inventory, and property, plant, and equipment) less satisfaction of debt. This method also produces a value that seems low. It represents a worst-case scenario.

Excess Earnings: Tangible assets are multiplied by the standard return on equity. Any money earned in excess of this value is considered excess earnings, which are then capitalized and added to the book value.

Multiple Models: This easy way to determine value is to take known value, earnings, or revenues and multiply that figure by the standard index. For example, the value of a business is worth between 10 and 20 times earnings or 1½ to 2 times revenues. The standard index for publicly traded companies is a price-to-earnings ratio of 15 to 1. This technique has some challenges, since profits and revenues can prove to be erratic and this method often fails to recognize debt or other intangibles because of its simplicity.

Cost Approach: The cost approach is based on what an informed buyer would pay for creating a substitute property with the same functionality. Actual constructions costs for a new golf course, as well as the furniture, fixtures, and equipment purchases costs are determined.

Comparative Market Value: The value is determined by a locating a recent transaction involving the sale of a comparable course in a local market.

Discounted Cash Flow: A forecast of the amount of cash the golf course will be able to generate in future years discounted to present value based on competitive rates of investment.

Of these seven valuation techniques, the two most frequently used are discounted cash flow (income approach) and comparative market value. But in spite of tried and true techniques for valuing golf properties, buyers (usually inexperienced and emotional) often pay inflated prices for golf courses.

Notwithstanding the popularity of these approaches, there are still plenty of intangibles: (1) each course provides a different experience; (2) the quality of management varies; (3) there are a plethora of different profit margins within the course's various departments; and (4) each course puts a different emphasis on strategies and tactics.

Appraisal is also subjective. The appraised value of a golf course hinges on the number attributed to three factors—income stream, capitalization rate, and market value—that are closely interconnected. You merely need to know two of the three components to calculate the third. To illustrate,

Income = Capitalization Rate × Market Value

Capitalization Rate = Income/Market Value

Market Value = Income/Capitalization Rate

Additional terms used to value golf courses include:

Discount rate: The discount rate and the capitalization rate are similar, but distinguishable. While both focus on the yield necessary to attract investors, the discount rate looks at projected cash flows, while the capitalization rate is based on data for a single period of time.

Net Income Multiplier: Revenues are multiplied by the standard multiple to approach the market value. It is a quick benchmark.

The interrelationship of these factors can be confusing.

As This Rate Becomes Larger	The Golf Course Market Value
Capitalization Rate	Decreases
Discount Rate	Decreases
Net Income Multiplier	Increases

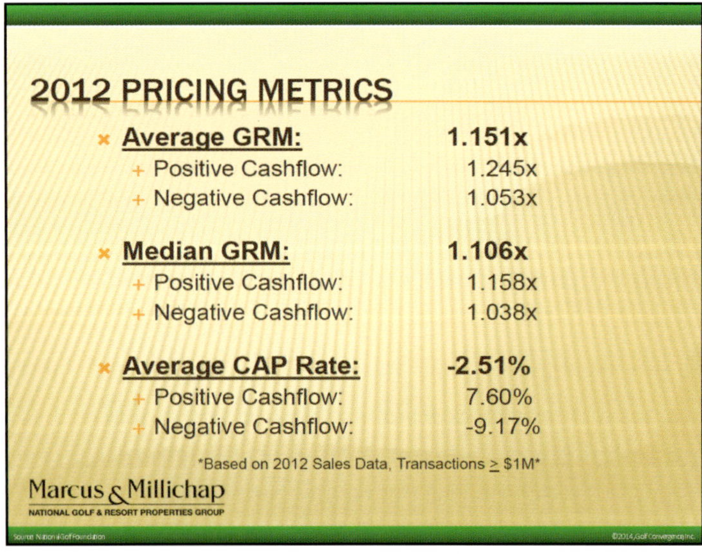

Confusing, yes. Simplistic, yes. Subject to market interruption, absolutely yes.

The capitalization rate, discount rate, and net income multiplier are constantly changing in response to economic conditions and alternative investment opportunities. Presented is a chart that highlights the current benchmarks to determine a golf course's market value.

Standard Index Method

For an appraisal, net income is not actually "net income" but rather a calculation that includes the following components: gross income less collection losses, allowable expenses, replacement reserves, and real estate taxes. Allowable expenses include management fees/expense, insurance, salaries,

Allowable expenses include management fees/expense, insurance, salaries, benefits, utilities, advertising, repairs, supplies, legal and accounting fees, and miscellaneous expenses. More important are the non-allowable expenses: depreciation, capital improvement, franchise fees and special corporation costs, owner's personal expenses, debt services, payment on loans for capital improvements, and real estate taxes.

Simply stated, divide net income by the capitalization rate to determine market value, as illustrated in the following table:

Net Income	Capitalization Rate	Market Value
$300,000	7.5%	$4,000,000
$300,000	9.0%	$3,333,333
$300,000	11.0%	$2,727,272
Note: Capitalization rates (or "cap rate") is the ratio between the net operating income produced by an asset and its capital cost (the original price paid to buy the asset) or alternatively its current market value.		

Discounted Cash Flow

Another method of valuation is discounted cash flow. A detailed analysis of the historical income statements is undertaken to prepare a projection of future cash flow.[4]

Discounted Cash Flow Analysis

ABCD CLUB GOLF FACILITY AS A 18-HOLE SEMI-PRIVATE/RESORT GOLF FACILITY — golf

		2008	2009	2010	2011	2012	2013
No. of Golf Rounds		20,000	22,000	23,500	24,000	25,000	25,000
No. of Members		250	275	300	325	350	350
Transfer Fee Income		250,000	257,500	265,225	273,182	281,377	289,819
Membership dues		$375,000	$424,875	$477,405	$532,704	$590,892	$608,619
Guest Fee Income		$1,050,000	$1,189,650	$1,283,689	$1,273,027	$1,316,845	$1,356,351
Cart Fee Income		$180,500	$204,507	$229,791	$256,408	$284,416	$292,949
Food Sales		$75,000	$84,975	$95,481	$106,541	$118,178	$121,724
Beverage Sales		$75,000	$84,975	$95,481	$106,541	$118,178	$121,724
Practice Range Income		$6,000	$6,796	$7,479	$7,868	$8,441	$8,695
Pro Shop Sales		$125,000	$141,625	$159,135	$177,568	$196,964	$202,873
Other Income		$15,000	$16,995	$18,698	$19,669	$21,103	$21,736
Total Income		$2,151,500	$2,411,900	$2,632,385	$2,753,508	$2,936,396	$3,024,488
DEPARTMENTAL COSTS & EXPENSES (Including Cost of Sales)							
Expense Multiplier	**103.5%**						
Golf Course Maintenance		$750,000	$776,250	$803,419	$831,538	$860,642	$890,765
Cart Maint. and/or Lease		$43,800	$45,333	$46,920	$48,562	$50,262	$52,021
Food & Bev. Costs	45.0%	$67,500	$76,478	$85,933	$95,887	$106,361	$109,551
Fd & Bev. Exp. (Incl. Payroll)	45.0%	$67,500	$76,478	$85,933	$95,887	$106,361	$109,551
Pro Shop Costs	70.0%	$87,500	$99,138	$111,395	$124,298	$137,875	$142,011
Pro Shop Exp. (Incl. Payroll)	20.0%	$25,000	$28,325	$31,827	$35,514	$39,393	$40,575
Total Dept. Costs & Expenses		$1,041,300	$1,102,001	$1,165,426	$1,231,685	$1,300,893	$1,344,474
Total Undistributed Exp		$392,575	$415,570	$436,918	$453,660	$473,864	$489,715
INC. BF FIXED CHARGES		$717,625	$894,329	$1,030,041	$1,068,163	$1,161,640	$1,190,299
Total Fixed Charges		$223,788	$236,247	$247,918	[illegible]	[illegible]	[illegible]
Total Expenses		($1,657,663)	($1,753,818)	($1,850,262)	($1,942,665)	($2,043,245)	($2,111,708)
NET OPERATING INCOME		$493,838	$658,082	$782,123	$810,843	$893,151	$912,780
Operating Expense Ratio		77.0%	72.7%	70.3%	70.6%	69.6%	69.8%
Reversion RT @	11.00%					$8,298,003.31	
Selling Costs @	4.0%					($331,920)	
Net Reversion						$7,966,083.17	
Cash Flows	$0	$493,838	$658,082	$782,123	$810,843	$8,859,234	N/A
NET PRESENT VALUE @	13.5%	$6,672,915					
Membership Sales		$420,000	$360,500	$371,315	$382,454	$393,928	$405,746
Refund Liability		($10,000)	($10,000)	($10,000)	($10,000)	($10,000)	($10,000)
Total		$410,000	$350,500	$361,315	$372,454	$383,928	$395,746
NET PRESENT VALUE @	15.5%	$1,248,288					
ESTIMATED VALUE		$7,921,203				Rounded to	$7,900,000

4 Larry Hirsch, Golf Property Analysts, "ABCS Golf Facility," September 2, 2008.

A Unique Valuation Alternative

The State of Indiana takes a novel approach to valuation. The formula consists of the following steps:[5]

1. Price by grade per hole
2. Delete land under course value @ $1,050 per acre
3. Add the appropriate physical and/or external depreciation
4. Add the value of improvements
5. Add land value
6. Adjust to market value-in-use

The key component is the "grades" assigned for the golf holes. The chart developed is very logical, and is represented on the following grid:[6]

	AA	A	B	C	D
Base Cost Per Hole	$163,000	$118,000	$73,000	$50,000	$23,000
Quality	Superior	Excellent	Good	Average	Fair
Design	Professional Championship	Championship	Private	Quality Public	Average
Acres	180	160	130	110	90
Terrain	Rolling and/or lake	Rolling and/or lake	Rolling	Flat	Flat
Length of Course	7,200+	7,200	6,400	6,000	5,400
Par	72	72	70	67 to 70	64 to 67
Sprinklers	Automated	Automated	Automated greens, manual fairway	Semi-automatic	Manual
Greens	10,000 square feet tiled	8,000 square feet tiled	5,000	Small	Small
Tees	3+ per hole	2 or 3	2	Small	Small
Bunkers	3+ per hold	Average 3	2	Few	Few
Roadways	Good quality paved	Good quality paved	Good quality paved	Average quality paved or gravel	Gravel

5 Department of Local Government Finance, "Golf Course Valuation—the Income Approach," March 2007, p. 13.

6 Department of Local Government Finance, "Golf Course Valuation—the Income Approach," March 2007, pp. 16–20.

Utilizing the State of Indiana formula, the valuation for a "B" grade golf course would comprise:

1. $73,000 × number of golf holes = 18 for a total of $1,314,000
2. 126 acres × $1,050 per acre = $132,300
3. $1,314,000 – $132,300 = $1,181,700
4. Depreciation Adjustment of 15%: $1,004,445

If an owner were in a battle with local government over property tax values, the State of Indiana would provide an interesting exhibit in a protest document.

In August 2009, the valuation methods for property taxes was expanded.

> "Indiana's part-time legislature passed a budget bill in August which included a provision for applying income capitalization appraisal to assessing golf courses for property taxes.
>
> 'This is a huge victory for course owners throughout the state,' exclaims Errol Klem, owner of Winchester Golf Club in Winchester, IN and IGCOA president. 'The value of a course will now be based on its earnings potential rather than comparable sales or totally arbitrary criteria.'
>
> About three years ago, Indiana's property tax assessments went from replacement cost value to fair market value, which allowed assessors to use a comparable sales, cost, or income approach."[7]

Interestingly, the State of New York has developed a similar grading system, classifying the state's golf courses into the following categories: GC 2—simple design, GC 3—private club, GC 4—championship, GC 7—pitch and putt, GC 8—range, GC 9—miniature.

Playing With the Numbers

Each golf course should obtain an appraisal at least every three years. An appraisal provides an indication of a golf course's value, and serves as a business tool that identifies weaknesses. Acting on the information gleaned from an appraisal, a golf course owner is likely to improve short-term income while increasing long-term value.

7 http://www.ngcoa.org/pageview.asp?doc=2248

End Notes

The lessons of this chapter are:

1) A golf course appraisal can cost from $5,000 to $50,000, take upwards of 90 days, and consists of 10 very detailed steps.
2) There are seven valuation techniques: book value, liquidation value, excess earnings, multiple models, cost approach, comparative market value, and discounted cash flow.
3) The two most frequently used methods to value a golf course are the discounted cash flow (income approach) method and the comparative market value method.
4) The appraised value of a golf course hinges on the number attributed to three factors, all of which are interconnected—capitalization rate, discount rate, and net income multiplier.
5) The capitalization rate, discount rate, and net income multiplier are constantly changing in response to economic conditions and alternative investment opportunities.

Concluding Thought

With good judgment, little else matters. Without it, nothing else matters.

Warren G. Bennis

SECTION 3

Operational Execution
Chapters 12 through 18

From a broad overview of the golf industry in Section 1, we transitioned in Section 2 to understanding the numbers at a golf course, learning how to increase and maximize revenue, increase operational efficiency, and enhance customer service.

In Section 3, we narrow the focus even more to the golf course, daily operations, and the golfer. The factors that influence the financial success of a golf course are as follows:

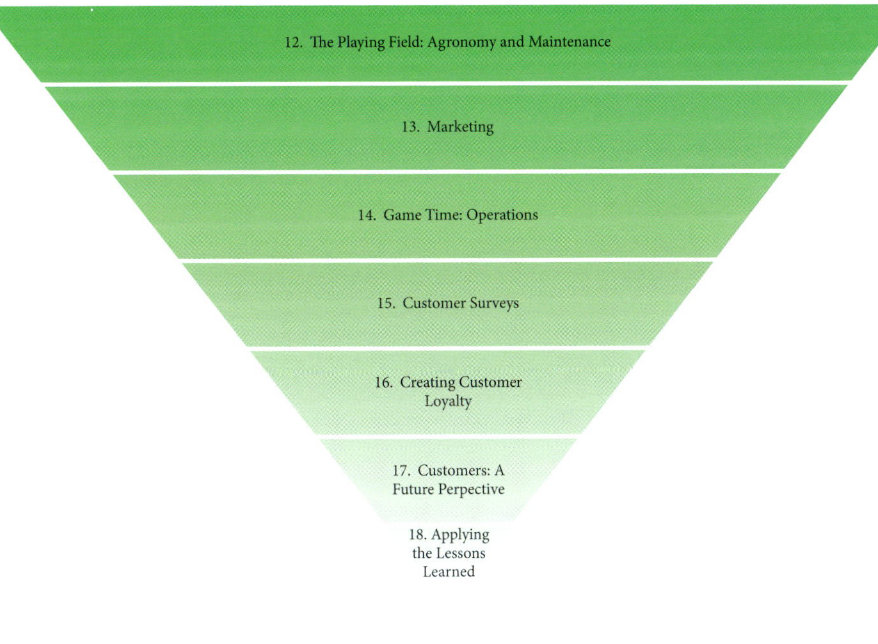

Knowing is not enough, we must apply.
Willing is not enough, we must do.

Goethe

Chapter 12

The Playing Field
Step 5 of Golf Convergence WIN™ Formula

Destiny is no matter of chance. It is a matter of choice. It is not a thing to be waited for, it is a thing to be achieved.

William Jennings Bryan

Chapter Highlights

In every customer survey, condition and price are consistently ranked as the most important components.

What does it take to be a "Top 100" facility, and is it important?

How are operators keeping budgets in check and still meeting customer expectations?

What is the "life cycle" of a golf course? And how does answering that question affect capital improvements, annual maintenance expenditures, and labor?

How important is the condition of tee markers, ball washers, and water fountains in enhancing a golfer's perceived value of a course?

This chapter will provide those answers.

The Endless Debate

One of the great things about the game of golf is the endless debate on which golf course is better. The discussion attracts people to the game, spurs many bar conversations, and serves as the incentive that drives certain golf course owners to seek and maintain excellence.

Many golfers and golf industry personnel attach great importance to the ratings given golf courses—the Top 100 in the World, the Top 100 in the United States, The Top 100 the Public Can Play, the Top 100 Golf Courses Prior to 1960, the Top 100 Golf Courses Since 1960, the Top 10 New Golf Courses, the Top 10 Golf Courses in the State; and the list goes on.

The first of these lists was created 29 years ago by George Peper, then editor-in-chief of *Golf Magazine*. In the March 2006 edition of *Links Magazine*, Peper writes,

> "Hey, it seemed like a good idea at the time. The magazine got great publicity and sold more ads and copies, and I was proud of our biennial list, the first to rank courses from one to 100. Over time, however, I realized I'd created a monster.
>
> 'You've done our club a tremendous disservice,' Pine Valley president Ernie Ransom told me after we pegged his course as No. 1 in the world. "Everyone wants to play here now, and 99 percent of the requests can't be granted."[1]

For a golf course, being ranked can have significant monetary benefits, from establishing lofty membership fees for the private club to attracting golfers at lofty green fees at the public facility. Being ranked also often enhances the brand image of the course.

Golf course rankings have become the subject of much debate and are an integral part of what makes golf so special. Like everything else, they should be viewed with a proper perspective and be properly managed.

The relevance of a top ranking is that it has positive financial implications for the golf course owner. All golf courses that are so ranked have one element in common—the maintenance conditions of the golf course are superior. In

---

1 George Peper, "Out of the Shadows," Linksmagazine.com, March 2006, p. 45.

determining a golf course's mission statement, a conscious decision is required concerning where on the spectrum it desires to be between low cost and high differentiator.

Types of Golf Courses by Categories

First, some basics on the type and nature of golf courses. Golf courses can be categorized as follows:

1. Ownership: private, daily fee resort, residential, military, private estate, industrial
2. Length: full-length, executive, par 3, pitch and putt, chip and putt, putting, Cayman
3. Design: core, integrated, hub and spoke

Types of Golf Courses by Setting

One of the biggest factors that influence maintenance costs is the type of vegetation on a golf course.

Golf course settings include:[2]

1. **Links** golf courses are seaside courses that look like those in the east of Scotland, where the game originated. They are grassy open expanses, with rolling hills, deep roughs, and no trees.
2. **Parkland** golf courses are characterized by lush, manicured turf, favorable weather, and significant tree cover.
3. **Heathland** golf courses are inland courses that are characterized by low-growing shrubs, gentle slopes, and few to no trees. They are made to resemble the inland golf courses of England and Scotland.
4. **Oceanside** golf courses border the ocean, but unlike links courses they are well above sea level.
5. **Mountain** golf courses often aren't in the mountains, but do have views of mountains.

2 http://golftrainingaidandteachingtool.com/Golf_Courses_01.shtml, July 4, 2008.

6. **Prairie** golf courses are usually located in the flatlands of the Midwest in the United States. They are flat, have few trees, and have views of the prairie.
7. **Desert** golf courses are usually located in the arid regions of the southwest United States.

The average cost of building a new golf course in the United States continues to climb, topping $8 million in some settings, according to a recently released survey of the Golf Course Builders Association of America (GCBAA).[3]

Within the confines of these types of settings, the artists of the game, architects, carve their masterpieces onto the landscape. Just as the paintings of Monet, Manet, and Picasso each have similar styles that can be identified, so do the works of classic architects such as MacKenzie, Ross, Tillinghast, or my favorite, Raynor. Add to those new architects such as Dye, Nicklaus, Doak, Jones (Robert Trent and Rees), Coore/Crenshaw, Hills/Forrest, Engh, and the very talented 200+ architects who are members of the Golf Course Architects Society. Many golfers have a favorite architect—old, young, living, or dead. Today's architects have become golf industry superstars.

Superstar status is a relatively new phenomenon. Architects of the past got very little attention. As architect Michael Rymer stated,

> "Golf courses were just places where you played golf. They weren't 'by' anyone and they weren't in any particular 'style.' Consider, for example, Bernard Darwin's famous *Golf Courses of the British Isles*, a book that brought attention to famous courses in England, Scotland and Ireland for the first time. Golf architecture is central to the book. There is, however, not a single architectural attribution anywhere to be found."[4]

In a similar vein, Pete Dye stated that while in the army during World War II he played Pinehurst No. 2 many times, never knowing who the architect was. He said he wouldn't have known 'Donald Ross from Betsy Ross' at the time."[5]

---

3 Keith Carter, "Average New Course Price Over $8 Million," www.golfmagazine.com, April 2008, p. 7.

4 Mike Young, Young/Rymer Designs, "Were the Old Architects Geniuses or Merely Practical?" *Divergent Views*, August 1, 2006.

5 Pete Dye, "ING Spring Conference speech," May 2008.

For the golf course owner, this current adulation of golf course architects often has significant financial consequences.

Mike Rymer believes:

> "... all of this adulation has gone too far. As good as the Golden Age architects were, the reverence for them can sometimes be over the top. Their courses are sometimes treated like sacred texts. Every swale, tree, and ridge (or lack of the same) is taken as a sign of the master and invested with deep architectural significance.
>
> The sanctification of courses designed by these famous architects can get in the way of thoughtful restorations. I've had people tell me that an architect carefully placed a tree behind a green for depth perception. The tree would have been no more than a two-foot sapling when the course was built in the 1920's. Swales in fairways, dug for drainage, are seen as marks of unsurpassed artistry. Odd bunker locations are taken to have deep aesthetic significance. I've come to think that Ross, Travis and others sometimes placed bunkers in certain locations simply to provide a source of fill dirt for nearby green pads.
>
> It's not possible to know all of the details of what an architect wanted for a course 75 years after it opened. Even if you are fortunate enough to have detailed drawings, it's still not possible. The fact that an architectural feature may have survived 75 years does not necessarily mean it was intended or desirable. It's very hard to know what details Ross would have wanted on the 300 or so courses he designed but never saw.
>
> Cults always get in the way of clear thinking.
>
> Thus, the relevance of all of this for today's golf course owner is simple. Golf course owners can waste hundreds of thousands of dollars while trying to restore a course to an image that even the original architect didn't have. A golf course is not a static being but a dynamic entity. With trees, shrubs, and ponds ebbing and flowing, perhaps those who attempt to preserve tradition take themselves too seriously and in turn fail to achieve their desired investment return."[6]

Golf course designers Bill Coore, Tom Doak, Gil Hanse, Kevin Norby, Mike Young, and many others realize that a golf course is an ever-changing entity

---

6 Mike Young, Young/Rymer Designs, "Were the Old Architects Geniuses or Merely Practical?" *Divergent Views*, August 1, 2006.

that requires continual maintenance in order to retain its essential values. A golf course, as designed by the architect, is only such on the day its opens. A golf course is a living organism that changes constantly based on the maintenance practices of the superintendent.

Maintaining the Playing Field

Turf grass is a living, breathing organism that will not stop growing. Courses face the challenges of proper staffing levels, adequate equipment to maintain prescribed levels of conditioning, and a budget that facilitates turf conditions and will attract daily play throughout the calendar year.

These challenges involve disease on the greens; daily turf grass cultural practices; out-of-service equipment, which may include daily equipment adjustments; irrigation leaks/repair; facility operations; tree management; and/or minor golf course construction work.

Any judgment regarding design is generally subjective, and little can be done to change the basic design without major expenditures. However, almost everyone can agree when a course is in good or poor condition.

A golf course can be divided into greens, tees and fairway, rough, water features, and sand bunkers, with an emphasis in these areas as follows:

Putting Green, Tees, and Fairway

- Soil structure
- Turf types
- Water quality
- Fertilizer, fungicide, and insecticide program
- Topdressing methods and sand quality
- Mowing operations and machine adjustment
- Putting surface preparation
  - Rolling
  - Mowing
  - Verticutting

- Aeration method and frequency
- Irrigation practices
- Tree maintenance

Sand Bunkers

- Sand quality and depth
- Shape and Depth
- Grass edges
- Method of maintenance
- Drainage

While hole locations are obviously an emphasis for the greens and marker locations for the tees, the list represents the critical areas of maintaining the playing field.

Costs to maintain a course vary widely, with labor being a significant component. Capital improvements can cost a fortune, and maintaining an equipment fleet is expensive.

Maintenance: A Wide Range of Costs

An average 18-hole golf course covers 150 acres, of which only 100 acres are maintained turfgrass,[7] and includes the following:

		Acreage	%
Turfgrass	Rough	51	34.0
	Fairways	30	20.0
	Driving Range/Practice Areas	7	4.7
	Greens	3	1.3
	Tees	3	1.3
	Clubhouse House	3	1.3
	Nurseries	1	.7
	Total	100	63.3

7 GCSAA, "Golf Course Environmental Profile," 2007, p. 12.

		Acreage	%
Non-Turfgrass	Non-turfgrass landscape	24	16.0
	Water	11	7.3
	Building	6	4.0
	Bunkers	4.5	2.9
	Parking Lots	4.5	2.9
		50	33.1
Note: In published report, averages were utilized which don't necessarily summarize to the total.			

The quality of the playing field can be reduced to four principal elements: (1) Labor, the largest expense; (2) water, fertilizer, chemicals, and utilities; (3) capital improvements; and (4) equipment required to maintain the facility.

The cost of maintaining an 18-hole golf course can range from $200,000 to more than $2.5 million. *Golf Course Industry* magazine reported the following maintenance expenses in 2013:

	18 Hole Facilities			18 Hole + Facilities		
	PUBLIC	PRIVATE	ALL	PUBLIC	PRIVATE	ALL
Total Maintenance Budget	458,071	848,961	651,392	1,173,164	1,752,183	1,387,918
Line Item Components:						
Water	12,484	20,390	16,499	27,387	50,884	36,258
Fuel	22,260	33,876	28,174	40,161	5,925	47,401
Mowing Equipment	25,335	50,649	37,644	70,484	105,303	82,464
Handheld Equipment	1,702	4,419	3,066	3,187	6,331	4,345
Course Accessories	3,804	5,294	4,561	5,182	8,963	6,550
Electricity and Natural Gas	17,990	20,088	19,046	35,238	46,537	39,357
Shop tools	1,878	3,284	2,568	3,482	7,922	4,962
Irrigation Parks, heads and maintenance	5,948	9,876	7,918	12,904	16,741	14,409
Fungicides	22,163	44,476	33,461	40,821	58,461	47,251
Herbicides: Pre-emergent	5,109	7,603	6,369	11,854	22,308	15,787
Herbicides: Post-emergent	3,613	4,144	3,869	5,221	10,577	7,269
Insecticides	3,694	6,570	5,141	8,128	14,883	10,645
Granular fertilizers	15,203	20,244	17,723	31,472	48,368	37,587
Liquid fertilizers	7,315	13,088	10,231	12,903	20,635	15,736
Wetting agents	3,129	5,669	4,399	6,113	7,854	6,764
Plant Growth regulators	4,309	5,982	511	5,122	12,905	8,140
Seed	4,127	5,138	4,620	10,639	10,637	10,638
Aquatic weed control water quality issues	1,635	2,145	1,890	2,754	4,385	3,370
Total Line Item Components	160,063	260,790	205,800	330,298	455,234	395,563

Are these annual maintenance numbers accurate? The GCSAA reports that the average annual maintenance costs for U.S. courses, including labor and water, are $690,206, $769,426, and $806,206 for public, municipal, and private courses, respectively.[8] How accurate these averages are is unknown, because accumulating accurate data within the golf industry remains a challenge.

Interestingly, 28% of private premium U.S. golf courses spend in excess of $1,500,000 per year for maintenance. The largest factor impacting the cost of maintenance is labor though water is an accelerating cost.

How many hours are required to maintain a golf course?

8 "Managing to Maintain," *Golf Inc.*, July 2007, p. 36.

The tasks involved administration, bunkers, cart paths, the course (irrigation, trimming, overseeding and topdressing, fungicides, herbicides, and insecticides), cutting (greens, 30" collars, tees, fairway, first-cut, roughs, native areas, aprons, driving range) greens (pins, ball marks, topdressing, rolling, brushing), maintenance (soil testing aerification, fertilization), ponds, the maintenance facility (cleaning, maintenance gardens), tees (markers, overseeding, topdressing), and trees (trimming).

Readers of this book can log onto www.golfconvergence.com and license an operational template that will assist you in calculating the hours required to maintain a golf course. You merely need to update your season length in weeks, and amend the frequency and hours per tasks you deem appropriate to create your operational hourly budget.

With 12,796 man-hours estimated to maintain a golf course for 32 weeks, the allocation of full- versus part-time workers is an art that can save significant capital, especially considering the differing benefits required for full-time rather than part-time employees. However, full-time workers, who cost more, often have a better understanding of the course's agronomic tendencies and take greater pride in ensuring optimum playing conditions.

The Natural Replacement Cycle

Since a golf course is a living organism, creating a capital budget and providing an annual reserve to replace the vital components is prudent.

Unfortunately, as golf courses begin losing money in a competitive market, the first cuts are always made by deferring capital expenditures. While understandable because of the large investment, these cuts are often made without the continuing recognition that the condition of the golf course remains the number 1 requirement of golfers.

The Golf Course Superintendents Association of America estimates that the amount of capital improvements required as part of a golf course's natural replacement cycle is $2,952,215, and that a prudent golf course should create an annual capital improvements allowance of $132,038.

On the next page are the estimated life spans of the various components of a golf course, as estimated by the GCSAA and Golf Course Builders Association of America.

Very few golf courses budget for capital improvements. Most courses incorrectly wait until the capital project is mandated and then often borrow to fund the costs.

Renovation Cost and Annual Capital Reserve

Component		Years Minimum	Years Maximum	Estimated Cost to Replace	Annual Capital Reserve
Greens		15	30	775,000	25,833
Bunker Sand		5	7	44,800	6,400
Irrigation System		10	30	314,000	10,467
	Irrigation Control	10	15	171,000	11,400
	PVC Pipe	10	30	329,600	10,987
	Pump Station	15	20	425,000	21,250
Corrugated Pipe		15	30	398,180	13,273
Cart Paths	Asphalt	5	10	93,350	9,335
Cart Paths	Concrete	15	30	146,685	4,890
Practice Range Tees		5	10	37,680	3,768
Tees		15	20	150,720	7,536
Bunker Drainage Pipes		5	10	65,000	6,500
Mulch		1	3	1,200	400
Grass		Varies	Varies	N/A	
Total Deferred Capital				2,952,215	132,038

Source: Golf Course Industry, February, 2013

The Equipment

Most golf courses operate with a potpourri of equipment. Surprisingly, heretofore, there has been no standardization of the ideal equipment standards and the investment mandated by a golf course.

Looking for a standard equipment list for your 18-hole golf course? The following list of equipment has been compiled to meet the general needs of a high-end public or an average private 18-hole golf course and should be used as a minimum guideline for reviewing equipment inventory. Keep in mind that a standard equipment list is as challenging to define as a "standard" golf course. Variations may occur, or additional pieces of equipment may be needed, depending upon an array of factors including golf course terrain, maintenance standards expected, and a range of regional requirements.

Also remember that, depending on the dealer your superintendent works with, bonus equipment may be included based on the amount purchased or leased.

Pieces of Equipment	Department	Total Cost
17	Greens	$87,500
2	Tees	24,000
4	Fairways	70,000
6	Rough	112,000
6	Transportation Vehicles	25,000
5	Tractors and Trucks	117,000
12	Sprayers and Spreaders	50,800
9	Utility Equipment	56,000
14	Tools and Small Equipment	850
	Total	$543,150

USGA agronomists suggest that 10 to 15 percent of the total equipment replacement value be spent toward purchasing new machinery each season to avoid losing valuable staff time and potentially, top course conditions, due to down time."[9]

The Superintendent's Impact

The golf course superintendent can have an incredible impact on one of the most important elements that has slowed the growth of the game—slow play. Research by the Golf Course Superintendents Association of America revealed that pace of play is largely a management issue.[10] Maintaining proper rough heights, trimming underbrush, marking the course, having tees properly positioned, rating the greens with a fair stimpmeter, and making sure pin positions are appropriate for the type and volume of play; all of these are controllable factors for the superintendent.

Proper equipment, adequate staffing, and ongoing capital improvements are necessary, and balancing the operational and capital expenditure requirements is always a challenge. Some operational guidelines include the following:

1. The staff training and advancement program should be reviewed to allow for cross training of higher-level employees. Individuals should be able to perform multiple functions. Having loyal and educated employees increases the level of quality for each golf course while having only one person do one specific job limits personal productivity and the enhancement of the golf course.
2. Supervisors and their staffs should be allowed the opportunity to encounter a broad range of educational seminars on local, state, and national levels. Ongoing education programs that provide high-quality professional instruction through regular meetings or conference attendance will provide relevant research data that will reflect positively on employees and their golf courses.
3. A full-time golf course mechanic needs to be exclusively dedicated to servicing and repairing equipment and helping with the maintenance of all golf department supplies.
4. The use of globally positioned satellites to map and locate all irrigation system piping, head locations, valves, and wiring is a huge benefit to expedite

9 Lynn Tumlinson, Golf Course Superintendents Association of America, "The Ideal Equipment Standards and Investment Mandated," *Divergent Views*, March 1, 2007.

10 Dan Gleason, "Shepherds of a Different Flock," *Golf Business*, April 2008, p. 42.

the repair process, to increase irrigation efficiency, and to avoid leaks and line breaks due to incorrectly mapped heads. Without proper irrigation line mapping, mistakes include regular leaks caused by the piercing of irrigation piping.

5. While it is clearly understood that every course has "local" environmental interests regarding specific tree management programs and operations, each facility should have sufficient information to institute an ongoing tree maintenance program and thereby protect the health of on-course tree populations while improving the turf through the increase of air movement across the property.

Beyond these basics of maintaining a golf course, facilities face increasing challenges with the cost and availability of fuel and water, often needing to take into consideration a trendier-than-ever green movement. With some golf courses in the desert southwest now spending more than $1 million annually for water, golf courses will be political enemies of some highly mobilized civic groups, especially in those desert areas where water is a most precious commodity.

Because of this, the industry needs to consider a redefinition of the maintenance standards for golf courses. A golf course can't continue to maintain 150 or even 100 acres of pristine, well-manicured turf. The redefinition of course conditions begins with the education of golfers.

Leaders in the golf industry need to become aware of the different maintenance standards in the rest of the world, particularly Great Britain, where facilities are maintained for far less money than U.S. courses. While the greens are routinely good, fairways, teeing grounds, and the rough are maintained at far lower standards.

Such should be the mantra for courses in the United States. To be effective, the entire industry will need to move in lockstep.

End Notes

The lessons of this chapter are:

1) Being ranked a Top 100 golf course has a financial benefit in terms of brand and fees that can be charged.
2) Golf courses are unique and can be classified by five categories: ownership, length, vegetation, design, and landform.
3) The typical golf course encompasses 150 acres, of which 100 are maintained.
4) Maintenance budgets within regions average from $377,000 to $1,412,000.
5) It requires over 12,000 man-hours to maintain a golf course that is open 32 weeks a year.
6) Golf courses have 11 depreciable components that require an annual investment exceeding $125,000.
7) The cost of an equipment fleet to maintain a golf course is $543,150.

Concluding Thought

For every complex and difficult issue, there is always an answer that is simple, easy, and wrong.

H. L. Mencken

Chapter 13

Marketing—Internet, Online Reservations, and Third Parties

Step 6 of Golf Convergence WIN™ Formula

You've got mail.

America Online, 1989

Chapter Highlights

Five percent of gross revenues should be devoted to advertising, public relations, and promotion.

Because golf courses are rarely adept at marketing, third-party marketing firms (last-minute tee time programs) have become a significant influence in the golf industry, changing the competitive landscape.

One of the most cost effective marketing programs is a Web 2.0 Internet site integrated with leading social networking sites.

The ability to market and create a positive brand is directly correlated to the financial success of the golf course.

Making the Complicated Simple

We have examined the golf industry, the local market, the financial benchmarks, and the golf course. But how do we use that information to capture the attention of golfers and motivate them to come?

Golf is not a "Field of Dreams." Just because you build it doesn't mean they will come. Millions of dollars have been invested in the course and the clubhouse, the management and staff have been hired, and the maintenance and cart equipment have been purchased. But until a customer walks through the door, the effort is all for naught. Marketing can be the key to your ultimate success.

Most golf course operators seem to believe that marketing consists of placing print ads in a local golf magazine and an advertisement in the Saturday sports section of the local newspaper, participating in coupon books, using third-party Web sites, and sending out discount coupons via e-mail.

In today's competitive economy, a highly targeted marketing approach is warranted as depicted on this page.

Let's start with the basics.

Marketing 101

Most golf courses spend about 2% of revenues on marketing. Most businesses spend about 5% of revenues on marketing. With the average daily fee course grossing about $1.5 million, the proper marketing budget should be $75,000. It should be noted that discounting price is not marketing.

With the evolution of technology, the ability to create a dynamic Web site, create a customer database, and communicate a consistent message to the target groups listed in the chart is the formula for success.

In essence, marketing comprises three elements:

- Advertising
- Public relations
- Promotion

Advertising is the foundation of a marketing campaign and has two components: awareness and recall.

Awareness is simply making a favorable impression on as many consumers as possible. Awareness, for a golf course, is creating sizzle by featuring the course's architect, the history of the course, the championships conducted there, the family experience, the best greens, and the unique selling proposition for the golf course. Awareness is getting your tagline firmly embedded in the minds of the golfers. When you realize that 90% of all marketing and 95% of all advertising is rooted in exaggeration, identifying the fundamental truth about your facility is important.

"Just do it," "Don't leave home without it," "Mmm, mmm good"—these immediately bring to mind Nike, American Express, and Campbell's Soup, respectively.

Fifty to sixty percent of the marketing budget should be allocated to the following electronic forms of advertising:

- E-mail marketing campaigns
- Social media via blogs, Facebook, Twitter
- Press releases to leading local golf publications
- Participation in the local golf consumer shows
- Creating links to golf marketing portals
- Creation of a community Web site, which costs in the first year no less than $3,000 and perhaps as much as $10,000
- Direct mail to patrons

- Advertisements in the sports section of the local newspaper to stimulate last-minute rounds
- Brand advertisements in regional and local four-color publications
- Loyalty programs and their implementation cost could also be allocated to a facility's marketing budget

The most effective advertisement is the simplest. A three-inch by two-inch ad printed in the local newspaper's Sunday sports section is always effective.

The best advertising programs are those that allow the customers to be proactive rather than only reactive.

When you advertise, consumers understand that you are paying to deliver the message, highlighting your strengths and not disclosing inherent flaws. As part of **public-relations**, an advertorial focuses on a supposedly disinterested third party who independently hails the benefits of your product. Since many publications and media outlets are at any given time seeking content, advertorials lessen your cost. Such publications will probably consume approximately 10% of your marketing budget. Public relations include sponsoring charity events and hosting writers and other groups to establish a basis for the message you are disseminating.

The final marketing piece is **promotion**, which is used to stimulate play on a specific day. Thirty to forty percent of a facility's marketing budget should be used for promotion, for example, a closest to the pin contest on Thursday in August with the winner getting a driver, or a hole-in-one contest with an automobile as the prize.

The guesswork of any golf marketing plan is determining how to allocate finite resources to each of these categories to achieve the optimal result with advertising, public relations, and promotion—different tools for different purposes.

Trial, repeat, tracking, and evaluation of a marketing program are necessary to position the course's brand. The astute golf course owner will allocate 10% of the marketing budget to this evaluation phase.

The importance of tracking and evaluation was evidenced at the Greenhorn Creek Golf Club in Angels Camp, California, where the course was losing more than $1 million per year.

Del Smith of the Grupe Company, a new development partner, commented,

> "When I arrived, the business was being run like a sport instead of the sport being run like a business. We found that there were no real measurements."[1]

Focusing on measurement, Smith made sure every print advertisement, radio spot, and direct-mail effort was tied to a unique code, phone number, or e-mail address. After 10 months the results indicated,

> "We saw that 99% percent of the money we were spending was only creating about 2% to 3% of our income. It was insane. With nowhere to go but up, the three- to four-person marketing department was dissolved and replaced by one person dedicated to growing an e-mail database and marketing to that list."[2]

Golfers are consumers, and consumers react to good marketing.

Four Mile Ranch on October 1, 2011 attempted to set a Guinness Book World Record for the most holes-in-one and the lowest "ringer" score on one day. The Jim Engh designed, Par 72, 7,033 yard golf course was set up with pin positions set in the bowl of each green making the course conducive to low scoring. The course marketed the event via e-mail to 12,000 golfers along the Front Range in Colorado. They filled the 144 player field at full rack rate and each participant was given a "Guinness Beer" upon completion of their record. The reaction of the participants was uniformly, "I had so much fun. You are going to do this again next year hopefully." Parenthetically, one hole-in-one was recorded and the ringer score was 52. More importantly, it was one of the highest revenue days for the golf course in their four year history.

A Marketing Component—The Internet

While brand marketing to create awareness will always be a valuable component to a marketing program, the creation of a dynamic 2.0 Web site is of growing importance, as is the correct use of e-mail newsletters, promotions, and value-based opportunities. A 1.0 Web site represents only static pages. A 2.0 Web site empowers the customer to engage in transactions and filter the

1 Craig Better, Golfbusiness.com, "Greenhorn Creek," April 2008, p. 26.

2 Craig Better, Golfbusiness.com, "Greenhorn Creek," April 2008, p. 26.

information they are seeking using search tools. Examples of Web 2.0 include Web-based communities, hosted services, Web applications, social-networking sites, video-sharing sites, wikis, and blogs.

Internet marketing is one of the most cost-effective, accurately targeted, and measurable ways to attract new golfers, retain existing customers, and reconnect with defectors. It is becoming the most important component of a golf course marketing effort.

Ten years ago, Web sites were in their formative stages. Think how far and how fast, as a society, we have adapted to the Internet. In an article in the May/June circa 1998 *Voyager Magazine*, author Quentin Cooper, a science journalist and well-known voice of BBC Radio, reported the following information that was gathered by a survey commissioned by the UK Government's "Information Technology for All" campaign:

- 20% of all people refuse to use a cash machine.
- 50% are unsure of the benefits of technology.
- 75% of all adults see no use to the Internet.[3]

It's sort of humorous—75% of adults saw no reason to use the Internet. In less than a decade, our society has been nearly completely transformed by technology we initially had no use for to one that is today an integral part of our lives. Today's golf courses have to keep pace in order to remain relevant.

A golf course Web site should provide clear statements that emphasize customer benefits by creating a community of dedicated visitors who have the opportunity to transact business on the site. They should be able to book reservations, register for events, and pay online.

The Web site should be focused on what entertainment and value the customer will derive both from that particular golf course and from the amenities that are available there.

A Web site must be consistent with the corporate strategy and do more than re-purpose existing static content. Quality execution in graphics, writing, and navigation are fundamental. Think of the Web site as a newspaper whose content is changed frequently, not a book with fixed content. The use of

3 Quentin Cooper, *Voyager Magazine*, circa May/June 1998.

third-party firms to create, host, maintain, and update your Web site is important; the ultimate measure of a course's site is how many customers actually bookmark the site as one of their favorites.

The highlights of a successful site will include:

- A hierarchical scheme that makes navigation intuitive to the end user.
- Speed of download. It cannot be quick enough.
- Simply yet elegant graphics. The pages should be clean and not cluttered, with no advertising or extraneous banners. "White space" is imperative.
- An effective e-commerce search engine should identify the golf course.
- The ability to quickly process transactions.
- The transmission of the transaction information along with the secured credit card data to the golf course owner.
- No meaningful content should be below the fold.

A differentiating factor for golf courses is the depth and breadth of their Web sites and their adoption of Web 2.0 technology. Embedding Google Maps, course flyovers, newsletters, online reservations, and demand pricing alerts will become standard fare over the next five years.

Not sure? Note the following video course flyover that has been embedded into the Web site of Four Mile Ranch in Canon City, Colorado. Impressive!

The greatest current online applicability for a golf course, beyond the display of static information about the facilities, rates, directions, and contact phone numbers, is a tee time reservation component that feature the "lowest price" that can be obtained from any source. OB Sports has it right. The OB Sports Web site offers a Best Rate Guarantee, as depicted on the next page.

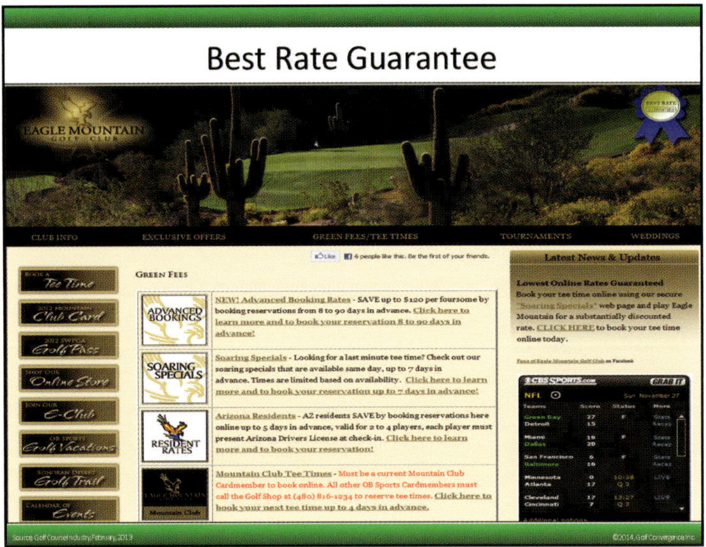

Also note the Facebook "like" link and real time NFL scoring over the Thanksgiving, 2011 weekend.

When Orbitz was constructed, it represented a consortium of airlines. Southwest Airlines declined to participate, indicating that the lowest Southwest rates could be obtained from the Southwest Web site. Southwest Airlines had it right. While Expedia, Travelocity, and Orbitz still offer the "lowest fares," each airline now offers its lowest fares only on its own Web site.

The number of golfers who book online continues to grow. The Internet is the most convenient method to book a tee time because a golfer can simultaneously view tee times on multiple courses. The recommended best practices for providing online tee times follow.

1. The purpose of a Web site is to create a "community of interest" that is dynamically changing. The following services should be available: advanced tee time reservations; last-minute tee times at either the rack rate or a discounted price, depending upon course capacity; USGA handicaps or scoring averages; upcoming tournaments and recent winners; an information board; etc. The site should also contain a "19th hole" at which links to other relevant sites are provided.
2. A course open to the public should feature a "database" that is open rather than closed. An open database allows all golfers to view available tee times prior to registration. Would you register in order to be able to shop at a department store? Not likely, so we don't believe requiring registration before viewing tee times is appropriate.
3. With an open database, upon selecting a tee time and seeing the price, the golfer should then be required to register, including entering a credit card number that is "lune test" checked (which is a sum of the digits verification) for validity and perhaps authorized.

4. A golfer should have the option of pre-registering in order to receive a potpourri of benefits, including advanced access and waiving the requirement to tender a credit card at the time of reservation.

5. When golfers register they should be encouraged to "qualify" themselves as to their preferences regarding:

   News—preferred golf courses, tee time confirmation notice, frequency, newsletters, lessons, tournaments, and merchandise specials.

   Preferred times divided into four alternatives—before 8 a.m., 8 to 12, 12 to 4, and after 4 p.m.

   Discounts—what percentage would they find attractive to entice them to play at the "last minute?"

   Merchandise—who are their preferred vendors?

   Qualifying customers greatly enhances the effectiveness of an e-mail campaign. Generic e-mail blasts to audiences that have not pre-qualified themselves have little value.

6. A golf course with multiple facilities should include a "map search" within the online tee time tab to help a golfer determine the location of the course within the city.

7. The site should include links to the golf course's social media resources. Social media are communications venues that rely on their audiences to create, modify, or distribute the medium's content. Examples of social media include forums, blogs, wikis, and instant messaging. Facebook, with 67 million unique visitors, and Twitter, with 17 million unique visitors,[4] are being used by leading golf courses to establish a dialogue with their customers.

Clients should view a golf course Web site as a newspaper at best and as a quarterly periodical at a minimum. Your Web site is not the Declaration of Independence, in which every word and graphic must be precisely correct before "launching." Instead, use the "POGE" principle—"principle of good enough." This principle warns that many projects can be over-engineered, creating delays in launch and accelerating costs.

---

4 Source: Compete, Comscore, April 2009, http://www.comscore.com/Press_Events/Press_Releases/2009/5/Social_Networking_Category_Has_Record_Month_Led_by_Gains_at_Twitter_and_Facebook/(language)/eng-

It is highly recommended that each golf course have its web site evaluated. There are several web sites that perform this complimentary service including: http://www.grademyseo.com/, http://www.mysitegrader.com/, and http://www.grademyself.com/. This site provides insights regarding the course's blog, indexed pages, readability level, metadata tags, images found, domain information, mobile optimization, twitter grade, RSS feeds, conversion forms and e-mail effectiveness. An example of websitegrader.com report is below:

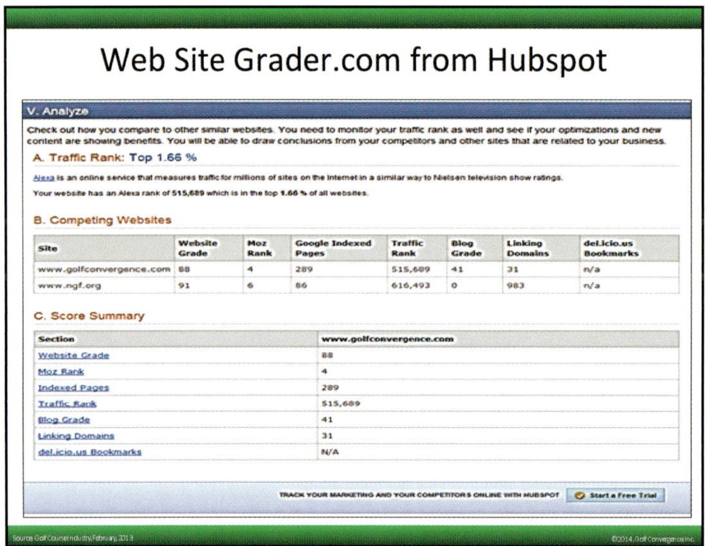

Web Site Grader.com from Hubspot

V. Analyze

Check out how you compare to other similar websites. You need to monitor your traffic rank as well and see if your optimizations and new content are showing benefits. You will be able to draw conclusions from your competitors and other sites that are related to your business.

A. Traffic Rank: Top 1.66 %

Alexa is an online service that measures traffic for millions of sites on the Internet in a similar way to Nielsen television show ratings.

Your website has an Alexa rank of 515,689 which is in the top 1.66 % of all websites.

B. Competing Websites

Site	Website Grade	Moz Rank	Google Indexed Pages	Traffic Rank	Blog Grade	Linking Domains	del.icio.us Bookmarks
www.golfconvergence.com	88	4	289	515,689	41	31	n/a
www.ngf.org	91	6	86	616,493	0	983	n/a

C. Score Summary

Section	www.golfconvergence.com
Website Grade	88
Moz Rank	4
Indexed Pages	289
Traffic Rank	515,689
Blog Grade	41
Linking Domains	31
del.icio.us Bookmarks	N/A

TRACK YOUR MARKETING AND YOUR COMPETITORS ONLINE WITH HUBSPOT Start a Free Trial

Source: Golf Course Industry, February, 2013

On December 6, 2011, HubSpot launched a totally free marketing tool: Marketing Grader replacing websitegrader.com. In under 30 seconds, it analyzes all of a company marketing—not just the web site—reviewing over 30 different factors and then providing a overall marketing grade for a company between 1-100. Since 2006 when Web Site Grader was introduced, a lot has changed and marketing now is about much more than just a golf course's web site.

All of this comes with a warning label. While the creation of a dynamic 2.0 Web site and the use of e-mail for communicating is recommended, the value of the Internet and e-mail communication is degrading, not improving. The Internet is no longer "good enough" to be the sole source of marketing. Identity fraud, viruses, worms, phishing, child porn, and endless piles of spam proliferate. It is unfortunate that what was great in concept has been taken to its lowest common denominator.

An Internet Marketing Component—Third-Party Online Reservations

Last-minute tee times raise the hair on the necks of most golf course owners. Golf course operators are forced to discount and participate in these local networks because they don't understand their "unique selling proposition." Just as important is the fact that many golf course owners understand neither their customers nor their booking patterns.

In a National Golf Foundation study, only 18% of golfers (regulars) decide a week or more in advance to book a tee time. A whopping 59% of golfers (exploiters) decide only a few days in advance and tend not to be loyal to any one course; they shop for deals. Twenty-three percent (opportunists) decide on the same day they play. As John Edwards, editor of *Colorado Golfer,* surmised, "The challenge for operators is to primarily work on the exploiters. The regulars are already captured and the opportunists are too fickle."[5]

Third-party marketers are springing up everywhere simply because they, and the customers, are savvy enough to use technology to fill a need course owners are either unwilling or unable to execute.

The pitch used by these third-party profiteers is quite convincing:

- Our services are FREE. Just give us one tee time per day you will not otherwise sell. Our service costs you nothing.

  As marketing experts, we will bring new customers to your course and help you create incremental revenue. We will provide your course exposure to our database of 30,000 local golfers.

  We will sell those hard-to-liquidate times on Monday–Thursday afternoons that you will otherwise not sell.

- Provide us a copy of your e-mail files and we will do a special custom announcement to your core customers.
- We will provide you with a website and/or electronic tee sheet to post tee times to your URL.

Sounds impressive, and if you know how to use the tools, it is a great deal for the golf course owner. But "using the tools" is a great big "if" that too many owners fail to comprehend.

Incredible Profits from Little Work

For those golf course operators seduced by the prospects of incremental revenue, here is what these entrepreneurs generate in revenue for themselves by running some ads in the local sports section, in regional golf publications, and in the yellow pages, while also posting some signs at your golf course and leveraging your customer database:

5 John Edwards, "59% of Core Golfers Wait for Deals," *Colorado Golfer*, June 2009, p. 2.

Description	Third-Party's Vendors Earnings
One tee time per day	1
Sold to a foursome	4
Rack rate	$30.00
For 30 courses	30
For 240-day golf season	240
Value of FREE golf "given" to him by golf courses	$864,000
Percent liquidated through Internet site	33%
Annual amount pocketed by entrepreneur leveraging course's tee time inventory in local market	$285,120

Considering that there are about 75 local markets that could be created, the annual profit potential might be more than $21 million per year. In 2011, we heard that one third-party marketing firm sold over $100 million in tee times.

Coupon books are also a lucrative deal for the third-party provider. Here is what we estimate the publisher of a Colorado regional magazine is generating in revenue from its coupon book:

Description	Publisher's Earnings
Number of coupon books sold	7,500
Price per book	$79.95
Publisher's gross income	$599,625
Courses participating	21
Total rounds donated (7,500 coupon books × 21 courses)	157,500
Average green fees of participating courses	$40.00
Value of golf given away by all courses	$6,300,000
Value of golf given away by one course	$300,000

Think about it. A marketer talks a golf course into giving away about 20% of its gross income potential for FREE; then the marketer makes $599,625.

A recent phenomenon that is drawing much attention is **Groupon**, a coupon e-mailed daily to subscribers.

According to Joe Assell, President and CEO, Co-Founder of GolfTEC, CEO of GolfTEC, "The jury is still out."

GolfTEC has used Groupon in 49 different markets, offering only a 30-minute swing diagnosis, in essence, a quick teaser for $35 (59% discount), or a 60-minute swing evaluation for $60 (60% discount). For each promotion, about 350 coupons are purchased. Despite proactive follow-up with coupon purchasers, the redemption rate is amazingly only 10-15%.

The key for GolfTECis that Groupon is selling introductory programs during the fall/winter when they have plenty of capacity. Only 30% of their lessons given by GolfTEC occur during September to February. The additional revenue has been welcome during the slower part of the year. The coupon offered does not offend their current customers, many of whom purchase 25+-lesson packages.

The downside, according to Joe Assell, "Groupon is very difficult to work with. They bump you if they have another promotion they believe will generate greater revenue, and they pay you over 60 days."

Though Groupon has assembled massive databases in nearly every metropolitan market, extreme caution in utilizing Groupon's services, in addition to the caveats advised by Joe Assell, is recommended.

Groupon requires the golf course sell its goods or services with at least a 50% discount from the rack rate. Groupon's commission is 50%. Thus, the golf course nets only 25% of retail. If a golf course were selling rounds of golf, they would have to increase play by 400% merely to break even – highly unlikely.

HighlandPacific, a new investor group, recently purchased Victoria, British Columbia. Seeking to attract new customers, the new owners tried Groupon with amazing success – sort of. Their coupon was for 50% of two green fees plus power cart and range balls. The program was suspended when 600 coupons sold by the morning of the second day. A small group of their Loyalty Program members complained that Highland Pacific did not let them know and participate—a customer service problem out of the gate.

A more amazing example of the perils of Groupon was seen over the 2010 holidays in Denver. A promotion for eight rounds of golf and 10 one-hour lessons valued at $1,080 was offered for $189, an 83% discount. The golf course manager specified that a cart was mandatory and that the tee times were only valid on Monday – Thursday, and Sunday after twelve.

Unfortunately, Groupon failed to list the restrictions until four hours after the promotion had been displayed. At that time, 543 coupons had been purchased.

Groupon's response upon learning of their mistakes was they would only refund the monies of disgruntled customers. No consideration was provided to the golf course and to the potential public relations nightmare created.

During the two-day promotion, 1,643 individuals (3% of the Denver database) purchased the coupon, representing $460,040 in tee times ($11.81 per round) and $924,188 in lessons. The revenue generated ($310,527) was allocated as follows: $155,264 to Groupon, an estimated $50,000 to Jintu, a marketing agency, and $100,000 to the City and County of Denver.

Incredible profit for Groupon for little work. The only possible upside potential is from the slippage – customers who pay and don't redeem the rounds or lessons. Amazingly, in some industries, the slippage is estimated as high as 40%. However, that still seems like a bad bet – selling merchandise to customers at a great discount hoping that they don't redeem the coupon purchased.

How are the marketers able to get away with their claims that they will produce incremental revenue for the golf course?

It is simple. Golf course operators cannot determine if the rounds sold by the third-party discounters would have sold otherwise. They can guess based on experience. If the 8:28 tee time on Mondays in November hasn't sold in previous years, the owners intuitively assume it won't sell now. So what's the harm in letting a discounter generate some revenue for those unused times?

The reason the course owners rely on instinct instead of data is because the direct tie from various marketing programs to the POS tee time reservation software systems is missing. Where the technology is in place, the staff is lax in tracking Web site booking and coupon redemption.

Research Study Demonstrates That Benefits of Discount Programs Are Negligible

A study of 30 golf courses in the Northern California comparing courses that discounted versus those that didn't revealed some amazing facts as shown here:

- The discounted golf course's "average daily rate" is lowered 31%.
- The golfer who receives a discounted round will spend less than $10 in the pro shop.
- The golfer who receives a discounted round has only a 16% probability of returning to that course and paying the rack rate.
- Thirty-eight percent of a course's core customers from a golf course that doesn't discount will migrate to the discounted rate plan within the first 12 months.
- Sixty-four percent of golfers who redeem a coupon usually bring only one other player.

The economics of discounting are not bright for the golf course. It is surprising that many general managers don't understand the relationship between discounts accorded and the increase in rounds that we discussed in Chapter 10, Pricing and Yield Management. Many discount programs, while stimulating rounds, more often than not result in a reduction in gross revenue.

Playing the discount green fee game is Russian roulette according to Andrew Wood, president of Legendary Marketing and author of two books, *The 12 Indisputable Laws of Golf Course Marketing* and *The Golf Marketing System*. As he says, "In the low price game there is only one winner—the company that can sell at the lowest possible price. And buyers who shop only by price have no loyalty. In any discount war, there can be only one winner, and that is usually the business with the deepest pockets."[6]

6 Andrew Wood, "Russian Roulette," *Golf Business*, May, 2005. http://www.golfbusiness.com/pageview.asp?m=5&y=2005&doc=1286.

Implications for the Golf Course Owner

The proliferation of technology companies poses a threat to golf course owners' relationships with their customers. The risks include:

- The erosion of green fees from net rates, standby bookings, and auctions
- Redirection of play away from their properties
- Siphoning of ancillary revenues associated with traditional merchandise
- Leveraging relationships to sell customers non–golf-related goods and services

However, if the golf course operator isn't smart enough to get off the heroin of giving away as many as two tee times per day, the beneficiary will be the third-party operator and the discount-seeking golfer. They will ultimately determine prices in the marketplace.

From an entrepreneurial and capitalist perspective, third-party firms should be saluted for identifying an opportunity, and providing the consumer a better alternative. As Mike Tinkey, Deputy CEO of the NGCOA, said during a phone conversation, "We clearly have lost the battle. Hopefully, we haven't lost the war for the livelihoods of golf course owners which are threatened by the third-party discounters."

Pariah of the Industry?

Last-minute tee time providers are viewed as the pariahs of the golf industry by the PGA, the NGCOA, and course owners. To properly frame the issue, you must understand certain fundamentals:

1. **Are last-minute tee time services going away? Never.** They are here to stay. At the end of the day, customers select the distribution channel for purchasing goods and services that provide them the greatest value.
2. **Are last-minute tee time services financially beneficial for the golf course owner? No.** While they can create incremental revenue, more often the core customer loyalty to a specific course is compromised by a last-minute service.

3. **Is it likely that a national reservation system for golf will ever be created? Not in the foreseeable future.** Golf is a local game. Ninety percent of all rounds are played within 10 miles of the golfer's residence.
4. **Will golfers be willing to pay a booking fee to reserve a tee time?** No, not unless demand exceeds supply for the date and time they seek to play. Golfers are not willing to prepay when they have no economic incentive to do so.
5. **Are golfers willing to accept non-refundable policies?** No, not unless they are able to book a specific day at a specific time that they would otherwise not be able to reserve through the normal reservation practices. For the customer, golf is a discretionary hobby, not a business. Golfers are rarely emotionally tied to a specific date and time.

The fact is golf courses are losing control of their ability to set prices. Thus, the ability of a course or an industry to rectify the current dilemma is nettlesome. The golf course owners in the United States should come to the realization that discounting is now standard practice.

Ultimately consumers will dictate what they are willing to pay. From the perspective of the 26 million golfers, technology has brought efficiency, creating data providing them the upper hand, and allowing the principles of capitalism and free markets to reign supreme.

Finding the Ideal Solution

Prior attempts by industry veterans such as the PGA and the NGCOA to organize the industry to thwart discounting have been unsuccessful. The perceived advantages and disadvantages of third parties are summarized below:

The *Perceived Advantages*	The *Disadvantages* of Third Parties
May claim to provide a means of marketing your facility at no direct out-of-pocket expense.	You lose control of managing the relationship with your customers. The golf consumer may be trained to look for and pay for only discounted golf. The perceived "value" of your golf course is diminished in the consumers' eyes and their willingness to pay full rack rate or book in advance is discouraged.

The *Perceived Advantages*	The *Disadvantages* of Third Parties
May claim to be a means to reach new channel of customers and fill holes in your tee sheet. Claims to bring in incremental business, e.g., out of town golfers that you would not normally see.	Some third party wholesalers/discounters in specific geographic areas have grown in such scope they control so much of the tee time inventory they have gained leverage over the owner/operator, similar to hotels.com, expedia.com.
In many cases, the third party will handle the technology needs of the program.	Third parties can and have separated the owner/operator from their customer base. Separation from your customer base may fracture any emotional ties and sense of loyalty that is key in establishing repeat business.
	Operating yields decrease. Third parties can and have generated advertising and other revenues by selling access to customers ("eyeballs") that come to their portals to book tee times at your course *and* this revenue is not shared with the golf course or courses in that market area.

The issues with third party tee time companies is highly contentious.

On November 18, 2011, the NGCOA issued a press release defining its role and issuing best practices regarding third party resellers. The press release stated,

> "In response to widespread concerns and questions expressed by golf course owners and operators regarding third party tee-time resellers, the NGCOA has developed a policy statement and issued a set of best practices to help members make informed decisions and optimize relationships with resellers. The policy, which was developed following input from the association's board of directors, local chapter executives, the NGCOA Canada and a survey of members, states that the NGCOA will provide information and education to help members decide if it is in their best interest to engage a third party. It has never been the role nor the intent of the NGCOA to prescribe how independent owners and operators should conduct business," said NGCOA CEO Mike Hughes. "But it is our responsibility to help members understand important issues affecting our industry and to give them information that helps them make decisions that are best for their business."

The NGCOA policy states the following:

- The NGCOA's role with respect to third party tee-time resellers is to provide information and education to its members so that they are aware of the key issues and can act in their best interests.

- Golf courses should promote (individually and/ or in groups) as many sales as possible directly through their own websites, pro shops, call centers and other outlets.
- If the golf course, using its own independent judgment, decides that it is in its business interest to engage the services of a third party reseller, the golf course should design plans and systems that position these resellers as supporting strategies, intended only to drive incremental business and fill in times of soft demand.
- Golf courses opting to use third party resellers should protect their business interests by utilizing best practices to manage their relationships with these entities.

The NGCOA's recommended best practices are designed to help members who engage third parties structure agreements that help them realize maximum benefits from the relationship. Best practices include: signed written contracts, clearly defined terms of agreement, best-rate guarantees, data ownership, payment terms, tee-time auctions, URL ownership, Search Engine Optimization, brand protection, tee-time inventory, loyalty and membership programs, indemnification and regulatory compliance, pricing, online links and transferability."

Rather than taking the leadership to create an alliance, the NGCOA's approach was to educate its members as to the benefits and risks of the best practices until late in 2013. The NGCOA then began evaluating their alternatives by the establishment of an exploratory committee to study launching a national tee time system to support their owners.

Making the Best of a Bad Hand

Who ultimately determines the fair price for a round of golf? The answer is the golfer. With supply exceeding demand by greater than 8%, and with the nation facing challenging economic times, there are no easy answers. Golf course owners will continue to forego long-term strategies for short-term profits. Discounting has become so pervasive that it is going to be difficult to eradicate.

Thus, developing creative ways to increase rounds through bundling or managed discounts without jeopardizing rate integrity remains a challenge; turning higher-paying customers into low-paying customers isn't a winning formula.

What then is the best solution in the current environment?

For the golf course owner, the formula is the Southwest Airlines model—your best price can only be available on your own Web site. This will allow you to capture (via the reservation system) the golfers' contact information and create an e-mail marketing campaign.

With respect to third-party tee time providers, golf course owners should proceed with caution and utilize these services only when they can: (1) avoid exclusive agreements; (2) require that the "best price" can only be obtained through the golf course's Web site; and (3) ensure that the golf course's database is protected from resale.

Thus, the ideal solution would be for the USGA and state golf associations, the NGCOA and the National Park and Recreation Association, or the PGA to identify and license a technology.

Such was advocated by the membership of the National Golf Courses Owners Association Canada during their annual meeting in November, 2010. Third party tee time resellers was one of the featured sessions at their annual convention.

Nothing has been done in response and frankly, the dominance of Golf Channel's Golfnow.com is so strong that it will remain a significant force as their initiatives are likely to have a profound and positive influence on changing a stagnant industry.

Perhaps the common good of the industry will at some time cause owners to create an alliance that will provide better service for their customers along with greater financial return to themselves.

But beyond the obvious, in the short term, realizing that a course can't be all things to all people is fundamental. To prosper, a golf course must create an appropriately conditioned course consistent with the fees established, identify core customers, and ensure loyalty.

In *Golf Business*, Phil Green, president and COO of OB Sports, stated that "the key to survival now and beyond lies in the ability to add value rather than competing solely on price. Central to this mission is the use of technology, as well as loyalty programs and superb service." The stakes are high in the battle for golfers, but, as Green believes, "there should always be a code of honor among those fighting on the front lines."[7]

---

7 *Golf Business*, "Up Close and Personal," January 2008, p. 22.

End Notes

The lessons of this chapter are:

1) Most golf course operators seem to believe that marketing consists of perhaps some print ads in a local golf magazine, an advertisement in the Saturday sports section of the local newspaper, participating in coupon books, using third-party Web sites, and sending out discount coupons via e-mail.
2) The strategic vision for the golf course is simply creating awareness of its brand image—its unique selling proposition.
3) The tactical plan involves the allocation of resources between advertising, public relations, and promotion.
4) Operational execution is focused on measuring the efficacy of a marketing effort by tracking results and adjusting the marketing programs proactively.
5) Marketing comprises three components:
   - Advertising
   - Public Relations
   - Promotion
6) The key to developing an ongoing successful marketing program is having real measurements to judge the efficacy of programs.
7) The creation of a dynamic 2.0 Web site is of growing importance, as is the correct use of e-mail newsletters, promotions, and value-based opportunities. Third-party marketing firms leverage the inability of the golf course to effectively market, earning incredible profits with little work.
8) These firms are viewed as the pariahs of the industry because the create the following risks for the golf course owner:
   - The erosion of green fees from net rates, standby bookings, and auctions
   - Redirection of play away from their properties
   - Siphoning of ancillary revenues associated with traditional merchandise
9) The benefit of third party marketing firms is negligible when the tool isn't used correctly.

10) Golf course owners should proceed with caution and utilize these services only when they can:

- avoid exclusive agreements
- require that the "best price" can only be obtained through the golf course's Web site
- ensure that the golf course's database is protected from resale.

Concluding Thought

It is a very cheap gesture to hit "send" on an e-mail. And it has risen to fill the variable time in our lives. I keep waiting for a shakeout, the supernova explosion that makes us stop and regroup and get back to the business of real life.

Brian Williams, *Men's Journal*, May 2008

Chapter 14

Game Time
Step 6 of Golf Convergence WIN™ Formula (continued)

The journey of a thousand miles begins with a single step.

Lao Tze

Chapter Highlights

The golf course experience could be viewed as an "assembly line process." The sun rises, the gates open, management and staff arrive, and another day begins. The golf course is like an amusement park that winds the customer from the entrance around a series of themes to a thrilling conclusion upon departure.

Every point of contact is important. The design and layout of the clubhouse and pro shop define the experience likely to be encountered. The bag drop, obtaining a cart, the range, starter, golf course, cart return, and the restaurant and bar—all are elements that provide the opportunity to define the customer experience.

Creating the superior customer experience through consistent execution is the only way to guarantee survival in today's competitive market.

All of the planning and all of the preparation are for naught if the experience received by the golfer isn't consistent with the price paid.

Creating the Superior Customer Experience

Golfers race from the parking lot and hastily put on their shoes, perhaps not even stopping to tie them. They walk into the pro shop looking at the staff person beyond the counter and think "They have such a life. They work at this beautiful golf course, play all the time, and they are accomplished golfers. They have it made. What a life!"

Few golfers know how much hard work is needed to create that efficient golf operation. The person behind the counter plays infrequently and rarely has time to hit balls at the range before or after his or her shift.

The Home Team

A golf course staff combines the talents of many different individuals. Staffing at a golf course, in terms of quality of the personnel retained and the number of individuals, both full- and part-time, can vary widely. The following table lists the typical positions filled at the golf course and the number of staff hired, both full- and part-time, for the peak season.

Job Title	Function	Minimum	Maximum
Bag Drop	Check in golfer to course	0	4
Starter	Start golfers on course	4	8
Ranger	Pace of play	0	4
Pro Shop Staff	Collect fees/act as starter	6	12
Director of Golf	Oversee golf operation	1	1
Assistant Golf Professionals	Customer service in pro shop	1	6
Director of Tournaments	Organize and administer golf programs	0	1
Director of Instruction	Create instruction programs	0	1
Teaching Staff	Teach customers	0	6
Food and Beverage: In Clubhouse: F&B Director, Chef, Sous Chef, Waiters	Sell food	4	8

Job Title	Function	Minimum	Maximum
Food and Beverage: On Course	Sell limited items from cart	2	2
Catering Manager	Arrange banquets and special events	0	1
Tournament Director	Groups and outings	1	3
Reservation Agent	Book individual times	1	5
Merchandise Manager	Select, arrange, and monitor inventory	3	3
Purchasing Agent	Purchase inventory	1	1
General Manager	Oversee general operations	1	2
Membership Director	Recruit members	0	2
Personnel	Retention of personnel	1	4
Controller		1	1
Bookkeeper	Account for activity	1	4
Receptionist	Handle telephone calls	1	1
Systems Administration, sometimes outsourced	Oversee systems	0	2
Superintendent	Oversee the turf	1	1
Grounds Crew, Mechanic	Maintain the turf	6	30
Total Staff		36	113
Note: Several of those positions, depending on the size of the operation, can be performed by the same individual; thus, some golf courses might operate with as few as 10 people.			

These averages of personnel retained vary widely between municipal, daily fee, resort, and private clubs. For example, at the Reignwood Pine Valley Golf and Country Club in Beijing, the grounds crew totals 292 people to maintain a 45-hole course. Why such a large crew? The average annual salary is only $2,750, and staffing levels have been suggested by the Chinese government.

The challenge is selecting, orienting, training, and educating both full- and part-time staff members. Most managers underestimate the complexities of the golf business. The motivations of the food and beverage personnel, the golf shop personnel, and the tournament coordinators are all different.

The key to the daily operation of a golf course is creating a "culture of discipline." When you have disciplined people, you don't need hierarchy. When you have disciplined thought, you don't need bureaucracy. When you have disciplined action, you don't need excessive controls. When a culture lacks discipline and has little emphasis on precise execution, it becomes a bureaucracy in order to compensate for the incompetence and lack of trust.

The key to operating a successful golf operation is getting disciplined people who engage in disciplined thought and take disciplined action. When expectations are clarified and the commitment conveyed, individuals will take their responsibilities seriously. The key for each employee is to turn common sense into common practice.

The Customer Experience Starts with Service

If a customer is treated really well and courteously, the cost often becomes secondary to the enjoyable customer experience.

Disney is a great brand that continues to thrive on the strength of exceptional customer service. Tom Connellan's book, *Inside the Magic Kingdom—Seven Keys to Disney's Success*, has great applicability for a golf course.

The seven keys to Disney's success[1] that should be integrated into the culture of the golf course operation are as follows:

- **Lesson 1: The competition is anyone the customer compares you with.**

  Your competition is anyone who raises customer expectations—because if someone else satisfies customers better than you, no matter what type of business, you suffer by comparison.

- **Lesson 2: Pay fantastic attention to detail.**

  If you knew that increased attention to some detail would improve customer loyalty, how much more attention would you be willing to give it? The devil is in the details. Execute, execute, execute.

- **Lesson 3: Everyone walks the talk.**

  Every time a customer comes in contact with your company, you have an opportunity to create value. Capitalize on that opportunity and you win.

- **Lesson 4: Everything walks the talk.**

  Everyone needs to focus on providing what customers want, even people who never come in direct contact with customers.

1 Tom Connellan, *Inside the Magic Kingdom* (Atlanta, Bard Press, 1997).

- **Lesson 5: Customers are best heard through many ears.**

  Listening posts are about the company listening to customers—as opposed to listening to itself. If you overlook information gathered by employees, you overlook probably the most valuable source of customer information you have.

- **Lesson 6: Reward, recognize, and celebrate.**

  The desire to be appreciated is one of the deepest of human yearnings. As management we need to focus on compensation that consists of two factors: economic income (reward) and psychological income (recognition).

  Practice a feedback ratio of 3 positive to 1 negative. The most common response to good performance is, unfortunately, no feedback. Getting no feedback is as devastating to employees and to the company as getting negative feedback.

- **Lesson 7: Everyone makes a difference**.

  To achieve good teamwork and optimize customer loyalty, you have to break down the silos. Each 1% increase in customer retention equals as much as a 7% increase in profits. Loyal customers are the result of detailed planning and flawless execution.

How can these seven keys to success be incorporated into the culture of a golf course? To begin with, digital speed—fully integrated golf management software—is the foundation on which a golf course can outperform its peers.

Preparing for the Visiting Team

What actually differentiates one course from another in terms of a customer experience? The factors include the motivation to play the golf course, the reservation process, signage, bag drop area, the clubhouse entrance, the pro shop, the range, the starter, the course, the locker/bathrooms, the cart drop-off area, and the restaurant—what is referred to as the "assembly line of golf."

The 13 Steps of Golf Operations

We have been fortunate to visit over 4,000 golf courses in 41 countries. During this journey around the world, the best management practices have been captured.

What follows is a template by which golf course personnel can ensure that they enhance the customer experience on the "assembly line"—regardless whether the economy is robust or languishing.

Step 1—Motivating the Golfer to Select Your Course

The 13-step program defines the total golf experience, which starts with a golfer's decision about "which course to play."

Though many golfers have a "home course," they are often influenced by other factors.

What Motivated Me to Play Course	Yes	No
Word of mouth from "respected friends"		
National ranking in *Golf Magazine*, *Golf Digest*, or *Golfweek*		
Yellow pages		
Literature at airport		
Literature at kiosk in hotel		
Phone listing on hotel phone		
Concierge		
Billboards		
Local referrals		
Invitation from friend to play		

The billboard on the next page is a good example of eye-catching advertising.

This billboard is effective for many reasons: (1) an appealing photograph that entices the avid golfer; (2) a sensational tagline—"Golf Heaven"; (3) announcement of the opening of the new course (a 54-hole resort); and (4) information that you are only 34 miles away from "Golf Heaven."

Most resort billboards are merely informational, providing contact information or directions. Some have compelling pictures, but few have compelling taglines. Another effective billboard was positioned leaving the San Antonio Airport, and promoted the Hyatt Regency with the tagline, "20 minutes but a million miles away—this fall enjoy the change of season with a change of pace."

The estimated cost of the billboard is about $2,500 per month.

Step 2—Making the Reservation Process Seamless, Quick, and Informative

The customer's first experience with the golf course usually comes while reserving a tee time. In most instances, the customer is put on hold—not a great first experience. We monitor the following when evaluating the process of reserving a tee time:

Reservations—Making the Process Easy	Yes	No
Touch-tone telephone?		
Was there a music on-hold system that played a message about course information?		
Phone answered by pro shop staff?		
Did phone ring more than three times?		
Touch-screen kiosks?		
Can a golfer book on-line?		
Was credit card guarantee required?		
Did agent get all players' names and e-mails?		
Were directions to course offered?		
Were the fees discussed?		
Were the amenities mentioned?		

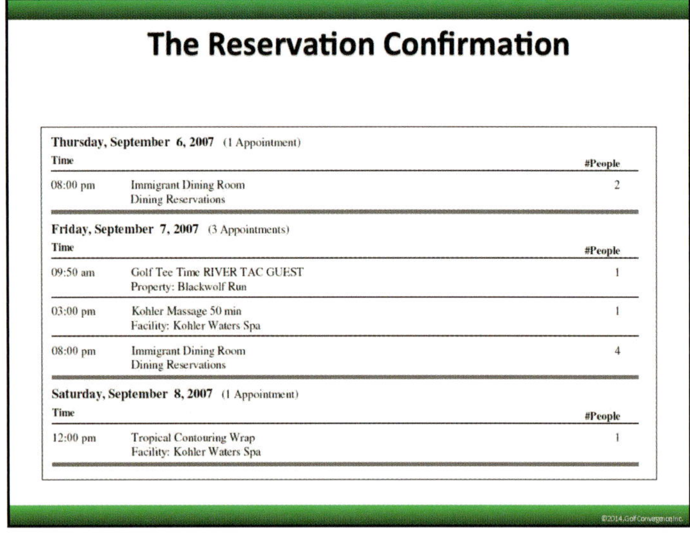

The Reservation Confirmation

Thursday, September 6, 2007 (1 Appointment)

Time		#People
08:00 pm	Immigrant Dining Room Dining Reservations	2

Friday, September 7, 2007 (3 Appointments)

Time		#People
09:50 am	Golf Tee Time RIVER TAC GUEST Property: Blackwolf Run	1
03:00 pm	Kohler Massage 50 min Facility: Kohler Waters Spa	1
08:00 pm	Immigrant Dining Room Dining Reservations	4

Saturday, September 8, 2007 (1 Appointment)

Time		#People
12:00 pm	Tropical Contouring Wrap Facility: Kohler Waters Spa	1

There are many golf courses that do a fabulous job at booking tee times. The American Club is at the forefront of that list. There are many that equal, but none that exceed, the quality of the customer experience at Kohler.

These written confirmations are effective because they: (1) provide details as to time and cost of pending reservations and when they can be confirmed; (2) provide the opportunity to upsell, and; (3) provide a link for directions to the facility.

Step 3—Providing Directions to the Golf Course

One of the great frustrations in playing golf at a course for the first time is finding it quickly and easily. Notwithstanding the use of Google maps or Mapquest, there is a high probability you will circle some golf courses for 10 minutes trying to find their entrances.

Thus, having some of the following signage is highly recommended.

Guiding the Golfer Smoothly to the Golf Course	Yes	No
Billboard on interstate?		
Sign on nearest exit?		
Directional sign at 5 miles?		
Direction sign at 2 miles?		
Direction sign at 1 mile?		
Flowers at entrance?		
Directional sign to facilities at club entrance?		
Sign for parking lot or valet?		
Sign for bag drop?		
Direction sign to clubhouse entrance?		
Welcome sign at clubhouse entrance?		

An example of the proper use of signs follows. This is World Golf Village's sign on Interstate 95.

With a tee time reservation in hand, the thought of being late because you got lost is aggravating. The golfer's goal should be to arrive 45 minutes before the scheduled tee time in order to practice, putt, and hit some range balls, especially when the golfer is playing a high-end daily fee course where the green fee is north of $100. Removing that angst from the golfer by providing directional signs creates comfort. In addition, these signs serve as "advertisements" for the golf course for every car that passes. It's a very cost-effective method to promote a facility.

Step 4—First Impressions Are Lasting

Another first impression is created at the entrance to the property. From attractive entrance signs welcoming golfers; flower gardens that are well maintained; directional signs for the bag drop, parking, and clubhouse entrance; to staff in uniform with name tags—all these indicate the experience is likely to be a good one.

In arriving at a golf course, the following are observed:

Club Entrance: The Bag Drop Area	Yes	No
Is staff in uniform?		
Does the desk say "guest services"?		
Is attendant available?		
Does attendant provide guidance as to next steps?		
Is bag tag affixed to bag?		
Is the bag tag personalized?		
Is course condition displayed as to green height, green speed, etc.?		

A Themed Entrance

Golf courses that have a theme and execute that theme throughout the property always heighten the customer experience. Depicted here are photos of the clubhouse and bag drop area at the Wizards Golf Course in Myrtle Beach. The neighboring course, Man of War, has a "horses" motif that is consistent with its branding. Wizards and Man of War are great names for a golf course and compelling.

The entrance at Yalong Bay on Hainan Island had this very innovative entrance.

In the middle of China on a remote island, this course features its Web site address in the flower garden at its entrance. How creative!

Flower Garden Entrance: China

The vast majority of golf courses don't avail themselves of the marketing opportunities that arise from having a great name and logo. Most golf courses have a first name that is a color (green is the most popular, followed by red, blue, white, and yellow) and a second name that describes a land feature (trees, water, hills, valley, etc.) or animals. Alternatively, naming the course after its location (Craft Farms, Highlands Ranch, Rio Grande Club) is boring. Names like the Sanctuary, the Bandit, or Devil's Thumb bring to life a golfer's imagination as to the challenge and customer experience that awaits.

Prior to the world recession from 2007 - 2013, four courses in the United Arab Emirates were to be named Fire, Earth, Water, and Wind. The Web site for the Fire course appears here:[2]

Capturing four of the five essential elements found in the creative elements of "Chi" forces, an Eastern belief system, and then hiring famed designers to execute the theme, ensures a curiosity factor and draws lots of attention and free publicity.

The names alone are enticing and suggest that all four golf courses should become becomes part of a golfer's lifelong bingo card.

Another opportunity for great marketing and brand recognition comes from the creation of a fabulous logo. Can you think of any course with a great logo? Think of Pebble Beach with the Cypress tree and Kapalua with the butterfly blended into a pineapple. Wailea on Maui had a great logo that was casually abandoned when the course was purchased over 15 years ago by foreigner investors. The property originally had the Tao symbol of the ying and yang, the blue for the water and the orange for the sun, blended perfectly. Unfortunately from a marketing standpoint, it was replaced by a sea horse, which is a special figure in Japanese culture but not directly relevant to the property itself.

Names, logo, clubhouse entrances, and the clubhouse all set the stage for what the golfer will experience. Staging the experience is an important element to a highly successful and profitable golf course.

One of the great advertising marketing opportunities that is often lost is putting a bag tag on the arrival golfer's clubs. Not only does it make each golfer

2 Leisurecorp, Jumeriah Golf Estates, http://www.jumeirahgolfestates.com/play/fire/

Branding Via Bag Tags

feel special, it provides a "souvenir" of the experience. The illustration here depicts the bag tag process used by the very well-run Barton Creek Resort.

It's great "free" advertising. The average golfer plays four to seven different courses a year. Bag tags beg the question: "How was your experience there? Is it a must-play course?"

Step 5—We Are Here to Enhance Your Experience

Golf has so many unwritten rules regarding etiquette and proper decorum that most players have a feeling of apprehension the first time they visit a course. Welcoming guests with warmth alleviates that anxiety and makes them feel welcome and refreshed.

The following are opportunities for a golf course to distinguish itself as the golfers enter the clubhouse before proceeding into the pro shop.

Clubhouse: Celebrate the Traditions as They Enter Your "House"	Yes	No
Flowers at entrance door?		
Symbol of pride and tradition by front door?		
Welcome mat?		
Mission statement displayed by front door?		
Sign that "dress standards apply"?		
Soft spike facility sign?		
Signage as to where soft spikes can be replaced?		
Plaques indicating heritage of course?		
Audubon Society awards displayed?		
Picture of animals to be seen on course?		
Display case with championship trophies?		
Display case with merchandise inventory on mannequins?		
History of site in hallway to POS area?		

As one enters the Hawk Hollow Golf Course in Bath, MI, the mission statement is displayed. The statement is a great reminder for the staff as well as displaying a course's commitment to the guest. Little things do matter. Hawk Hollow also constructed a white picket fence between the highway and several adjoining holes. The white picket fence extends from the club entrance to near the clubhouse, perhaps ¼ mile. Expensive, probably, but it creates a special feeling about the upcoming experience.

A picture is worth a thousand words. The photograph shown here was located inside the men's locker room at the famed New South Wales Golf Club in Sydney, Australia. It highlighted the club's regulations with respect to trousers, shirts, shorts, shoes, socks, and shoes permissible within the clubhouse. The pictures left no ambiguity as to acceptable attire.

Step 6—Think Nordstrom

If entering the clubhouse creates an anxious moment, entering the pro shop is even more intimidating. A lot of this phobia stems from the attitude of golf staffs. If you are greeted with, "Welcome, glad to have you visiting with us. How can I help you?" anxiety will evaporate like morning dew. But too many golf employees are unwelcoming. Many women comment that they feel like they are an imposition on the young male staff pounding the computer at the check-in station.

The following is a checklist used to measure the consumer friendliness of the pro shop experience.

The Pro Shop: Welcome with Warmth	Yes	No
Does the pro shop have a theme?		
What ambience is created within the shop to hold the customer?		
PGA plaques of staff behind counter?		
Course awards displayed behind counter?		
Name entered into computer?		
Were you upsold: merchandise, membership, range?		
Yardage book?		
Tip sheet on how to play the course?		
Are tees colored to represent a theme?		
Logoed balls?		
Logoed merchandise?		
Logoed gloves?		
What is the distribution of soft goods (men's and women's) versus hard goods?		
Women's inventory commensurate with percentage of rounds played?		
Fees posted?		
Two POS registers available?		
Was there a wait at counter?		
Candy bin upon departing?		
Customer service monitor poll?		

Making the pro shop warm and welcoming is an understandable challenge. Undertaking a repetitive task 300 times a day is boring to nearly everyone. How can you make what is a repetitive experience enjoyable for the staff? The picture depicted here from Chateau Whistler reminds the staff as to their role in serving the customer.

Shakespeare stated in "As You Like It," Act 2 scene 7,

"All the world's a stage, And all the men and women merely players. They have their exits and their entrances; And one man in his time plays many parts. . ."

There's a well-known story about the frog in water on a stove and the temperature increases gradually until the frog is cooked. The tale is analogous to what happens at a golf course. Staff easily becomes complacent and in some cases argumentative with customers, which results from the assembly line mentality of moving customers through.

There is no lack of self-help books, but while they all offer simple advice, implementing sage advice is not easy. Reminding without offending, coaching without becoming pedantic, leading versus managing—are all constant challenges. The previous sign serves as an effective and tactful backstage reminder that the staff of the golf course is on the "world's stage."

One of the best gestures of warmth displayed within a pro shop was evidenced at Lost Tracks in Bend, Oregon. Brian Whitcomb, the owner and former president of the PGA of America, has the philosophy that a golf course is his home, and those who visit are treated with the same respect as those who visit his house. Brian loves candy. At the exit of his pro shop he offers his "house guest" a big vase of Tootsie Rolls to select from.

The total cost of giving away candy? Brian indicated it was less than $200 per year. The value in terms of the experience created: priceless.

Step 7—Chariots of Fire: Earth Calling Satellite

While the best golf experience is found while walking with a caddie, carts have become de rigueur, both for their economic benefit to the golf course and their convenience to the golfer. Because of carts and the mobility they provide, some who otherwise might not play the game have the opportunity to enjoy the sport. Ironically, however, the cart doesn't appear to speed up play in general.

Any golfer will surely expect water, ice, towels, and tees in the holders once the price of the green fees exceeds $100. The fundamental cart services and provisions should be as follows:

Carts	Yes	No
Cart washed and clean?		
Clean towels in cart?		
Seed mix bottle full?		
Full ice chest?		
Scented mango towels available in ice chest?		
Tees in rack both long and short?		
Bottles of water?		
GPS?		
Carts reflect theme of course?		
Golfer's name in placards when advanced reservations have been made?		

GPS: Enhancing the Customer Experience

While GPS has been a fixture in the golf industry since the early 1990s, the technology has advanced remarkably since those days. The golf course GPS that began life as a toy has evolved into a business tool that some courses find indispensable.

The technology has evolved to assist in pace-of-play, fleet rotation, and customer-to-pro shop communications.

As the technology is expensive, with the annual cost exceeding $50,000, recently the introduction of advertising on the GPS has been incorporated to lower costs. The course and the GPS vendor split the advertising revenues after an agency fee is paid.

GPS is almost becoming "standard" for golf courses whose green fees exceed $150, especially those that are resort-oriented. Unfortunately, GPS is of limited value on golf courses that require golf carts to stay on the path. Carts on paths only increase the length of the round and create golfer frustration. GPS, when used correctly, however, enhances the golf experience by allowing the golfer to select the proper club quickly, order food, and record their score.

Carts will remain a mainstay of a golf operation because they can generate revenue and they are used by upwards of 75% of golfers who are given the choice of riding or walking.

Step 8—Fire Until the Blisters Burn

A golf course that has a well-designed range and short game area can be a pleasant addition to the golf experience. At the range, having golf balls aligned, tees available, and a bucket with water and a towel to clean your clubs all adds to a pleasant golf experience. Such is the case at the Broadmoor, where two individuals "walk the range" and clean the golfers' clubs while they practice.

The following criteria are used to evaluate the adequacy of the range and practice facilities:

The Range: Warming Up in Order to Chill Out	Yes	No
Stations with benches properly spaced for safety?		
Stations rotated frequently to ensure good turf conditions?		
Is the range in the aggregate in good condition, level teeing grounds with identifiable greens and target flags?		
Type of golf balls and color—good quality, white?		
Balls aligned—course logo foil used?		
Free tees?		
Correct distances to flags displayed from current tee markers?		
Driving range fees assessed by minute or number of balls? Or not at all?		
Putting green available?		
Short game area with bunker available?		
Seed mix in buckets on range?		
Water bucket/club cleaning machine?		
Clock on the range?		

At the home of golf, St. Andrews, the importance of pace of play is first subtly communicated to the golfers by the imprinting on the range balls, which notes the pace of play goal.

Pebble Beach and Desert Mountain also stamp their balls with the desired pace of play. The time on their golf balls is 4 hours 30 minutes, which says something

The Ultimate Driving Range –
Pods of 4 with Music

about the different cultures. It makes you wonder how many more people would play if a round could be completed in less than 4 hours.

It is always a mark of distinction when a golf course makes the effort to indicate accurate yards to the various flags on the range, based upon a range finder that a staff member uses each day to measure distances from the hitting stations. Having a clock prominently displayed on the range also tends to ensure a smooth flow of players to the first tee.

On of the best range experiences can be found at Diamante in Cabo San Lucas, Mexico. Each foursome is grouped together, with tables fully stocked, i.e., sun tanned lotion, tees, divot repair tools, and your choice of music: Sade, Sting, Bono, etc. What a great experience.

Step 9—Get Ready, Get Set, On Your Mark, Go!

Can I see your receipt? Where are the other players? I need to see their receipts now. You have to play in 4 hours and 30 minutes. Keep up the pace. Keep you carts on the cart path. Wave to the group in front of you on Par 3's. Fix your ball marks. Replace your divots. Rake the bunkers. And oh, by the way, have fun.

How many starters come across as drill sergeants? Way too many.

The alternative experience is the starter at Doonbeg in County Clare on the West Coast of Ireland. When that starter approaches a group, the standard "keep up" responses are expected, but instead, the friendly Irishman opens a humidor and says, "What are we smoking today, boys?"

Don't you wonder why a golf course puts its most inexpensive labor (likely a volunteer who is working for perhaps minimum wage and/or for the opportunity to play golf for free) as the key customer contract before teeing off?

Imagine checking in, being already registered in the golf course database, having your name automatically appear as fully paid when you approach the starter, and being greeted with a Ritz-Carlton style treatment of, "Mr. Keegan! Welcome." The only question you might have is, "How did they do it?" I am still wondering, and amazed, how an A&W clerk near Cedar Rapids Airport said, "Mr. Keegan, enjoy your root beer float" when I paid with cash.

Or imagine if you were to hear "Mr. Keegan, it's great to have you here today. Thank you for coming. You're going to have a great time. This is an exciting course. The architect is _____. His philosophy was _____. I want to ensure that you have a great time. Here are my suggestions for your consideration: _____."

The opportunities to make favorable impressions are endless. So why do so few courses avail themselves of the opportunity?

The following checklist can be used to measure the friendliness of the experience.

The Starter: Welcome with Warmth	Yes	No
Sharpie and ball marks provided?		
Divot repair tool?		
Free fruit, water?		
Scorecard: color printing?		
Scorecard: routing map of course?		
Scorecard: slope, pace of play, etc.?		
Instructions on pace of play, rules of course given?		
Is starter wearing a headphone connected to POS counter?		
Did the starter recognize the golfers by their first names?		
Does the starter take receipt and enter it onto the tee sheet?		

On the first tee at the Old Head of Kinsale, in Cork Island, Ireland, a ritual "stone of accord" is displayed bearing the following account:

> *"In ancient times when Celtic people (the Eireann) lived on this headland, friendships were acknowledged, arguments settled and bargains and marriages were sealed by joining hands through the Stone.*
>
> *This tradition may be up to 6,000 years old and can still be practiced. As we set out to enjoy the Royal and Ancient game let us continue this ancient tradition by shaking hands through the Stone to symbolize camaraderie and goodwill."*

The little things often make a big impression.

Step 10—18 Tees, 18 Fairways, 18 Greens: The Thrill Ride

The golf course is like a great book. It excites in the beginning, engages throughout, and disappoints and brings heartache when least expected. As the end approaches we hope for a fabled ending, and even if the fable isn't to be told on that day, the golfer, upon completing the round, immediately wants more.

Each round is a story to be remembered and told, and no two games are identical. Most golfers realize that golf is the devil's game, and they know it can never be conquered, that any good shot can be followed by despair. The putt made may be followed by the drive that is likely to end up anywhere but where the golfer had hoped.

History museums are popular. Golf courses are, in essence, history museums. How better to convey that thought than to design a golf course that describes and demonstrates the theories of the world's great golf course architects. Not only is the round fun, but it's also highly educational, as the golfers gain an appreciation for the game and its complexities. What is the origination of double greens

The Tract: Each Course Is Unique	Yes	No
Tee signs with yardage guidance?		
Unique tee markers depicting a theme?		
Elevated multiple tees with "sticks" indicating tee positions?		
Tee signs suggesting where a golfer would have the most enjoyable round?		
Flowers on some tee boxes?		
Seed mix on every tee next to tee markers?		
Food and beverage cart available?		
Lightning warning signs and notification of what to do?		
Heart defibrillator available at the course?		
Pace of play clocks on the golf course?		

and pot bunkers? How many different styles of courses are there: fire (desert), water (rivers, ponds and creeks), wind (links), earth (tree-lined)?

Thus, courses that have a theme that is carried throughout, like an entertainment park, should be celebrated. The Architects Golf Club, in New Jersey, uses those theories of the greatest architects, and educates the golfers as they play the course.

Each golf course should tell its own story and provide bookmarks on which your enjoyment can be measured.

Presented here is how Pronghorn makes its thrill ride unique and distinctive: golf course flags with the signature of the architect, Tom Fazio.

Celebrating History

An Architect's Signature on Flag at Pronghorn

Step 11—When You Have To Go, You Have to Go

Is there anything more disgusting than a filthy bathroom? Is there anything more disgusting than a golf course where you pay $78 in green fees and are required to use a Porta Potty, or worse, yet, one that hasn't been cleaned recently? Years ago at Philmont Country Club, Pennsylvania, one of the finest woman amateur golfers carried in her golf bag a rubber plastic toilet seat that she used in the bathrooms on her home course as well as others she visited.

A golf course restroom should not resemble a Tijuana gas station. Bathrooms are graded based on the some of the following criteria:

Bathrooms: The Dump Should Not Be a Dump	Yes	No
Fragrance acceptable?		
Carpeted?		
Toilets clean and modern?		
Paper toilet seat covers available?		
Lockers available?		
Flowers by basin?		
Candles by basin?		
Soap fresh?		
Cloth towels?		
Sunscreen?		
Deodorant?		
Mouthwash?		

The Facility's Facility

The importance of bathroom facilities is recognized by some. The on-course restrooms at Red Sky Ranch in Vail cost nearly $1.5 million each. Whistling Straits is to be lauded for hiding its bathrooms within the dunes on the course, as depicted here or at Diamante in Cabo San Lucas, Mexico as shown on the next page.

Step 12—The Mad Dash to the Finish Line

What seems so simple can be such a confusing process for the customer. Upon completing the 18th hole, do I drive the cart to the car and unload? Are the carts even allowed in the parking lots? Whose liability is it if the cart is damaged in the parking lot? If I return the cart to the clubhouse, is there an attendant on duty to clean the clubs? If the round cost in excess of $200, should I tip the attendant or presume that it is included in the green fee?

The process can be simplified for the golfer with signage from the 18th directing the desired flow of carts and with a clean staging area with logical "parking" positions for the carts. A tip jar sends a clear message as to whether gratuities are appropriate. More than half the golfers in America do not tip, and when they do, it's only a dollar or two. That lack of response from the golfers could reflect their frustration with their game, their desire to quickly depart, or the realization that the clubs aren't going to be cleaned very well. Most golfers have experienced all of these.

What if an attendant asks, "How was your round and what could we do better to heighten your customer experience?" Rarely is that second question asked, but what better time is there to get a snapshot of the golfer's experience?

More checkpoints for a course to consider are:

The Finish Line	Yes	No
Free club cleaning?		
All clubs cleaned or just the irons?		
Garbage cans nearby to allow customers to dispose of "junk" while gathering belongings?		
Carts allowed in parking lot?		
Clear signage where to return carts?		
"Thank you" sign for playing?		
A sign showing the replay rate to encourage further incremental play?		
Upon departing property: "thank you" sign and directions to other courses?		

When the golfer returns the cart and gathers belongings, the course has one last opportunity to make a favorable impression. Look at the photograph to see how Hualalai creates a lasting impression. The cart return attendant has cool, moist towels ready for the golfers as they return to the staging area, and uses the Hawaiian sign for "hello/thank you" as they approach. What a nice customer service gesture.

Of all the closing guest experiences, one of the most impressive is at Coeur d'Alene, Idaho. The 14th hole on the golf course is a floating island to which golfers are shuttled by boat. At that course, a walking caddie is assigned to the foursome. Upon completing the round, players who make par are presented with a certificate.

This touch demonstrates that when a guest's expectation is exceeded, the story gets retold many times as free advertising.

Step 13—Chow Time

No aspect of a golf operation is as scattershot as the food and beverage experience.

The Famed Castle Pines Milkshake

Some courses confuse food service with selling implied sex masquerading as "marketing." At these courses, skimpily clad ladies parade around the course in beverage carts, offering beer that is often warm and coffee that is often cold. The smiles are usually nice, though.

Other golf courses provide grilled brats and hamburgers at the turn. Is there a better smell to stimulate a golfer's appetite?

With respect to restaurant dining, Castle Pines Golf Club has great milkshakes; turtle soup is a staple at Pine Valley; Southern cooking is available at Sage Valley; fish chowder is on the house at the turn at Caledonia Game and Fish Club; and fish tacos are almost obligatory at the Ocean Course at Cabo del Sol, Baja California Sur, Mexico.

Many courses lose money from their food and beverage operations. The standard fare at nearly all municipal golf courses and low-tier daily fee courses is just that: standard. The key to a food and beverage operation is to have sufficient tournaments and a catering operation to create the volume necessary to provide the economies of scale in a food operation.

Items to watch for at on-course food service include:

Fine Dining or Chow Time?	Yes	No
Sign that states "Guest Services" rather than "Halfway House"?		
Ability to pre-order food mid-round to keep from delaying the round?		
Four essentials available (club sandwiches, burgers, hot dogs, and salads)?		
Outside grill with brats, dogs, and burgers being cooked?		
Diversity of beverages, from athletic to soft drinks to beer?		
Crackers, snacks, and small assortment of candy?		
Ice machine to allow carts to refill ice buckets?		
Chilled bottled water available?		

The Customer Experience—Great Game Plans Are Meaningless Unless Execution Occurs Every Day

A Leading Department Store?

The process of creating the perfect golf experience for the customers seems never-ending. Like football, in which every play has the theoretical possibility of resulting in a touchdown, the operational plans created by a golf course are implemented in the form of numerous make or break moments.

Great golf experiences are treasured. Think Sea Island. The following photo highlights the special experience created there, where dress shirts, Polo blazers, and ties are available in the Pro Shop!

By stocking contemporary yet traditional clothing in its pro shop, Sea Island helps the forgetful guest comply with the policies of the facility. This creates a new revenue source and offers gentlemen a line of sportswear of the quality and distinction usually found in leading clothing stores. At Sea Island, we were informed that the dress clothes outsell the golf attire.

Another great off-course experience is available at Bandon Dunes by visiting its labyrinth in the forest as illustrated here.

This memorial was visioned by Mike Keiser to his good friend Howard McKee. As you enter the area, a message on a stone reads,

> "The labyrinth is a metaphor for our journey through life. Its path leads toward an inner light, to the center of our self and the center of the sacred, one and the same. its directions, at times, is confusing, taking us around, and then back again. Yet it through this circular journey of discovery and growth that we reconnect where we once began.
>
> In memory of Howard McKee, whose own journey through the labyrinth contributed to the vision and experience that is Bandon Dunes.
>
> This is a replica of the labyrinth in Chartes Cathedral, France dated 1194-1220."

I would guess that less than 5% of Bandon's visitors know the labyrinth exists and far fewer has visited it. It is truly special.

This kind of creative thinking meets and exceeds the expectations of customers, creating valued memories and the likelihood of more guests wanting to return.

Great golf experiences can also be achieved at municipal, daily fee, resorts, and private clubs. That great experience happens when employees take pride in their work, have a hospitable attitude, and see the customers as guests.

End Notes

The lessons of this chapter are:

1) Creating a superior customer experience requires careful thought, preparation, and consistent execution.
2) The staff at a golf course can vary widely from as few as 20 individuals to upwards of 200, depending on the diversity of activities and service level objectives.
3) Disney has seven keys to success that should be emulated at a golf course:
   a. The competition is anyone the customer compares you with.
   b. Pay fantastic attention to detail.
   c. Everyone walks the talk.
   d. Everything walks the talk.
   e. Customers are best heard through many ears.
   f. Reward, recognize, and celebrate.
   g. Everyone makes a difference.
4) The golf course experience is like an assembly line and comprises 13 steps:
   a. Motivating the golfer to select the course
   b. Making the reservation process seamless, quick, and informative
   c. Providing clear directions to the course
   d. Creating a positive first impression
   e. Welcoming the guest into the pro shop
   f. Creating a department store, not a penalty box
   g. Carts: clean, properly stocked
   h. Range: a place to learn and practice
   i. The warm start
   j. Ensuring the golf course is like an amusement park thrill ride
   k. Keeping the bathroom facilities consistently comfortable and clean
   l. The finish line: greet, serve, and ensure a friendly departure

Concluding Thought

Excellence is doing ordinary things extraordinarily well.

John W. Gardner

Chapter 15

Who Are Your Customers?

Step 7 of Golf Convergence WIN™ Formula

My job would be perfect if I didn't have a boss, I didn't have a staff to manage, and I didn't have to put up with the customers.

Unknown

Chapter Highlights

Does the average golf course owner and manager know and understand his or her customers' needs, wants, and desires? Customer feedback is an important resource.

A survey is an incredibly valuable tool in determining a golfer's perception differentiating their satisfaction with regards to a transaction vs. how they perceive their relationship with the golf course. Surveys can also help you determine the most cost effective marketing programs.

With the electronic tools available, it is cost effective and easy to understand who your customers are and what they seek.

The Motivations of Golf May Not Be What We Perceive

Understanding the underlying motivations of golfers is essential. You must identify the real reason a consumer decides to come to your facility to spend upwards of six hours of his or her day to play: for sport, for competition, for exercise, for leisure, for recreation, for networking, or merely to enjoy the outdoors.

What is the game's attraction? Consider this:

A private club in Texas had lost $7 million over the prior seven years. Its membership had fallen to less than 200. The 228 acres of land it owned was worth $20 million. If the club were to be sold, each member would have netted in excess of $100,000. The average age of the members was 72. The cost of joining a comparable club in Dallas was about $30,000.

Instead of selling, 150 members elected to put up an additional $27,500 each to continue operation. They moved out of a 43,000 square foot clubhouse into trailers so they could renovate the building. They made what was a sectarian club non-sectarian. They closed the swimming pool. They closed the fine-dining restaurant. They converted the tennis building into the men's locker room. They rebranded the facility and hired new leadership to assist them as they pursued their vision.

Why?

A five-some was playing the tenth hole and I walked out to the tee to talk to the members. I was serving as Interim General Manager for six months, guiding them through the strategic plan they were implementing.

One of them, a 71-year-old doctor who was a member of the board of directors, approached me and commented, "Playing so far above my head, I can't stand it. I'm six under net."

As I stood there, he got nothing but grief from his player partners, who called him a sandbagger and chided him that they were going to increase their bets past his choking point.

After hitting his drive long and far, into the heart of the fairway, he came to me and said, "This is why I play. It's not the course; it's not the club; it's not the game.

It's merely the opportunity to spend four hours with people whose friendship I value. I've played with these bandits for 25 years and hope to do so for another 25. They are very special friends. If we sold the club, they wouldn't all transfer to the new facility, I'm afraid. So I'll pay the assessments, whatever they may be, to keep our current club as it is, where it is."

Golf, at its best, blends friendship, entertainment, and social competition in a framework of an outdoor recreational sport. What a great venue to attract and retain customers.

Customer Key Benchmarks

Understanding who is actually utilizing the facility and the actual potential for rounds and revenue and translating that potential into reality requires understanding the motivations of those attracted to the facility. Why? Products and services can be tailored to conform to their specific needs, wants, and desires.

Billy Casper Golf Management,[1] a golf course management company that serves more than 100 public golf courses, has identified certain predictable characteristics as to the volume of individual customers at a golf facility and their behavioral tendencies:

1. A golf course, on average, has 8,000 distinct customers, from a minimum of 3,500 to a maximum of 11,000.
2. 10% to 20% of those customers are "initiators" and make the tee time.
3. 50% of those customers play the course merely once per year.
4. 50% of those who play will not return next year.
5. Only 13% will play six or more times.
6. Customers average four rounds played at a specific course.
7. A golf course will have a 20% wallet share of core golfers who each play 40 rounds per year.
8. Customers become at risk of not returning when they haven't played your course in 90 days.
9. The response rate from customers offered a 20% off coupon, a 10% off coupon, or merely receiving acknowledgement that they are missed is nearly the same.

1 Peter Hill, Billy Casper Golf Management, "Programming for Profit," presented at NGCOA Multi-Users Conference, February 4, 2009.

Another closer look at the golf course customer database produces some additional insights. Following is the detailed analysis of a golf course managed by the Sunrise Capital Group:

Measure	Value[2]
# of Unique customers current year	4,776
# Retained from same period one year ago	1,257
Retention quotient of prior year customers	35%
# of Acquired customers during period	3,465
# of Defectors during period	2,361
Acquired/defector ratio (>1 is good)	1.4
% of Customers comprising top 60% revenue	23%
Customers who generated top 60% of revenue—e-mails addresses obtained	34%
Customers who generated top 60% of revenue—addresses obtained	53%
Customers who generated top 60% of revenue—phone information obtained	96%

A misconception exists throughout the industry that the typical golf course may have 15,000 unique customers. Gathering the demographics of the golfer—that is, name, address, phone, and e-mail—is a very manageable process due to the small number of unique individuals that a golf course serves annually.

Unfortunately, this is one area where golf course operators have struggled. A survey of 994 golf courses by Golf Convergence concluded that while 93.6% of golf courses maintain a database of customers' names, only 8.3% of those golf courses were able to capture more than 50% of the e-mail addresses of golfers who played their golf course.

The challenges to creating a customer database can be traced to several sources: use of a cash register, lack of an integrated tee sheet, and the attitude that the facility didn't feel identifying customers was important or thought the process was too cumbersome for staff and inconvenient for the customer.

I am always humoured how difficult a golf course staff can make a simple task. Note how efficiently a golfer's e-mail address can be captured as illustrated in the slide on the following page:

2 Sunrise Golf Group, "Golf Inc. Presentation," October 3, 2007, Slide 1.

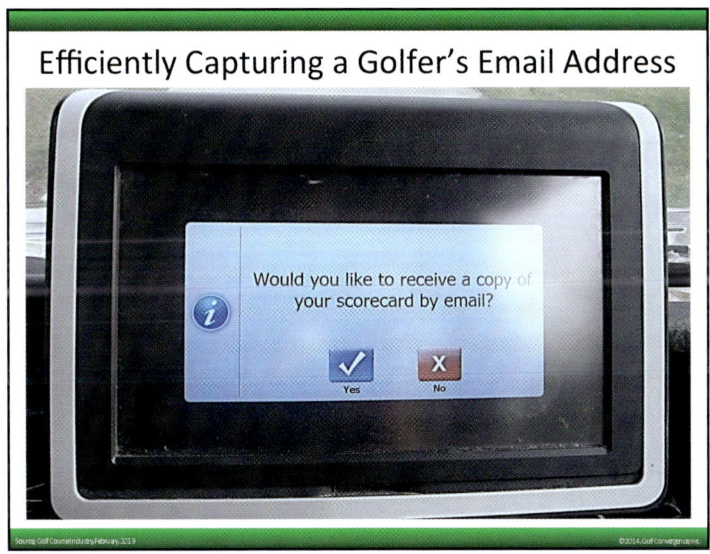

Customer Feedback

Information about your customer can be obtained in several ways:

1. Customer surveys, which serve as the electronic bridge linking golfers to golf course facilities
2. Volunteer programs
3. Advisory councils

All three are vital and augment the value of an integrated golf management solution described in Chapter 7, Technology—The Foundation.

The Mechanics of Surveys

There are many ways to construct, issue, and tabulate surveys. They can be lengthy paper forms that are manually tabulated. Long and cumbersome surveys come with many inherent risks. Satisfied customers are not likely to invest the time to complete them, and the results tend to be skewed towards the dissatisfied customers when the overall response rate is low.[3]

3 www.questionpro.com, "Measuring Customer Loyalty and Customer Satisfaction," July 11, 2008, p. 1.

The most efficient survey method is to create a brief, 25-question survey that is electronically distributed from one of the many Internet survey sites (such as Survey Monkey or Survey Gizmo). For reasonable fees, Survey Monkey issues, filters, and tabulates the results.

An effective technique is to retain a third party to undertake a survey on behalf of the course. The fees assessed (between $1,500 and $3,000) are reasonable. The use of the third party eliminates survey bias as customers can be completely candid because the promise of treating their responses confidentially is more credible.

Using a third party has another benefit—they can often add to your customer database a large sampling (5,000 to 10,000 golfers' names within 10 miles of your facility) through acquisition via third parties on a one-time use or by obtaining the cooperation of nearby golf courses to participate in the survey and provide confidential access to their customer database. The ability to compare and contrast the views of your patrons with the views of area golfers is often very informative.

The measure of a well-constructed survey is the completion rate for those who start the survey. A completion rate of greater than 90% on a 25-question test would indicate that the survey was compelling. Caution should be heeded in that for each question added, the completion rate after 25 questions begins to drop significantly. The use of incentives can create a positive bias in the response.

Questions to Pose

A customer survey should comprise four components: learning about the golfer, where they play, their opinion about your facility, and their golf spending habits and practices.

Questions about gender, age, household income, ethnicity, zip code, how many times they play golf each year, their barriers to playing more often, how many different courses they play annually, and the factors that they consider important in selecting a golf course are usually included in the survey's first section.

To begin the second section of the survey, the question "Would you recommend the following courses to a friend, colleague, or family member?" should be asked. A 10-point rating scale ranging from "Extremely Likely to Extremely Unlikely" is appropriate. Which courses in the area are their favorite, and which courses they play most often also provide insights as to their playing patterns.

The third section of the survey provides the opportunity for respondents to opine on the facility as to how they rate the various aspects of the golf course; condition, layout, customer services, food/beverage, merchandise, pace of play, price, proximity to home/work, range, tee time availability, etc. Their evaluation of course conditions can be further analyzed by their opinion on the condition of bunkers, fairway, greens, rough, and tees. Questions asking whether they are likely to play the course again and the primary barriers to playing there more frequently provide insight on challenges to increase rounds and revenue.

Finally, learning what they perceive to be a good value, whether they make tee times on the Internet, and where they search for special prices are beneficial.

A well-crafted survey should reveal:

1. How does the value your course creates compare to your competitors?
2. At what price points would your competitors' customers become your loyal customers?

Following are the results from four randomly selected questions that highlight the disparities that can exist between a facility, the local market, and national averages.

The first question usually pertains to gender. Nationally, according to the NGF, the distribution of players is 76% male and 24% female, compared to the national population of 51% female and 49% male.[4]

What Is Your Gender?	Atlanta	Denver	Grand Rapids	Pacific Grove	San Antonio	Winnipeg
Male	92.80%	83.10%	52.30%	79.90%	91.60%	77.5%
Female	7.20%	16.90%	47.70%	20.10%	8.40%	22.5%
Only Grand Rapids mirrors the national market while Pacific Grove and Winnipeg resemble the typical gender demographics in golf.						

Note that in this illustration of six different cities, only Winnipeg comes closest to following the industry averages.

4 Source: Golf 20/20, NGF analysis (PGA TOUR Segmentation Research Sept. 2004).

Age is another factor that determines playing frequency; the older the clientele, the greater the probability that they will play more rounds per year.

What is Your Age?	Atlanta	Denver	Grand Rapids	Pacific Grove	San Antonio	Winnipeg
Golf Course Demographics						
Junior (up to age 17)	0.70%	0.50%	0.80%	0.60%	0.00%	0.40%
Student (18-23)	1.20%	1.00%	1.30%	0.30%	0.80%	2.40%
Young Adult (24-34)	24.10%	16.30%	20.80%	5.80%	3.10%	9.70%
Adult (35-59)	53.50%	53.50%	63.60%	48.00%	52.70%	59.70%
Senior (60 and older)	20.60%	28.70%	13.60%	45.40%	43.50%	27.70%
Median	45.83	48.80	44.71	53.76	54.08	49.46
Local Market Demographics						
30-Mile Radius	94	98	103	93	89	98
Note that the population in San Antonio (11% younger than the national average of 37.1 years of age) would suggest sensitivity to green fees. With such a young population, who often face the pressures of supporting a young family, attracting them to play with increasing frequency will be a challenge. It should be noted that the golfer survey should confirm the results of the geographic local market analysis discussed in Chapter 5.						

The third criterion is to measure the annual income of the golf course's customers, as reflected in the following table.

What Is Your Income?	Atlanta	Denver	Grand Rapids	Pacific Grove	San Antonio	Winnipeg
Golf Course Demographics						
$0-34,999	4.10%	4.30%	11.40%	1.70%	3.90%	6.50%
$35,000-49,999	6.60%	8.20%	17.10%	3.20%	12.50%	14.60%
$50,000-74,999	17.40%	21.10%	21.30%	12.70%	18.80%	25.90%
$75,000-99,999	18.70%	21.90%	19.70%	18.80%	20.30%	24.90%
$100,000-$249,999	44.70%	41.80%	16.40%	37.90%	25.00%	27.00%
$250,000 or more	8.50%	2.80%	0.30%	8.10%	0.00%	1.00%
Median	136,441	118,723	67,366	118,179	79,238	95,952
Income						
Income Index	114	127	101	117	95	96
The median household income in the United States is $53,908. This chart clearly demonstrates that golf attracts citizens whose median household income is significantly above national average.						

It is always amusing to listen to this same group of golfers whine that they couldn't afford to play golf if the green fees were raised, even slightly. The Director of Parks & Recreation, Charles Sablen, relayed a story that one of his senior golfers in November, 2012 commented, "If you raise the rates in 2013, I may have to give up golf." The golfer was getting into his Mercedes Benz car to drive to his winter home in Scottsdale, AZ.

Spare me. Golfers, as Shakespeare once stated, "Thou doth protest too much." (Shakespeare's *Hamlet*, Act III, Scene II)

The fourth fundamental question regarding playing frequency highlights the potential opportunity to increase rounds.

How Many Rounds Do You Play Annually?	Atlanta	Denver	Grand Rapids	Pacific Grove	San Antonio	Winnipeg
1 - 4	3.10%	2.10%	18.90%	4.50%	2.30%	2.00%
5 - 7	7.10%	7.40%	16.90%	5.30%	1.50%	18.60%
8 - 19	21.30%	24.90%	18.90%	15.20%	13.00%	44.10%
20 - 40	33.60%	38.40%	21.40%	28.00%	29.00%	22.00%
41 - 60	19.50%	17.80%	14.00%	21.30%	23.70%	8.50%
Over 60 Rounds	15.40%	9.50%	8.60%	25.70%	30.50%	4.80%
Median Rounds Played	34.73	31.32	24.42	42.09	45.32	20.98

The National Golf Foundation defines the core golfers as playing 8 or more rounds. The median rounds played in these market highlights: 1) the concentration of rounds amongst few less than 2,000 golfers; 2) the peril of season passes which are offered by 70% of public courses; and 3) the risk of not identifying your core, acquired and defectors.

The combination of age, income, and playing frequency form a Bermuda triangle that needs to be carefully analyzed to determine programs and rates.

Why Are These Insights of Value?

The correct formation of a strategic business plan is dependent upon an analysis of a golfer's historical spending patterns and obtaining a current

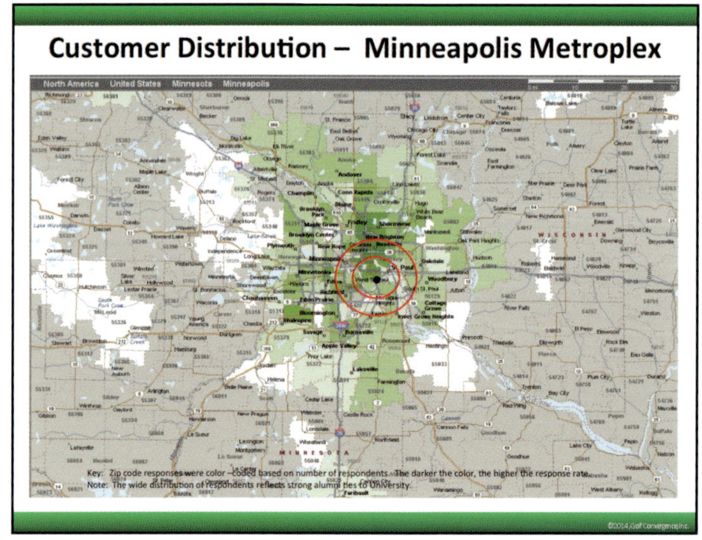

perspective by identifying customer age, gender, net income, ethnicity, playing frequency, favorite golf courses, and price point barriers. The key point being measured is the variance between a golfer's expectations and the level of satisfaction received. Understanding that variance ensures that the facility is serving the proper market segment (i.e., platinum, gold, silver, etc.).

For one client, the survey remained open for 11 days and yielded 703 completed surveys, providing a 97% confidence factor and a margin of error on the results of ±4%, which indicates that the results achieved are reasonably accurate. The zip codes of respondents were as depicted above.

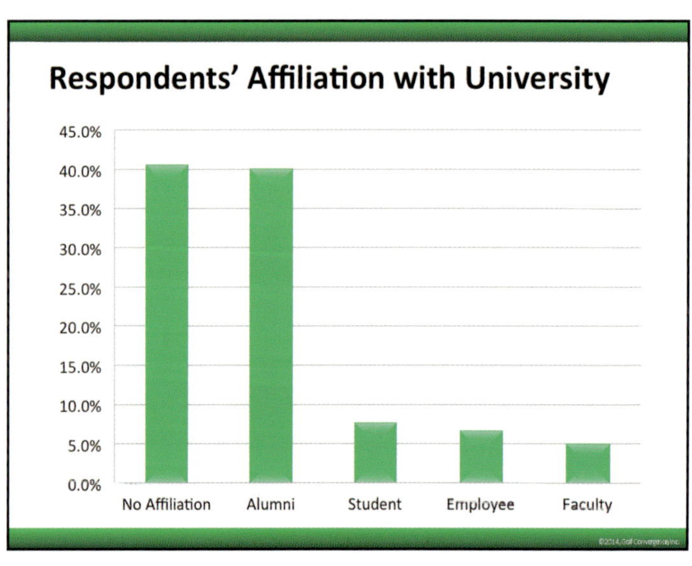

Using only a cash register at the time, the survey provided valuable data as the course was unsure who its customer was. The survey revealed that a significant portion of its frequent players had ties to the University (see chart).

That statistic raised the question, "Is the public perception that the golf course is open only to those with affiliation to the University?" For example, the University of Michigan and Ohio State golf courses are not open to public play. The University of Minnesota survey revealed that the public perception that their facility was private was incorrect. Those who frequent the facility clearly realized the facility was open to public access, as 94.9% responded that they knew that the golf course was open to the public. Only 5.1% thought the golf course had limited access.

The survey also asked these customers, "What matters in course selection?" They responded as depicted here.

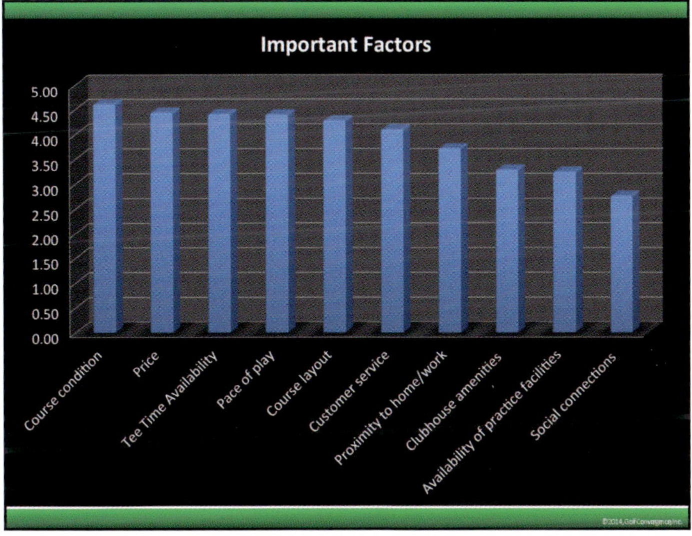

The results of the survey were consistent with other surveys conducted by Golf Convergence and by leading trade organizations such as the Golf Course Superintendents Association of America shown here. Conditioning and value (experience > price delivered) predict success. Since a large part of the "experience" equation is the conditioning of the golf course, this should be no surprise.

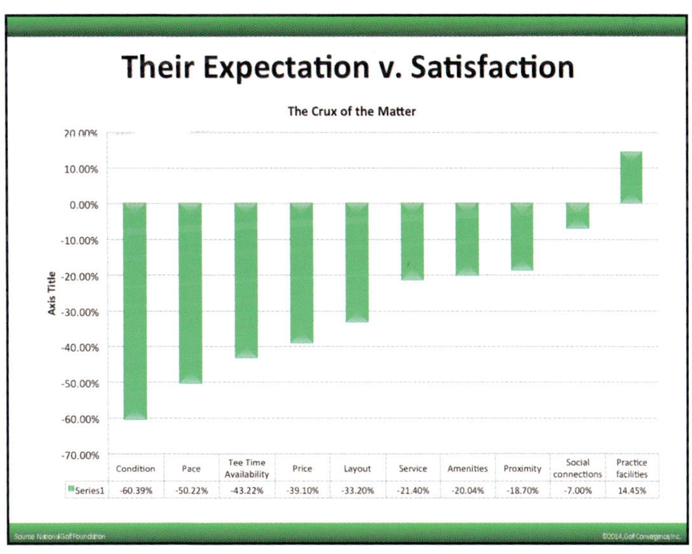

For another client, The Trails at Chickasaw Point, we conducted a survey of 14,000 public golfers within Anderson-Clemson-Westminster, South Carolina market.

The survey remained open for 10 days and yielded 803 completed surveys providing a 95% confidence factor and a margin of error on the results of plus or -5%.

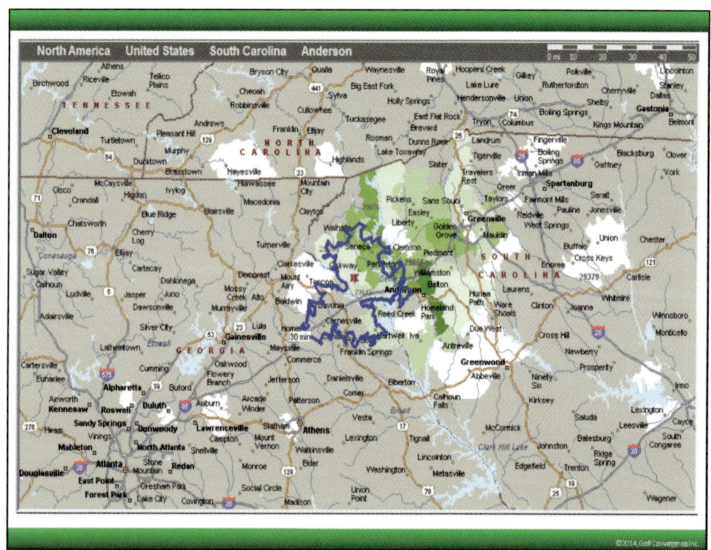

The distribution of public golfers outside the 30 mile drive time circle (blue jagged line), indicates the challenge the course will have in attracting and retaining public golfers. The opportunity for growth at this golf course is based on the 1,600 lots and 400 homeowners and ensuring their expectations and satisfaction are in balance.

Mirror, Mirror on the Wall, Which Course Is Best of All?

In undertaking a survey, golf course managers can measure the quality score of the facility compared to its local market set.

Presented is a chart on the favorite golf courses in the Greenville, NC market.

It is no surprise that the private clubs rank higher than the public facilities. What is encouraging for Bradford Creek that is located within that the City of Greenville, it is the highest rated public golf course. What is also positive is that the nearest other public golf course is 15 miles away. Thus, there is an opportunity for this golf course to become economically sustainable.

Survey Says?

Surveys can be a two-edged sword. Asking golfers what they believe is the appropriate green fee rate, for example, will always produce a misleading answer; golfers will understate what they are willing to pay. With respect to fees, a better question is: "What is a good price for a golf experience (18 holes of golf, excluding cart)?" Also, the question "What is the appropriate price for an unlimited season pass?" always gets a ridiculously low answer. Less than 10% of respondents will provide an answer that is near the fair market value. Most golfers will respond with the option that represents one category higher than the lower price so as not to look cheap but wanting to influence the determination of setting a lower rate.

Asking golfers who have little golf business experience or who rarely care about a course's policy a question about course policy can be problematic. Thus, a client posed the following question: "No-shows at a golf course average 7% of total rounds, costing the facility about $150,000 per year in lost revenue. What is the appropriate policy a golf course should implement to control the growing problem?"

Answer	Percentage
A cancellation (no-show) fee should be charged for golfers who cancel less than 24 hours prior to the scheduled tee time.	37.9%
A fee should be charged for every reservation made to compensate for the anticipated loss.	8.7%
Credit cards should be taken to secure tee times and charged for any no-shows.	47.8%
Greens fee rates should be increased to compensate for the anticipated loss.	5.6%

Notwithstanding the results of the survey, should a credit card be taken or a cancellation fee charged, a decrease in rounds is likely.

Surveys have provided some other fabulous insights regarding golfers' behavior. One course was struggling to boost weekday play and was contemplating numerous incentives, from discounts based on temperatures under 55 degrees or over 80 degrees; a value package of green fees, cart, and range balls; or discounts on the number of players who purchased green fees (buy 3 get the 4th free).

Two things were learned. First, over 30% indicated that their work schedule prevented them from playing during the week, and no incentive was enough to get them to the course. Secondly, those who could play were seeking as much as 50% off the rack rate to increase their playing frequency or to switch to a tee time to fill a consistent opening at the course.

Volunteers and Advisory Councils

Another form of feedback that is available comes from volunteers and advisory councils.

The concept of the volunteer program is a valid one, if properly implemented. Usually, a volunteer program provides free golf during non-peak times to individuals who perform valuable services for the golf course. From a volunteer program, management can also garner meaningful feedback on the strengths and weaknesses of the operation.

A typical volunteer program would include:

- In order to be eligible for discount golf, an individual must volunteer for a minimum of eight hours per week. A formal time-keeping system to measure hours worked is usually necessary; the "honor system" often leads to chaos.
- The number of volunteers should be limited to 15.
- For working such hours, volunteers are provided the opportunity to play golf at a 50% discount off the established rates at off-peak times. It should be noted that volunteers should pay the posted golf cart rates.
- Volunteers should only be able to play on a walk-up basis, occupying a tee time that would otherwise not be sold.
- Volunteers, if they play in regular groups or outings, should be required to pay the same green fees that a regular patron would pay.

Volunteers do come with risks, starting with the IRS. Further, volunteers are difficult to hold accountable and keep responsible. Volunteer programs can create a sense of entitlement; individuals can be difficult to terminate, they sometimes discuss the course's business with the customers, and managing them can be like herding cats.

The program can become abusive. Note the bragging blog of a social and marketing Internet whiz:

> "I've been volunteering at a local municipal golf course here in Lake Oswego (Oregon) in exchange for free golf. I work only 3 hours a week . . . but get free golf the whole summer. Pretty good trade off for me."[5]

Notwithstanding the challenges of administering these programs, it is recommended that each golf course explore the potential of this program.

Another kind of volunteer program is the Golf Advisory Council. The concept of this body is to advise golf management on plans, policies, and procedures, thereby providing an effective forum for customer feedback prior to

---

5 Trevor Mauch, "While I've Been Away" blog, http://www.trevormauch.com/why-ive-been-away-not-a-good-excuse/102/, July 25, 2008.

the implementation of major initiatives. These Councils come with risks, as members of the Golf Advisory Council often perform frequent oversight of the facilities, asking questions and perhaps even giving orders, thereby taxing the resources of the staff who must attempt to respond courteously.

Implications for Today's Golf Course Manager

Customer feedback that is unbiased is of tremendous value. This feedback reveals:

- Why golfers choose a golf course.
- How your course stacks up against the competition.
- The fair value of your course.
- Your unique value proposition message to your customers.
- Your competitors' weaknesses.
- At what price points your competitors' customers become your loyal customers.

Online tools make surveys easy and they make it possible for you to measure the successes and failures of your relationship with your customers within a day.

End Notes

The lessons of this chapter are:

1) Obtaining customer feedback is essential to create a valued experience for the golfer.
2) Customer feedback can come from surveys, volunteer programs, advisory councils, or surveys.
3) While volunteer programs and advisory councils can be beneficial, both have significant risks.
4) While many golf courses are maintaining a customer database, most are lacking sufficient names to make this a valuable tool.
5) Electronic surveys offered by third-party Internet firms are very cost effective.
6) There are four required questions in each survey: gender, age, income, and frequency of play.
7) A survey of customers regarding potential course policy usually reveals that they will be self-serving in their answers.

Concluding Thought

Almost all conflict is a result of violated expectations.

Blaine Lee

Chapter 16

Creating Customer Loyalty

Step 7 of Golf Convergence WIN™ Formula (continued)

A single conversation across a table with a wise man is worth a month's study of books.

Chinese Proverb

Chapter Highlights

It is easy to believe that satisfied customers are valid predictors of future customer behavior. Such is not the case.

The value of any business to ensure sustainable growth is based on the promoters, which can be measured by the "net promoter score." This index measures the relative strengths of a facility's franchise. Enterprise, Intuit, and Costco have all embraced this concept.

This chapter embraces the concept of customer loyalty and the importance of identifying customers as core, acquired, or defectors to boost growth.

In the golf industry, usually 12% of the golfers generate a majority of the revenue. Identifying, measuring, and rewarding those golfers is imperative. In creating a strategic plan, the value of the golf course can be significantly impacted by the commitment of management to understanding their customer.

Customer Loyalty

After identifying the customers and their preferences the question now is how do you create customer loyalty and increase your wallet share of each golfer at your facility when there is little connection between satisfaction rates and actual customer behavior?

While some golf managers seek to "introduce new players" to the game, emphasize tournaments among local corporations, or broaden marketing efforts to attract first-time visitors, the more sophisticated managers are taking a different tact: they are trying to identify their most frequent visitors and serve them better. Promoters of a facility can stimulate revenue growth. But for an individual to become a promoter and make a referral, the individual must believe the company offers a superior value (price, quality) and must feel good about his or her relationship with the facility.[1]

Loyalty Programs

It should be obvious, but knowing your customer is critical to success in any business. That sounds trite, but the mechanics of managing customer service are detailed and, often, difficult. Airlines, hotels, merchandisers, and many other retail businesses have been capturing customer demographic information, aggregate spending, and frequency of their use for at least three decades.

The power of customer information is incredible. Note an e-mail sent from Marriott Corporation to its valued customers:

> "As a Platinum Elite member of the Marriott Rewards program, we value your business as well as your opinion. We've noticed you've not stayed with us in recent months as often as you had in the past. If there is anything we can do to better meet your needs or improve the program for you, or if there is a reason you're staying with us less than you had in the past please reply to this email to let us know. If you prefer to call instead feel free to do so at your convenience by dialing 1-800-442-9929. We hope to hear from you soon. Thank You

---

1 Fred Reichheld, "*The Ultimate Question*," (Boston, Harvard Business School Publishing Corporation, 2006), p. 28.

Maxine Lozano Figueroa Back-Up Team Facilitator & Marriott Rewards Representative"

Marriott understands the importance of customer loyalty. An April 2008 promotion gave Platinum members a free one-year membership in Clear, the fast pass for airport security.

The Marriott Rewards promotion, titled "you travel more—you need less hassle," is reproduced as depicted here.

Not only does Marriott get it, but so does United Airlines, as noted in the following.

The rewards? For crossing two million miles, United provided the following benefits: complimentary annual membership to the United Red Carpet Club for life, four (4) system-wide upgrades to use for a one-class, one-way upgrade on United or United Express flights to any destination they fly, and your choice of the following:

1. A custom-engraved classic 80 GB iPod.
2. A monogrammed Tumi portfolio case.
3. An engraved business card case from Tiffany's.
4. A $200 gift certificate for the selection of premium wines.

Why do these programs work? They feed on the ego of each customer, making them feel recognized and appreciated. Customer loyalty programs pander to our desire to be recognized as special.

They are very successful in building the wallet share they earn from the customer.

Program Mechanics

The components of a customer affinity program are best exhibited by Vail Resorts in Colorado.

Every purchase made by the customer is tracked. Quarterly newsletters are sent to customers in an electronic format. Rewards are also an attractive part of the program. They include free lift tickets, ski lessons, and discounted food and accommodations. These rewards are mailed automatically to customers, who don't need to monitor their accounts to be rewarded.

The process of becoming a part of Vail Resorts' affinity program is easy. Each skier completes an application. The skier is then given a photo identification card. Less than one minute has elapsed from the time the photo is taken to the time the card is in the skier's hand. These cards can be purchased at many sporting goods stores throughout Colorado. Cards are updated and reissued annually.

The card is used by the skier to "purchase" a lift ticket, pay for food, and take advantage of other services on the mountain. The skier merely goes to the chairlift or a cashier and presents the card. The card is scanned with a Symbol Technologies (http://www.symbol.com/) hand-held wireless scanner. Customers are billed on their credit cards. By empowering the chairlift personnel to "check in" a skier, Vail Resorts has been able to reduce its ticketing staff.

The result? Reduced labor costs and improved customer service.

This is the resort equivalent of Hertz's "Gold Club" membership. Vail makes it easy for the customer to receive the "preferred rate," and resort managers can identify a skier at the ticket counter should he or she forget to bring the card. Those with lost cards check in at the ticket office rather than the lift; a credit card is not required as it is "on file."

Golf Technology Strategies—An Oxymoron?

Very few golf courses effectively engage in customer relationship management. Facilities have historically faced four barriers:

1. Lack of insight regarding their customers
2. Inadequate tools to cost-effectively market
3. Marketing inexperience
4. Inconsistent execution of programs

First, it is important to recognize where golfers typically come from. For the typical golf course, golfers' play can be segmented as depicted here.

Until a decade ago, it was impossible to accurately track player demographics. The critical record of customer activity, the tee sheet, was a paper-based product. Point-of-sale systems were cash registers. If a computer-based system was used in the 1990s, rarely was an electronic tee sheet integrated.

While the logistics of golf were a challenge, the attitudes of many golf course employees were just as problematic. Under the guise that they were slammed at the POS counter and not wanting to extend the processing time for a customer, staff would resist even capturing the basic data—name, e-mail, and zip code.

"What gets measured gets done." That quote was first uttered by Tom Peters in the 1980s, but it is an opinion often expressed by Mike Rippey of Kitson & Partners. When counter staff understand the importance of data collection in generating facility revenue, collection rates will improve.

Measuring Customer Loyalty

Of all the benchmarks that measure a customer's satisfaction, one measure that is evolving is "word of mouth." In a new study, "How Valuable Is Word of Mouth," Dr. Robert P. Leone of the Neeley School of Business at Texas Christian University writes,

> "Most companies with statistical models for customer valuation focus only on customer spending and don't factor in a customer's word-of-mouth value. We demonstrated that when companies try to ascertain how valuable individual customers are, it's not just about how much the customer spends but whether that individual can bring in new business.
>
> But if a company creates a priority list of customers based solely on how much those customers spend, they risk focusing on the wrong individuals. This is because high-volume spenders and good referrers are not generally the same people, and the value of the best referrers can far exceed that of good spenders."[2]

For the study, participants were divided into four classifications: champions—those who spent a lot and regularly referred others; affluent—those who spent a lot but seldom referred others; advocates—those who spent little, but regularly referred others; and misers—those who neither spent much nor referred others.

As Dr. Leone concluded, "Mass marketing is very costly and inefficient with low rates of response from prospective customers. But referrals from existing customers are personalized, so the odds of response are much greater. The more targeted a company's marketing is, the more efficiently they can spend their marketing dollars."[3]

Other entities have labeled the metric for measuring customer loyalty as a "net promoter score,"[4] which was developed by Fred Reichheld and first used by Enterprise

2 Robert P. Leone, "How Valuable Is Word of Mouth," *Neeley Intelligence,* Spring 2008, p. 1.

3 Robert P. Leone, "How Valuable Is Word of Mouth," *Neeley Intelligence,* Spring 2008, p. 2.

4 Bain & Company, "NPS: The Next Six Sigma? http://www.bain.com/bainweb/publications/.

Rent-A-Car. Results have consistently shown that companies with high customer loyalty typically increase revenues at more than twice the rate of competitors.

In measuring wallet share, a *Business Week Online* article highlighted that "detailed analysis of individual customers shows that between 60% and 80% of defectors pronounce themselves 'satisfied' or 'very satisfied' before they defect." Moreover, satisfaction data is impractical for driving daily managerial priorities and tradeoffs. To manage for loyalty, managers need timely, granular, and actionable data, the kind they see on their financial statements.[5]

The fundamentals of customer relationship management are listed here:

- Identify customer success factors.
- Create a customer-based culture and adopt customer-based measures.
- Develop an end-to end process to service customers.
- Recommend ways to help customers solve problems.
- Offer a complaint resolution process.
- Track all aspects of selling to customers and prospects.[6]

Results have consistently shown that companies with high customer loyalty typically increase revenues at more than twice the rate of competitors.

Applying Customer Loyalty Models to the Golf Industry

The National Golf Foundation initially incorporated this concept into its online Voice of Customer Operating Model, dubbing the results a "loyalty index score." Other entities have labeled the metric for measuring customer loyalty as a "net promoter score."[7]

5 Fred Reichheld and Rob Market, "NPS: The Next Six Sigma?" *Business Week Online*, September 25, 2006. http://theultimatequestion.com/bainweb/publications/publications_detail.asp?id=25271&menu_url=publications%5Fresults%2Easp

6 "CRN Defined," *Golf Business*, August 2006, p. 44.

7 Bain & Company, "NPS: The Next Six Sigma?" http://www.bain.com/bainweb/publications/.

Intrigued by the impact of word-of-mouth on golfer loyalty, the NGF surveyed 100,000 people, asking, "How likely are you to recommend the golf course to a friend or colleague?"[8] The answer to that question is the best indicator of customer loyalty as well as future revenue growth, according to NGF officials.[9] The program collected customer feedback in 22 different areas in which golfers rate those factors on a 1 to 10 scale, as follows:

Criteria	Description
1	Overall Value of Golf Course
2	Convenience of Course Location
3	Tee Time Availability
4	Overall Course Conditions
5	Condition of Greens
6	Scenery and Aesthetics of Course
7	Pace of Play
8	Condition of Golf Cars
9	Amenities
10	Friendliness/Service of Staff
11	Food and Beverage Service
12	On-Course Services
13	Overall Experience
14	Affordability
15	Condition of Tees
16	Condition of Bunkers
17	Condition of Fairways
18	Overall Quality of Practice Facility
19	Golf Course Design
20	Overall Quality of Golf Shop
21	Overall Quality of Golf Shop Apparel
22	Overall Quality of Golf Shop Merchandise

In 2011, the NGF introduced a new golf satisfaction that measures course conditioning, pricing, service, layout and pace of play. This survey as provides a golf course unique performance benchmarks to compare its customer satisfaction rating with other local courses.

8 Golfbusiness.com, "Rating Your Customers," April 2008, p. 17.

9 "Strategy for Improvements," *Golf Inc.*, June 2008, p. 22.

Measuring customer loyalty is an integral step of the Golf Convergence WIN™ process. Through a series of interlinked questions, the National Golf Foundation and Golf Convergence are able to measure each golfer's loyalty to a specific golf course. With a national average of 26, the following client received a score of –21, as determined by the formula discussed following the table.

Golfer Type — Average	Promoters	Passives	Detractors	Total
Local player/Area resident	14%	32%	26%	72%
Non-resident player	1%	3%	2%	6%
Discount card holders	0%	1%	2%	2%
Member of our club	3%	4%	4%	11%
Member of other area club	0%	1%	4%	5%
League player	1%	0%	2%	3%
Business/corporate outing golfer	0%	0%	0%	0%
Loyalty Index	**19%**	41%	**40%**	

Another example of the powerful insights that can be obtained through this question is illustrated here highlighting golf courses in Chicago metroplex.

Loyalty Ranking – Suburban Chicago

Loyalty Score	Promoters	Detractors	Loyalty Index
Cantigny	57%	7%	50
Mistwood GC	43%	8%	35
Heritage Bluffs	39%	6%	34
Arrowhead	41%	8%	33
Fox Bend	42%	11%	31
Bolingbrook	43%	14%	30
Cog Hill #3	38%	9%	28
Prairie Bluff	33%	8%	26
Tamarack	43%	19%	24
Cog Hill #1	32%	10%	23
Carillon	33%	11%	21
Seven Bridges	38%	17%	21
Broken Arrow	24%	9%	15
Naperbrook	32%	17%	15
Springbrook	32%	19%	13
White Tail Ridge	19%	8%	11
Village Greens	26%	18%	8
Settler's Hill	20%	14%	7
Phillips Park	20%	14%	6
River Bend	18%	19%	(1)

The net loyalty score is obtained by subtracting the detractors (40%) from the promoters (19%). With the possible range of answers from 10 (strong promoters) to 0 (strong detractor), usually those answering 1 to 6 are subtracted from those answering either 9 or 10.

In undertaking this analysis for another client, ascertaining the loyalty of local area golf courses provided an insight into the facility's relative strength in the market. A competitive review of the courses on the Monterey Peninsula

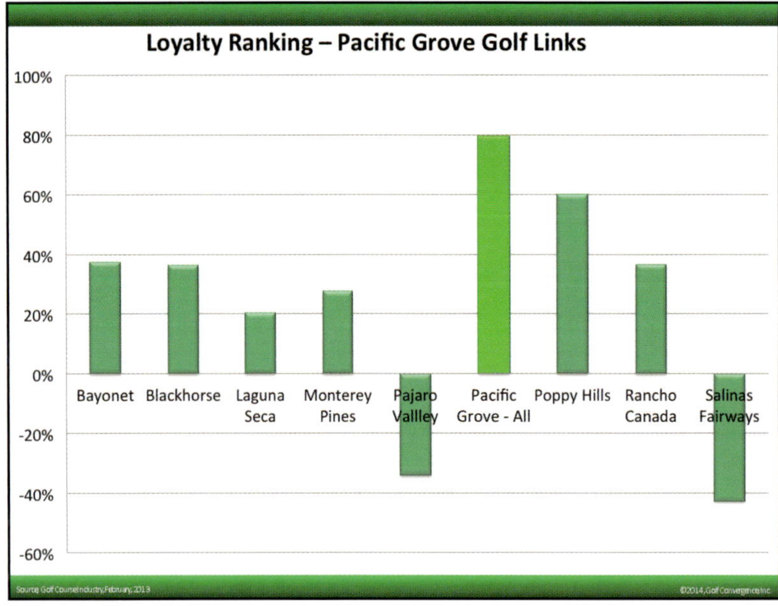

frequently played by local residents revealed the information depicted here.

Why are those loyalty share numbers important? Loyalty correlates to wallet share, and the percentage of wallet share a course receives from the golfer is a highly predictive factor of success. Higher wallet share equals higher revenue equals higher net income. Wallet share represents the percentage of a golfer's money spent at each golf course versus the total amount spent annually by the golfer.

The national average of wallet share is 34.0%. The lower the green fee, the higher the wallet share percentage a course generates. The reason why is when the green fees are low, it attracts a core element of golfers who play there frequently because of the low price point. In contrast, at a course that has a high green fee, i.e., a resort, golfers only play there once or twice because of the high price point, otherwise, they would likely join a private club.

It is so much easier to attract a greater wallet share of the customer through building loyalty than it is to attract a new customer to the golf course. Promoters refer five golfers per year to the facility, while strong detractors can provide up to five negative references.

E-mail Marketing: Panacea or Hoax?

Creating customer loyalty starts with developing a dialogue with the customer.

Course owners are currently trying a smorgasbord of options. It is clear that e-mail serves as an effective tool when the message is unique, exclusive, and of high quality. To be effective, an e-mail has to be relevant to the reader. Junk information and over e-mailing will drive away clients. The e-mail needs to come from a "friend" who cares.

Specifically, e-mail blasts have been found to be effective in three specific circumstances:

> **To build a brand.** A monthly e-Newsletter to members/golfers styled with the ability to click *More* for information on topics that may interest the reader. Not only does this keep the e-mails short, it drives traffic to the course Web site. Additionally, if the e-mail system can log clicks, readership, and members' reports (nearly all do), it will provide valuable member information.
>
> **To offer a significant discount.** The operative word here is "significant." Discounts of less than 30% are not significantly attractive to warrant an e-mail.
>
> **To eliminate the bias in surveys.** Most customers are more comfortable providing negative feedback online rather than in person or over the phone.

Within the caveats just defined, e-mail can work if precise guidelines are followed, which at a minimum include undertaking the following:

1. Utilize the course Web site as a revenue-generating tool with online store, e-Club, contests, and search engine optimization.
2. Build an opt-in list by using surveys with incentives to create a qualified list.
3. Develop compelling subject lines.
4. Ensure the "FROM LINE" is immediately recognizable by all your recipients.
5. Ascertain the appropriate frequency and don't over mail. E-mails sent on Tuesday through Thursday tend to generate the highest open rates. At a minimum, your database should be contacted monthly.
6. Segment your databases (such as core, acquired, defectors, or promoters; passive and defectors) to increase the efficiency of e-mail, rather than delivering a broadcast message to a wide audience. Communicate only to the interest level of the member; an exaggerated negative example might be sending Junior Golf materials and notices to members who told you they hate kids.
7. Evaluate the results of each e-mail sent. A second e-mail should be sent to the 15% who opened the first e-mail. Understanding the behavior of your customers and modifying future e-mails is important.

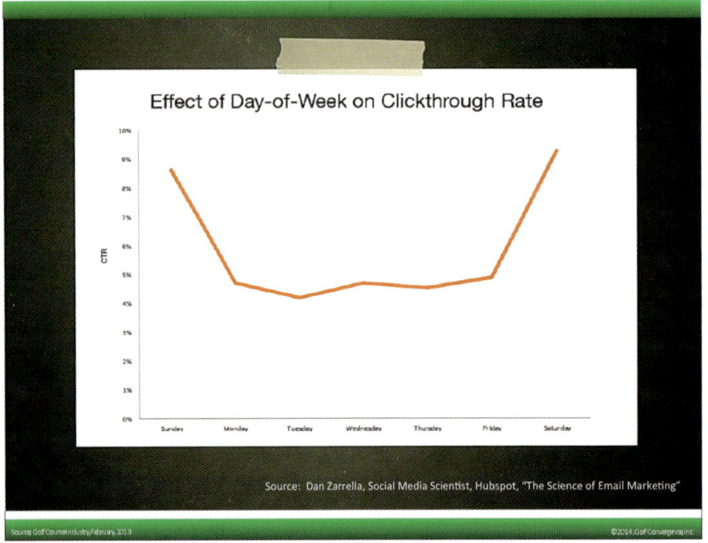

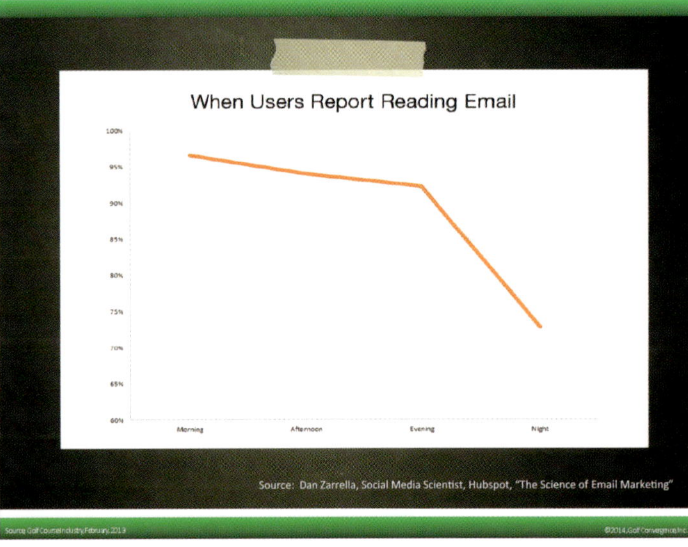

8. Be spam compliant.

9. Never sell peak tee times most popular with core golfers at a discount. Only allow reservations for off-peak times via e-mail.

10. Add a "Send to a Friend" button at the bottom of each e-mail.

11. Consider outsourcing data sources and participating in "data alliances" with non-competitive facilities.

With those fundamentals in place, the benefits of e-mail marketing is increased knowing the preferred day and time to send e-mails as illustrated in the two charts depicted here.

It is highly recommended that individuals seeking to perfect their e-mail marketing campaigns study the many masterful information brochures available at hubspot.com.

What Results Should You Expect?

A golf course owner can anticipate the following results from a well-constructed e-mail to the existing client base:

- Between 15% and 22% of recipients open the e-mail and read it.
- Less than 1% act on the offer.
- About 1.6% are out of office and not receiving e-mail.

- 1.2% unsubscribe, even though they opted in.
- 0.4% of e-mails will be blocked by a "spam arrest" filter in which reconfirmation of the sender's e-mail address is required for the recipient to view the e-mail.

Why are the open rates so low? Even though most encourage recipients to use "white" or "safe" lists, more than 25% of e-mails sent to corporations are blocked by spam filters. E-mail is best used as a communication tool between friends. However, technically your promoters, passives, and defectors have provided their e-mail addresses voluntarily.

Thus, defining your expectations is key. E-mail is not a panacea and remains one of the components of a golf course's marketing program.

Who Are the Leading Firms and What Do They Cost?

The software tools needed to undertake e-mail marketing can be obtained from several sources: golf management firms, golf discount brokers who create a local community, or third-party marketing specialists focused on the golf industry.

Some golf management software firms, have integrated this feature into their core application. Jonas Software offers a robust Clubhouse Online product that features tee time reservations, tournament registrations, newsletters, and more. Clubhouse Online also includes a "smart" e-mail engine from which numerous data elements can be extracted to create highly customized e-mails categorized by events, birthdays, status, interests, age, or purchasing activity. However, most golf management software firms integrate with third-party providers.

The majority of golf courses have selected one of the leading providers focusing on the golf industry, including 1-2-1 Marketing, Club Essential, Course Trends, Cyber Golf, Golf e-Mailer, and Legendary Marketing. Each of these firms serves over 150 clients and provides services including:

- Broadcast e-mail
- Marketing
- Photography, in a few cases

- Public relations
- Web site design: template and custom design
- Web site hosting

The software tools these firms use are much the same. The difference between firms can be measured by:

- Price
- Access to a proprietary database the vendor has created
- Level of software support
- Whether or not the vendor assists in the execution of the marketing program.

Prices start at $99 per month.

If you have a very talented software-savvy staff, and if you have created your own proprietary database, I would start off with one of the more inexpensive e-mail tools, i.e., Vertical Response. However, most golf course staffs fall short in their abilities to utilize these tools. Therefore, utilizing an outside firm, especially one that has aggregated a large customer database, can create the accountability you need for success.

There are risks in using outside firms. During the past 12 months, "firewall" holes have been detected with one vendor, whose customer e-mail databases were exposed and could be copied. While the ability to do this is an exception rather than the rule, the golf course managers thought the risk was zero.

Finally, each of these software firms is a small entrepreneurial organization. They will always claim that their support is responsive, but responsiveness can vary.

How to Increase Customer Loyalty

Creating a dialogue with the customer is fundamental. Valuable recommendations for those golf courses undertaking such a dialogue with their customers include:

1. Improve contact information breadth (number of customers) and quality (both address and e-mail by:
   - Simple business card drawing; counter people mention at every check-in
   - Web site registration
   - Newsletter subscription
   - Loyalty program; information is part of registration

2. To grow the customer base, the first and often easiest step is to establish regular customer contact by setting up an e-mail system to automatically generate a "return" offer from the POS data.
3. Analyze and set up your integrated POS system to target messages to appropriate golfer segments. Messages are automatically created and delivered monthly.
4. For a retained customer base that is spending less, put a continuity program in place to increase loyalty to the facility by identifying those whose spending decreased.
5. Increase contact with customers who bring in 60% of revenue. "Get intimate" with your highest-value customers. Put a bounty on knowing who they are by rewarding those who provide residential and e-mail addresses with small preferential perks.
6. As a general rule of thumb, a course should only blast to its entire list of golfers two or three times per month.
7. A survey should be created to identify specific golfer interests, such as last-minute tee times, tournaments, etc.
8. Create an online presence. Give directions; enable the booking of secured online tee time reservations, the purchase of prepaid gift cards, etc.

In 2014, 50% of the marketing budgets of the leading management companies were devoted to creating a meaningful and strong online presence.

During the next one to three years, "winners" and "losers" in the facility management arena will be strongly influenced by their ability to manage and build customer franchises. This task can be outsourced to firms such as Golf Convergence. Outsourcing the analysis and tracking component of facility customer franchises is a more efficient and effective way of getting meaningful results.

The facility general managers and their staffs are more effectively utilized when they execute plans rather than collect and analyze data.

A Golfer's Strategic Value

A lot of maxims ring true for the operation of any business or golf course. For the golf course, a strategic but often overlooked maxim is that each customer has a different value. While all customers have "cash value," some customers may also have strategic value. For example, the director of marketing for a corporation may have huge strategic value. By identifying such customers quickly and courting them wisely, you can capture their corporate outing business.

To identify strategic customers, you need to engage them in a dialogue to obtain the knowledge from which loyalty programs can be built.

By identifying your customers, you can increase the amount of revenue you generate from each. Plus, finding a new customer to replace a lost one is about five times more expensive than maintaining the loyalty of an existing customer. However, losing customers, the right ones (those who play an excessive amount, yielding little per round during high-demand times), is usually not a bad deal.

The challenge of the golf course owner is to make a distinction between features that people desire so much that they are willing to pay for them, and those that are desired but don't bring in extra profits. No market is so mature that a golf course can't further differentiate its customer value experience.

End Notes

The lessons of this chapter are:

1) The motivations to play golf are likely to be different than perceived by the golf course owner.
2) Fundamental to any business is knowing your customers.
3) Customer loyalty programs are extremely successful.
4) The challenge of customer relationship management is registering the customer by capturing the requisite and relevant demographic information.
5) Customer franchise analysis involves four steps: collection, analysis, execution, and monitoring.
6) Most golf course managers don't fully comprehend how much the balance of retained, acquired, and lost golfers affects the volatility of their revenue base.
7) A golf course typically has about 8,000 distinct golfers playing an aggregate 31,500 rounds.
8) The retention of golfers year to year for a typical facility is under 50%.
9) The identification of customers as core, acquired, or defectors with timely and precise e-mail messages to those customers can impact positively gross revenue.
10) There are more than a half dozen firms offering the following services to the golf industry: broadcast e-mail, marketing, photography, public relations, Web site design, and Web site hosting.

Concluding Thought

A luxury once sampled becomes a necessity.

Andrew Tobias

Chapter 17

Customers—A Future Perspective

You can tell whether a man is clever by his answers.
You can tell whether a man is wise by his questions.

Naguib Mahfouz

Chapter Highlights

The golf industry is in flux. The needs, wants, and desires of golfers are rapidly changing based on societal factors.

This chapter postulates how the ownership, management structure, and operational policies of golf courses will evolve over the next two decades based on economic, societal, and business trends that impact golf. Within the context of a discussion regarding why people buy real estate, we present the concept of creating sustaining golf communities regardless whether they are surrounded by real estate.

Ultimately, changes are forecast with growth in municipal courses slowed, daily fee owners likely to sell, the role of low-end private clubs diminished, and the mid-tier clubs having to diversify their services and activities to remain competitive. It is speculated that the future for the remote high-end club that represents a members' third or four facility will become challenged and be deemed not to be economically viable on a self-sustaining basis once initial appeal of bigger, better, greater wears off.

What Will the Golf Club of the Future Look Like?

In the early 2000s, most new golf courses were built as amenities to support home sales. That trend stopped almost completely in 2009 due to the difficulties of the global credit markets. Nothing has changed since.

Will this downturn last? Will the trend toward golf-related real estate projects forever end? Probably not; the aspects of community represent a core value that to some extent will be pursued regardless of economics.

When is the reversal likely to occur? Henry Delozier, past president of the National Golf Course Owners Association and principal of Global Golf Advisors, feels "Golf-related real estate has held its value better than the residential communities without golf. Second, more European investors, emboldened in part by the strength of the Euro, have started showing an interest in recreation-related U.S. property."[1]

All of life is a cycle, and history does repeat itself, but there are certain values that have transcended time. Community is one of those values.

The Coming Evolution in Golf Courses

As people evolve, society changes. The pressures of time, money, work, and family we now face will change. Why and how we work and play will change.

Golf, at its core, is a business, usually a small business. Many who are involved in the business of golf think and operate as small businesspeople.

Golf, at its core, will evolve to reflect the needs and desires of its customers. The traditional, almost antediluvian thinking regarding golf results in slow change. As a business, golf is perhaps as many as two decades behind other industries, such as the hospitality industry. But the number, ownership, and motivations of golf course operators are likely to change over the next two decades.

1 David Owen, FT.com, "Into the Rough," June 11, 2008.

Here is what we predict about forthcoming changes in the ownership and management structure of golf courses. This analysis focuses on the following types of facilities:

1. Municipal
2. Daily fee
3. Low-end private clubs
4. Mid-tier private clubs
5. High-end/exclusive private clubs
6. Resorts

For municipal golf courses, the challenges that lie ahead are not trivial: "there is blood in the streets in the operation of most municipal golf courses." Just set up a Google alert on golf courses losing money, and the daily influx of e-mails highlighting the woes in the industry are overwhelming.

Since 9/11, the pecking order for the allocation of municipal funds has been entrenched, providing police and fire with the highest priority, with other municipal services competing for the remaining resources. A golf course that is cash-poor but asset-rich will, in order to balance the budget, ultimately be required to liquidate assets or privatize services.

A substantial number of citizens believe that golf, like tennis and swimming pools, should be supported by the taxpayers, and that a profit focus for golf is inappropriate. Other activities, such as tennis and swimming pools, are not adequately provided by the private sector. However, golf is adequately handled in the private sector at a wide range of price points. If taxpayers subsidize the golf operations, that benefit will be for approximately only 9% of the taxpayers.

Thus, we expect to see a reduction in the number of municipal courses as a percentage (it's currently 15%) of the total number of golf courses. The construction of new municipal courses will be rare, with any growth in this sector coming from new cities that may incorporate or daily fee operators who fail. In the latter example, the municipality may decide for the protection of green space to acquire and operate the golf course. Investment in required capital improvements and renovations should outpace new course construction 3 to 1.

Municipal golfers (senior and pass card holders in particular) are always looking for someone to subsidize their leisure.

However, submitting a Google alert for "golf courses losing money" or a Google search under the same phrase generates a list of municipalities whose golf courses are facing challenges: Alameda, CA; Alton, IL; Augusta, GA; Bloomington, IL; Broken Arrow, OK; Cedar Rapids, IA; Charleston, SC; Columbus, OH; Erie, PA; Grafton, WI; Houston, TX; Lake Country, MN; Lansing, MI; Lexington, KY; Little Rock, AK; Macon, GA; Menlo Park; CA; Osceola, FL; Passaic County, NJ; Roanoke, VA; Sumner, WA; San Francisco, CA; San Jose, CA; Shreveport, LA; Tempe, AZ; Topeka, KS; Twin Falls, ID; Walnut Creek, CA; and Waukegan, IL, begin a long list of cities.

Adding to the unstable future for municipal golf courses is what Golf Inc. refers to as "municipal madness." The cost of a golf course should be about $8 million. Some cities are now investing more than $60 million. Golf Inc. reported that Carlsbad, California, "spent $68 million during an almost 20-year period on The Crossings at Carlsbad. Pierce County, Washington invested over $21 million to build Chambers Bay after buying an abandoned sand and gravel mine for $33 million. Dinuba, California purchased about 350 acres at $6,000 per acre ($2.1 million) and then built a $26 million, 250-acre golf course plus clubhouse. Other luxury-priced, government-owned courses have been built in Bolingbrook, Illinois and Anne Arundel County, Maryland."[2]

Notwithstanding these lavish municipal developments, a strong case could be made that the primary role of municipal golf is to serve as the entry door to the game of golf.

For those cities that opt to remain in the golf business, privatization will receive increasing emphasis, and management companies will be awarded the rights to operate the facilities subject to ever-loosening contracts. Ultimately the green fees will rise to be competitive to the market in order to allow for profit.

A form of privatization that may receive increasing attention is the creation of 501(C)(3) non-profit companies to manage the facilities. The City of Baltimore has used this model well for more than a decade. The City of San Antonio in

---

2 Rebecca Larsen, "Municipal Madness," *Golf Inc.*, August 2008, p. 31.

2007 funded a 501(C)(3) with $10 million to completely renovate, upgrade, and operate its fiscally draining golf courses.

Perhaps the plight of municipal golf courses is becoming so dire that "branding" them might be necessary to save them. Mike Rosenberg of Examiner.com writes, "Pepsi Central or eBay Poplar Creek Golf Course may sound like far-fetched names, but officials say company branding rights could turn out to a savior for San Mateo during trying financial times."[3]

An interesting but disturbing thought. Municipalities, because they have, in essence, unlimited access to capital, will likely acquire the low-end daily fee golf courses who struggle and are unable to further leverage their assets as part of their open space initiatives.

For daily fee golf courses, the growth in profits will come with the growth in population necessary to sustain the facilities.

The profits of a daily fee course, after capital investments and repayment of debt, are basically the owner's salary. With diminished margins and set standards of living, liquidation of the asset becomes likely.

What I fear might likely happen is that respected people in the business (like Kathy Aznavorian and Sandy Mily of Fox Hills Golf Club of Plymouth, MI, or Walter Lankau of Stow Acres in Stowe, Massachusetts) may sell their golf courses to fund lucrative and well-earned retirements that would last their families for generations. In many cases, the smart investment decision would be to sell the golf course to either commercial or real estate developers. The proceeds from these sales would be far greater than the present value of the projected cash flow at an appropriate discount rate.

Many golf courses owners appear to be unprepared for their inevitable inability to run their business—they don't have a succession plan.

The largest influx in the daily fee category is likely to come from private clubs that open their doors to offset declining membership rosters.

As for **private clubs,** the National Golf Foundation believes that "10% to 20% of private clubs are at risk." While the NGF reports that the "majority

---

3 Mike Rosenberg, "Brands Could Save Parks," www.examiner.com/a-1527238~Brands_could_save_parks.html, August 8, 2008.

of operators say they are doing OK financially, one in five are seriously challenged—that projects to 750 clubs nationwide. On average, all clubs, regardless of financial health, have seen a drop in membership and rounds since their peak (2000)—members are down 13% and rounds are down 17%."[4]

The good news is that the NGF report also found that "most of these at-risk clubs will convert to public rather than close."[5] Generating an average $3.9 million in revenue, private clubs average $150,773 in property taxes.[6]

Interestingly, many private clubs are lowering their initiation deposits in hopes of increasing monthly dues to cover operating overhead. Unfortunately, this strategy eliminates the barrier of exit so member turnover can actually accelerate. When exiting an equity club, members will calculate the cost of monthly dues versus the equity refund that they might receive upon the sale of their membership. To the extent that the dues they will incur exceed the potential equity refund, they will "walk from their equity deposit." Thus, the lowering of membership equity deposits is not without consequences.

Low-end private clubs have suffered the largest decline in recent years. Many have large deferred capital investments and will most likely need to become public or liquidate. The only possibility of survival is for them to completely reconstitute their charters.

An example of this may be the Harmon Club in Rockland, Massachusetts. While only a 9-hole facility, the club attracts "busy, upper-middle-income golfers who consider golf and fitness an important part of their lives but who can only spend so much time and much money pursuing it." Just as importantly, this new breed of members wants to extract some health benefit from their memberships as well.

---

4 National Golf Foundation, "Golf Industry Report—The Future of Private Golf Clubs in America," Summer 2008, p. 4.

5 National Golf Foundation, "Golf Industry Report—The Future of Private Golf Clubs in America," Summer 2008, p. 2.

6 Club Managers Association of America, "Who We Are," http://www.cmaa.org/who/index.html.

The management of the Harmon Club uncovered a new revenue model that works. It is a $150 per month individual membership with no money required in advance. Interestingly, the General Manager who oversees the operation, commented, "We don't want a great golf course. Too many people wouldn't pay to play here. It would throw the operation out of balance. It isn't a grand slam, but we can go places with this. It's a nice product that recognizes market realities and holds out a lot of positive for the future of golf."[7]

Mid-tier private clubs are likely to hold their own, but will also need to greatly diversify the activities and services offered to remain competitive. The mid-tier club will need to refocus on becoming a family activity center to which all members are drawn. This model is now being successfully implemented by ClubCorp. The company's CEO, Eric Affeldt, stated, "The concept of people wanting to become members of a place where they can hang out with other people who share similar interests has as much merit as it always did."[8]

ClubCorp was the vision of Robert Dedman, Sr. His "vision was to offer private club membership opportunities with broader amenities (including tennis, swimming, and better food and beverage service). At the same time he wanted the club to be less exclusive, and more affordable, than the more prominent old-line, pure-golf properties. Even more daringly, he would do so with a clear profit motive—famously declaring that while most clubs at that time were run like they were 'nobody's business,' he would succeed by first expanding the market to draw out pent-up demand, and then, through sound management practices, make sure that revenues covered capital and operating expenses."[9]

But that's only half the equation. The other half is making sure the places consumers join remain relevant. Today, relevance comes from a wider range of recreational and entertainment options."[10]

---

7 David Gould, "Getting Harmony," *Golf Inc.*, January 2008, p. 64.

8 Joe Barks, "How ClubCorp is Defining the Market—Again," Club and Resort Business, http://www.clubandresortbusiness.com/article/4693/how-clubcorp-is-defining-the-marketagain.html, August 15, 2008.

9 Joe Barks, "How ClubCorp is Defining the Market—Again," Club and Resort Business, http://www.clubandresortbusiness.com/article/4693/how-clubcorp-is-defining-the-marketagain.html, August 15, 2008.

10 Joe Barks, "How ClubCorp is Defining the Market—Again," Club and Resort Business, http://www.clubandresortbusiness.com/article/4693/how-clubcorp-is-defining-the-marketagain.html, August 15, 2008.

"The working concept we use now is the 'sports resort'," ClubCorp CEO Affeldt continues. "It's a term we got from Western Athletic Clubs [an operator of luxury health and wellness clubs in the San Francisco and San Diego areas that was acquired by KSL], and it connotes a completely different lifestyle. We think our success will hinge on how we can turn country clubs into sports resorts."[11]

Thus, mid-tier private clubs appear to have the choice of selling, converting to public, or reinventing themselves.

High-end private clubs will always have a market. At these exclusive facilities, membership is not about golf but about social status and prestige within the community. For the wealthy businessperson who likes golf, collecting memberships in golf clubs is akin to collecting merit badges in Boy Scouts.

There is an exception to the high-end private club market in which troubled times are likely to come: the remote golf club built as a hunting preserve (Ballyneal, CO; Black Rock, ID; Dismal River, NB; Sutton Bay, SC). The entry fees for these facilities are $50,000 and higher, and they serve as weekend retreats for the "guy's club." But I don't think these courses are sustainable long-term, despite the facts the courses and facilities are fabulous.

The Likely Trend: Consolidation of Management

The consolidation of owners and golf courses is likely to continue. The consolidation in the management of the remaining properties will likely be based on a "cluster strategy," in which common administration, management, marketing, and membership sales are leveraged to increase the operating income of the courses.

An example of this is the Canongate Golf Clubs, which offers reciprocal playing privileges at all of its clubs for members. While some industry experts didn't believe that the concept would work, based on small fees and dues, the concept is appealing.

---

11 Joe Barks, "How ClubCorp is Defining the Market—Again," Club and Resort Business, http://www.clubandresortbusiness.com/article/4693/how-clubcorp-is-defining-the-marketagain.html, August 15, 2008.

The chart depicted here is the collection of courses assembled by Canongate.

What speaks well to the concept is the high customer satisfaction of members like Steve Eubanks, the well-known writer. Steve comments, "As a member, I am impressed with the capital investment that they are making and the benefits they are offering. They conduct during the summer a Canongate Junior Tour in which over 100 players up to age 15 play weekly in what has become a great venue for kids to learn the game and compete."[12]

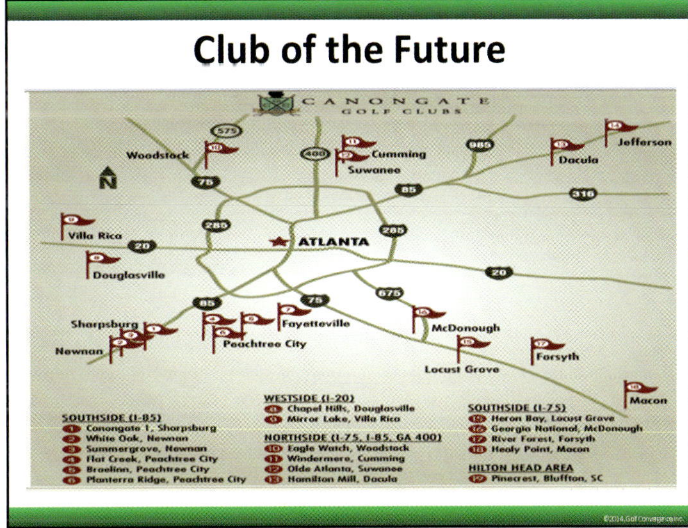

The concept of a cluster is also evidenced in the Akron and Denver markets. In North Carolina, Pinnacle Golf Properties seeks to "improve the bottom line by using national pricing for supplies and sharing resources among its six nearby clubs. Because six of its courses are in the same area, it can offer reciprocal play to members of individual clubs, a great benefit in marketing memberships."[13]

For golf courses that have a limited season (generally those north of Interstate-70 that crosses the entire United States), paying salaried staff for an eight-month golf season just doesn't make sense. Many workers use the off-season to take "accrued comp time" earned during the busy season for their long days, or planning for the next golf season. Does it take four months to plan how to execute a repetitive task for the next eight months?

The consolidation of private clubs under one management structure makes sense. Does each property need a general manager? For example, in the Denver market several mid-tier clubs are struggling. Those clubs could align and offer reciprocal playing privileges with a single consolidated management team overseeing the multiple properties; this would seem to be very cost efficient.

---

12 Steve Eubanks, e-mail to author, July 15, 2009.

13 Rebecca Larsen, "Turnaround Artists," *Golf Inc.*, January 2008, p. 14.

With new management companies hailing this concept, it appears the economic merits of a cluster strategy are well grounded.[14]

However, cost efficiency is unfortunately rarely the deciding factor when the egos of private club membership are involved. Members most often feel, because the club is manifestation of themselves, that the financial challenges are a result of poor management rather their insisting on a high level of service and a quality experience without the offsetting appropriate fee structure established.

What Is Assured?

The service standards at a golf course will greatly influence the success of the facility, whether it is an entry-level daily fee course or the most exclusive club.

As Daniel Pink writes in *The Whole New Mind*,

> ". . . over time, we moved from the Agriculture Age (18th century—farmers) to the Industrial Age (19th century—factory workers) to the Information Age (20th century—knowledge workers) and are now transitioning to the Conceptual Age (21st century—creators and emphasizers) fed by affluence (the abundance that characterizes Western life), technological progress (the automation of white collar work), and globalization (certain types of knowledge work moving to Asia)."[15]

This trend puts a premium on high concept and high touch that will be increasing at golf courses as included in the customer's definition of value.

Recently, I was vacationing at the Hayman Island Resort located in the Great Barrier Reef in Australia and experienced a marvelous client service standard. It was perhaps as good as any service I have experienced in all my travel. For every request made, the response from the staff person was consistent:

- Absolutely.
- Right away, sir.

14 Jim Dunlap, "There's no place like home," *Golf Inc.*, July 2008, p. 30.

15 Daniel H. Pink, *A Whole New Mind* (New York, The Berkley Publishing Group, 2006), p. 49.

- Of course.
- Certainly.
- It would be my pleasure.
- I will take care of that immediately for you.
- No problem at all sir.

More important than the words, they truly were sincere and immediately completed the task.

At dinner one evening, our main course was taking a little longer to be delivered than expected. I asked the waiter if he would check on its status. The restaurant's manager immediately came to our table. He expressed his regrets regarding the delay.

I asked if the wait was unreasonable based on their defined service standards. His reply was classic, "Our standards are determined by your criteria—not ours. I am only here to see that you get what you want, when you want it. It is truly our pleasure to serve you."

What a great line. Could you imagine how successful every golf course would be if that service philosophy was their mantra?

I inquired how the Hayman Resort was able to consistently deliver such a high-quality product.

He said that it was quite easy, after they got the system defined. Each person spends two days in training before meeting any customers. During that time, they are introduced into the culture of the resort, the expectations held for each employee, and the service standards that are to be maintained. Each employee is given a manual for his or her position that "details" every task they will complete, every client interaction they might encounter, and a formula for resolving those unforeseen circumstances.

The Hayman formula had three parts. The client is always told: (1) What will be done or how to do it for themselves (such as directions to a location); (2) when it will be completed (time frame, as in "it takes about five minutes to walk there"); and (3) the cost of the service (in this case it's free; "it is our pleasure to assist you"). Theirs is a simple formula. Every communication is couched in "positive syntax," with those three basic parts included.

This formula can be seen in the new FedEx campaign. When I called to track a package, the live person greeting me said, "I am glad you called FedEx. This is Jacqueline Robinson. What can I do for you today? I am here to assist you."

Great line, "I am glad you called . . ." Golf clubs would benefit from implementing that mantra in the future to improve their investment return, regardless of whether targeting the low price point or the differentiated experience.

What Motivates the Golfer to Come to the Course?

The fundamental building blocks of the future golf course, whether it be a municipal golf course or a high-end private club, will be creating a community of golfers that share (1) common interests and (2) similar core values.

People naturally want to be with others who share an interest in the same activities—be they playing golf or reading books. And they seek out a "tribe" that supports their values. We in the club business tend to focus on externals—the tangible "stuff" of buildings, menus, driveways, and irrigation systems. But all of that "stuff" is essentially provided in order to facilitate relationships—on the golf course, in the clubhouse, over dinner.

These relationships satisfy the psychic needs of people everywhere—the need for tribe, the need for team, the need for community. These relationships are the ultimate magnet for new customers, the ultimate cement for continued loyalty. People may come to a golf course for "stuff," but they stay for people reasons; that is, they genuinely enjoy the company of their fellow golfers, they like the way they think on critical issues, and they enjoy the service community that's been assembled. Bricks and mortar attract but don't sustain. In the final analysis, the sense of community wins; thus, programs and activities that are family oriented are likely to be successful.

End Notes

The lessons of this chapter are:

1) Community is about creating shared experiences and stores, generating familiarity between people, and acknowledging and embracing family through diverse activities.
2) Programs created for woman, juniors, and new entrants to the game increase rounds incrementally, not exponentially.
3) The golf course of the future will look vastly different.
   - **a.** Municipalities will again concentrate on the low-end market. Their recent tendencies to create high-end daily fee complexes will abate.
   - **b.** Low-tier private clubs will see significant contractions, with many becoming self-private golf courses.
   - **c.** The mid-tier private clubs will diversify their offerings of activities to attract and retain families as a center of their social lives.
   - **d.** The high-end private clubs will continue to cater to the wealthy. However, the waiting list will grow shorter, initiation fees will remain static, and the trend to build new remote clubs will abate as the capital required to support such facilities will be constrained. The success of these golf clubs will likely mirror the national economy.
4) Management of private clubs will likely be consolidated within local markets to achieve the economies of scale available. With such consolidation, the opportunity for reciprocal playing privileges will likely grow.
5) As we enter the conceptual age, the golf course of the future will feature community.

Concluding Thoughts

Conformity is the jailer of freedom and the enemy of growth.

John F. Kennedy

Change has a considerable psychological impact on the human mind. To the fearful it is threatening because it means things may get worse. To the hopeful it is encouraging because things may get better. To the confident it is inspiring because the challenge exists to make things better.

King Whitney Jr.

Chapter 18

The Courage to Change—A Short Tutorial

Far better it is to dare mighty things, to win glorious triumphs, even though checked by failure, than to take rank with those poor spirits who neither enjoy nor suffer much, because they live in the gray twilight that knows not victory or defeat.

Theodore Roosevelt

Chapter Highlights

What does today's golf course owner and manager need to compete?

While focusing on the importance of brand image and providing a low-cost solution or a differentiated alternative, it is important to understand the current state of the industry.

The seven steps outlined in these pages, when implemented with a firm grasp of the business's major themes, will move your operation closer to your ultimate goals.

What Is Your Brand Image?

Are you a platinum-, gold-, silver-, bronze-, or steel-branded golf course?

This book has emphasized the creation of a strategic vision, creation of a tactical plan, and operational execution to form a golf course's brand image. While a brand image can't be touched or felt, it largely determines the financial success of a golf course.

We all understand what a brand image is: Think of Ritz-Carlton, Mercedes, or Nike. Images evolve. Value propositions are well defined. A course's image and value proposition should also be well defined.

The components of a brand are the by-products of the course's name and logo, the facility (the course and clubhouse), the pricing, and the depth and breadth of staff—all controllable factors. A course's brand isn't too different from the brand a rancher puts on his cattle: once it's there, it's all but impossible to change.

What Are the Owner's Options?

Each week from late August to January, college and professional football teams create "game plans" to ensure their victories. Fifty percent of those game plans fail; some fail because of poor strategy, some because their tactics are incorrect, and others because their execution is lacking. Whether because of the lack of attitude or aptitude, their efforts result in teams that fail to achieve their objectives. Rarely does a team make it through the season undefeated.

As it is with football coaches, every golf course operator who creates a business plan will not win. Without a vision, the course will flounder. With only a great vision and detailed tactical plans, the course will suffer. The finest tactical plans without a talented team are meaningless. It takes all three components: strategic vision, tactical planning, and operational execution to be successful.

A Winning Game Plan: Golf Convergence WIN™ Formula

This book is a simple message for the golf course owner. Using the Golf Convergence WIN™ seven-step formula will differentiate your facility from local competitors and greatly enhance the probability of financial success. As the saying goes, "luck favors the prepared."

To implement this formula, well-intended golf course owners or management teams that seek to bolster their investment returns must answer, examine, and explore the following questions.

Creating a Strategic Vision

1. **What Business Are You In?** Deciding what your unique niche is and what role your business serves to the golfer is the foundation for creating a mission statement. Is your facility meant to be the entry door to the game for the masses, a park to entertain the taxpaying citizens, a forum for businesspeople to meet and greet, a private enclave, or a resort that attracts a certain clientele as defined by net worth and residential location?
2. **The Macroeconomics of Golf 101—Is This an Industry You Should Be In?** The worldwide supply of golf courses versus the demand for them defines the growth or contraction of the industry. What effects are the convergence of rounds, courses, and players having on utilization? What factors are impacting the current climate in golf? Who is playing the game, and how can your course retain those customers? How are time, money, and skill impacting the brand image of the game? Is golf truly a game of the elite, by the elite, for the elite?
3. **The Players—What National Influences Are Affecting Local Golf Course Operations?** How are the trade associations—the Club Managers Association of America, the National Golf Course Owners Association, the National Golf Foundation, the Professional Golfers' Association of America, and the United States Golf Association—impacting the growth of the game? Are these groups producing qualified business managers and teaching professionals at competitive wages? Does the USGA/R&A's rigid stance on equipment standards adversely influence the growth of the business? Are equipment manufacturers creating barriers for entry into the game through their arcane and highly technical descriptions of their products? Do these national organizations foster elitism or send a message that attracts the masses?
4. **The Forms of Ownership—What Are the Economic Advantages and Weaknesses?** The ownership of a golf course—municipal, daily fee, resort, or private—and the great divisions in organizational structure,

management philosophies, and operating policies between these different types of ownership produce economic advantages and weaknesses that need to be recognized. Comparing your facility's ownership structure to the different and proportional mix of courses in the local market defines your target market and the opportunities it holds. You may find that the cost of retaining a professional management company is offset by increased profits. Even if retaining a management company is a cost rather than an obvious financial benefit, the intangible benefit of not having to worry about running the course is fair compensation itself and should be evaluated.

5. **The Local Market—Is the Market Oversupplied? Are There Opportunities for Growth? What Is the Impact of Weather?** All golf is local, all golf courses are unique. Age, income, ethnicity, and the population within 10 miles of the golf course are the most influential macroeconomic predictors for 95% of golf courses.

   The mix of supply versus demand changes for each market. Obtaining the answers to the following supply and demand questions determines the economic opportunity that exists:

Questions Regarding Supply

1. What is the competition: how many courses by type and price?
2. How many annual rounds are being played on those courses?
3. What is the potential demand of rounds?
4. Does your market show a normal "demand curve"?

Questions Regarding Demand

5. How many golfers are in your local market?
6. How many rounds per year do they play?
7. What is the per capita "play rate"?
8. What is the household income, age, and ethnicity of the population?

The answers to these questions provide the opportunity. The answer to how weather has impacted the operation provides insights on the quality of a facility's management team. If rounds are higher than suggested by the number of playable golf days, the team should be lauded. Conversely, if rounds realized don't equal the potential, that gap reveals that a comprehensive examination of pricing, marketing, and staffing may be appropriate.

Developing Tactical Plans

While the definitions of which plans are strategic, tactical, or operational can be debated, the delineation drawn here focuses on defining the golf industry and the local market (strategic) in relation to your facility and its unique customer base (tactical).

6. **Technology—Is This Viable Tool Effectively Being Used to Boost Your Club's Investment Return?** The foundation of every successful golf course, particularly those open to the public, is a technology platform that seamlessly integrates the elements of all profit centers into a streamlined information and reporting system with which managers can proactively manage based on current financial data.

   Has the course acquired, implemented, and trained the staff to use a comprehensive golf management system that serves as a management tool?

7. **Are the Key Financial Metrics Understood?** The financial statements are the goalposts of a business.

   Do you understand the key financial ratios, comprehend the standard industry definitions? Do you contribute to and benefit from the valuable research data amassed by Golf Datatech and PGA PerformanceTrak? How do your key operating statistics, (course utilization, revPAR, EBITDA, staffing levels, capital budgets, and deferred expenditures) compare to local and regional course profiles?

   Are you using the latest management tools in financial data streaming to be alert when financial thresholds are crossed, requiring management decisions to maximize revenue?

8. **Financial Modeling—How Does the Course's Financial Performance Compare to Industry Averages?** While you are focusing on details, often a clear picture is lost. Some courses have more than 80 different fees and 250 general ledger accounts. In the resulting confusion, a course's financial performance isn't gauged accurately.

   Have you developed accurate financial models that can support management decision making, or are the financials merely a tool that reflect historical results?

9. **Yield Management—Is Each Tee Time Properly Priced to Ensure Revenue Is Maximized?** Tee times are like airline seats. Once the time has passed, once the plane has departed, their value becomes zero.

   While it is an oversimplification to say that there is no number in the golf business more meaningless than the rack rate, very few courses know their effective yield in the aggregate or by player type. What is the gap between your fees and the value experienced by your customers? Are your course's prices set by guessing, by using yield management techniques, or are they based on local market rates?

10. **Valuation—What Is the Course Worth If You Should Opt to Sell?** The axiom is money is made when a business is bought, not sold. Are you operating the golf course today in a way that will improve its long-term value from the original purchase price? A golf course is a depreciable asset that requires constant reinvestment, and its brand image is constantly changing based on the value created for the golfers.

    What are the current capitalization rates? What is a fair price for your course today? How have the key indices on which price is determined changed in the past year? Which of those statistics can you focus on to most favorably boost your valuation? What are your deferred capital expenditures? Which investments would have the greatest impact on the valuation?

    Given that the value of a golf course is determined by a precisely defined formula, is the land value greater for commercial or residential real estate development, or is it greater based on its current operating performance? Who are the likely buyers for your course? Who should be retained to appraise, list, and sell the golf course?

Operational Execution

Once a strategic vision and tactical plans are in place, operational execution follows, ensuring consistency in the products and services offered.

11. **The Playing Field—How Do We Properly Maintain a Living Organism that Requires Constant Maintenance and Capital Investment?** Golfers consistently cite the condition of the golf course as one of the leading factors in their selection of which course to play.

The level of playing conditions expected by golfers, relative to the price point charged, is a large component in establishing the brand for the facility. Defining the need and frequency of capital improvements, annual maintenance expenditures, the equipment required, and the associated optimum labor is required to maintain proper course conditions.

Once management has ascertained the level of playing conditions desired, is it the desire of management to invest in equipment, staff, and capital reserves to adequately fund the inherent replacement cycles at a level consistent with industry standards?

12. **Marketing 101—Is the Investment Properly Allocated and Well Tracked?** Most golf courses approach marketing reactively rather than proactively. With investment dollars allocated between advertising, public relations, and promotion, what was done in the prior year becomes the benchmark for the current year's spending. What if a golf course used zero-based budgeting for its marketing program?

    Of those investments, how much should be spent on a Web site and what features should be incorporated therein? Are customers being organized and connected based on common interests such as course reviews, instruction, tournaments, and social activities? Are the most loyal customers recognized? Does the Web site have blogs, forums, and other interesting and appropriate content? How effectively are Twitter, YouTube, and Facebook being utilized to attract the Gen Y golfers?

    Third-party marketing firms are emerging. What is the financial and social cost of participating in these networks? Should the relationship with third-party firms be continued? If so, under what terms and conditions? How can the golf course leverage the extensive e-mail databases amassed by these vendors to the benefit of the course?

13. **Best Management Practices—Does the Course Provide Value Equal to or Better than the Fees Charged?** The golf course is like an amusement park that winds the customer from the entrance around a series of themes to a thrilling conclusion upon departure. Every golf course is unique. What are the industry's best management practices and how many have your course adopted relative to the price point being offered?

    There are thirteen customer touch points. Creating a superior customer experience requires consistent execution.

14. **The Customer—What Are Our Customers' Value Perceptions?** This question must be answered so correct pricing can be established. Golfers

consciously base their decision as to where to golf on many factors, including the overall experience, course conditioning, and price. Subconsciously, that decision is made on the perceived value derived.

What are your customers' value perceptions and what is the related brand image of your golf course compared to its competitors? Has your golf course developed an extensive e-mail database in which local golfers can be effectively polled using electronic survey tools to obtain enlightening insights regarding barriers to increased play, motivating price points, and your course's brand image in the local market?

15. **The Customer—Enhancing Loyalty to Acquire and Retain Core Customers While Minimizing Defectors; Is That Possible?** The strength of a golf course's customer franchise can be precisely measured. In the current environment, with the only growth in a facility's customer base likely to come from "stealing the customers" from another golf course, have you identified your core customers and the turnover of the golf course's client base? Customer loyalty serves as an accurate predictor of a golf course's financial success.

    A facility needs to identify both its best customers and those likely to depart. A plan that includes precise messages directed at each of these types of customers is necessary to ensure that the battle for market share is won.

16. **The Customer—Who Is the Customer Likely to Be? What Are the Customers' Needs? Are We Fulfilling Those Needs?** The golf industry continues to evolve. Likely changes include slowing growth in municipal golf, selling by daily fee owners, diminishing role of low-end private clubs, and diversifying of services and activities by mid-tier clubs to remain competitive by becoming a sports resort. The future for the remote high-end clubs that represent a members' third or fourth affiliation will become challenged and be deemed not to be economically viable on a self-sustaining basis once the newness of bigger, better, and greater wears thin.

    How are the ownership, management structure, and operational policies of golf courses likely to evolve during the next two decades? What economic, societal, and business trends will impact the game of golf?

    Dependent upon the motivations to buy, how does the golf course become a sustaining business enterprise? Is it through the creation of community?

Success Stories—Does the Formula Work?

Consider for a moment what happens if the formula doesn't work. At a minimum, what would be obtained from the process would be valuable insights into methods for improved operational performance. Knowing your facility's strategic vision, developing a tactical plan, and forming some commitment to consistent operational execution would produce benefits. In other words, the process of merely working through the formula has value.

And what if the formula works? A golf course could significantly enhance its operations in relationship to its competitors, boost its profits in the short term, and increase its value in the long term. Again, great benefits result. We believe, and have proven, that application of the formula has the potential to increase your EBITDA by at least 12% of gross revenue.

But, the skeptic might ask, do you have any examples of where the seven step formula has been executed to great benefit?

Following is an excerpt of an article from the *Ann Arbor News*; in this case, short-term results were evident.

Ann Arbor's Leslie Park, Huron Hills Courses Are Rebounding by Lon Horwedel | *The Ann Arbor News*[1]

It's no secret that Ann Arbor's two municipal golf courses, Leslie Park and Huron Hills, have struggled financially in recent years. So much so that there was talk of selling Huron Hills, or at least a portion of it, to stop the financial bleeding. It got so bad, a consulting firm was called in to assess the situation. Their report of the city's two courses was bleak at best.

According to the report, green fees were too high, customer service was not up to par and both courses had maintenance issues. To make matters worse, Leslie Park and Huron Hills had to try and reverse their fortunes as gas prices began to soar and Michigan's economy continued to plunge. In addition, this year's golf season started two weeks late after

1 Lon Horwedel, "Ann Arbor's Leslie Park, Huron Hills Courses Are Rebounding," *Ann Arbor News*, July 31, 2008.

an extremely long winter. These factors would make it understandable if both courses continued to spiral into a financial abyss.

Now for a surprise. Halfway through the 2008 golf season, both Huron Hills and Leslie Park are doing well.

How did the City of Ann Arbor do for the 2008? The results are now in.

	Huron Hills	Leslie Park
Rounds	Up 14%	Up 37%
Revenue	Up 7%	Up 22%
Food/Beverage	Up 82%	Up 106%
Merchandise	Down 6%	Up 30%

Revenue potential: $234,500

Policy
Monday Morning: open at 6:00 a.m. versus 8:00 a.m.
Fivesomes on Monday – Thursday
Raise Resident Rate at Springbrook $3
Specials – Internet/Coupon (12% of total play) curtailed on Friday/Saturday/Sundays
Rain Checks (3 ½% total rounds) restricted to Thor Guard or Superintendent's approval
Twilight Hours changed from 3 to 5 and Super-twilight from 5 to 7
Wave Implemented (off-peak historically – may be incorporated during peak season)
Friday charged at weekend rates at both golf courses
Complimentary and Employee golf restricted to Director of Golf, Golf Professional and Superintendents (5% of total play). Yes – that includes Park District Council retroactively
Senior Moved from 12 back to 11

These impressive financial gains were made in spite of the fact that both courses opened two weeks late.

The skeptic might say, you got lucky. Any more examples?

The Naperville Park District applied the process, identified its financial potential, and implemented changes that will increase EBITDA from a loss of $280,000 in 2008 to a potential profit of $130,000. The revenue component is identified as depicted on this page.

Expenses could be trimmed without impacting service, as determined by management and staff as depicted on the next page.

Upon reopening the Ocala Municipal Golf Club after a course renovation that was recommended by a strategic analysis of the City's alternatives to return to profitable, the assistant city manager commented regarding the Golf Convergence WIN™ process that it "was the genesis for the success we all feel. It is even more evident that your vision and recommendations have been accurate, reliable, and most importantly, helpful."[2]

2 John Zobler, Assistant City Manager, Letter dated October 26, 2009, to Golf Convergence.

For the University of Minnesota—Les Bolstad golf course a $600,000 positive change in EBITDA was documented by application of the Golf Convergence WIN™ process. For the City of Winnipeg, the strategic plan created by Golf Convergence revealed how they could reverse their financial fortunes by over $8.5 million within the next five years through privatization. Merrill Hills achieved organizational stability and increased membership.

Expense Savings: $162,000

Policy	Impact
Reclassify 1st Assistant from exempt to part time at Naperbrook & Springbrook Staff: 08 83k total 50% savings in 09 = 42K SB + 50K 1st asst.	90,000
Introduction of loading schedules into Kronos for accurate timekeeping reducing overtime Staff: $19,100 / 2 = 9K per course	18,000
Reduction of 1 ½ positions at each golf course Staff: 6 shifts = 2 staff $10,000 per course (Outside & Counter)	20,000
Reduce role of starter introducing PA system on some occasions Staff: Agree…occasional PA system (limited shifts 5K per course)	10,000
Modify work schedules eliminating guaranteed and overtime hours Staff: 2 hrs x 5 emp x 7 days x 4 wk x 5 month x $8 = $11,200 x 2	20,000
Reduce maintenance winter staff by 1, changing exempt to part-time Staff: Reduce PT labor in winter	4,000
Total Expense reductions Staff: Total Expense reductions	$162,000

For the fiscal year ending June 30, 2011, the Pacific Grove Golf Links achieved gross revenues exceeding $2.7 million with a resulting net loss of $446,000. They are one of the highest-grossing municipal golf courses in America, yet they are struggling to break even. They have reported net losses for four of their last seven years.

Simply, Pacific Grove is the finest links course owned by a municipality in the United States. By applying the formulas contained in this book, we clearly demonstrated how they could increase revenues by over $250,000 and reduce expenses by more than $650,000.

Will they achieve those goals? I hope so. If they don't, as the expression goes, the fault is with the archer, not the bow.

However, I find their forum dominated by a group of 35 golfers wanting unlimited play season passes for $1,200. The Men's Club "demands" to reserve weekly the 8:00 a.m. tee time for their 28 members. They are willing to pay just $20 per golfer. The cost to produce a round of golf at that facility last year was $45.09 prior to interest, depreciation and amortization. I will never understand how selling your most valuable tee times at the lowest price to the golfers who create the most distractions and dominate the discussion is a good business practice. Though I have a BBA, MBA and was a CPA, I must have missed that finance class when that subject was covered.

During the summer of 2011, we illustrated to the City and County of Denver, after extensive research and fieldwork, how they could turn a $750,000 profit into a $2.0 million positive cash flow with judicious investment. We demonstrated to an exciting 36-hole resort in the middle of nowhere how they had a shot at breaking operationally even on their $30 million investment with proper management and targeted marketing. Truthfully, the resort probably should not have been built but having been built, there is hope. In 2013, they generated EBITDA of $250,000 versus a loss in 2013 of $1.161 million.

For a Jim Engh designed course that was emerging from receivership and is located 45 miles from any city with a meaningful population, we guided them in raising rates, providing value and turning an annual loss exceeding $200,000 into a possible small profit in 2013.

For an exclusive club that is a venue for major golf championships, we advised a group of members during their perilous transition from developer ownership in May, 2011. For the first time, member surveys were conducted, Board meetings held, lines of communication opened, democratic elections to the Board of Directors completed, the concern of dissident groups threatening litigation addressed and resolved. The formula for success clarified through consensus. As importantly, we demonstrated that a golf course is a living organism and that their nationally acclaimed course had become overgrown, difficult and the playability was a challenge. In September, 2011, Bill Coore masterfully presented a photo essay of the agronomic changes and maintenance practices needed to secure this course's future on the national stage, validating our research.

In 2012 and 2013, those who executed the principles contained in this book evidenced enhanced knowledge and perspectives creating a platform for financial stability and increased customer value, whether it be in Atlanta, Becker, Brookings, Casper, Clemson, Durango, Hillcrest, etc. For those willing to challenge the status quo, to seek creativity rather than accept conformity, the business of golf can be enjoyable and lucrative.

The bottom line is that those who diligently apply the principles in this book will increase their net income by greater than 12%.

Challenges Beyond the Grasp of One

While the primary focus of golf course owners and managers should be on their own facilities, such focus should come with a broad perspective on understanding what the game of golf is and what it represents to our society.

There are five major themes to golf that each individual in the industry should know. These themes direct us to the future of the golf industry:

1. **Industry:** The days of "build it and they will come" are over. The industry has remained stagnant since 2005, in part because the prices are currently overvalued by 10%, resulting in discounting of up to 30% at many facilities.

   The short-term solution is effective marketing based in technology; golf has historically lagged behind its peer industries in the use of technology.

2. **Consumers:** Golf is a game "of the elite, by the elite, and restricted to the elite." Golf will never be a sport for the masses. Like polo and 12-meter yachts, it is expensive to play golf, and unless you are good, frankly, it isn't much fun. Sir Charles Barkley, as he stated on the Hank Haney project, is correct.

   Golf provides recreation and entertainment, but its real benefit is in the values developed in those who participate. Failure to attract new golfers is serious, but Public Enemy Number One is attrition. Participation rates continue to decline, in no small part because almost 50% of population growth in the United States is due to the influx of people of Hispanic ethnicity, and they play at only 50% of the frequency of Caucasian Americans.

3. **The Environment:** Water is a critical resource, and its threatened supply greatly affects the golf industry. Many courses should focus on reducing the size of the playing field, thereby reducing the requirements for irrigation and fertilization. Curtailing water consumption would also reduce expenses. The industry needs to transition from emphasizing a manicured experience to a natural experience.

4. **The Golf Course:** During the past two decades, courses that have been built are more difficult, more expensive, and more time-consuming. One way to measure difficulty follows:

Slope Rating	Pre-1990	Post-1990
Mean (average)	120	127
Median (midpoint)	121	129

Consistent with these trends is the construction of large clubhouses exceeding 40,000 square feet, which are expensive to operate. The cost to maintain these facilities is exorbitant and the costs are passed on to the golfers; this is another negative influence on the adoption of golf by the masses.

The daily fee course should create an experience through which golfers feel they have been challenged, but one that through their own efforts they have conquered.

For example, bunkers could be placed where few golf balls will get in them, creating the illusion of difficulty and ensuring that these hazards don't adversely affect the pace of play. If the round takes too long or the golfers feel beat up, they aren't likely to return. As PGA Past President Brian Whitcomb once taught me, "Golf courses should be made to look hard and play easy."

The golf course competes for the entertainment dollar of the consumer. Creating a theme for a golf course differentiates a facility from a typical daily-fee course. For example, the Lost Tracks golf course in Bend, Oregon, has the theme of a railroad.

Here are pictures of how this theme was flawlessly executed from tee markers to island greens, with a railroad car serving as a bridge.

Brian Whitcomb ingeniously implemented the railroad car concept. He furnished the railroad car with dining/ parlor furniture and tables. Then, he hung a single bag tag. It seems that every golfer who plays the hole leaves a bag tag affixed somewhere to the rail car. Brian correctly discerned the human trait that each of us is trying to create an identity as to where we have been, marking our place in time for those who follow.

5. **Management and Staff:** To remain relevant, individuals within the profession and those entering the profession need to acquire the requisite

business skills in accounting, management, marketing, and technology to appreciate the complexities of successfully running a golf enterprise.

Successful business operators are never satisfied with the status quo. They are near perfectionists seeking to constantly improve operations, for leading is a journey not a destination," Tomorrow's leaders will share their information, provide expertise, and clearly articulate their values and standards.

The axiom is, "Is it easy for customers to do business with us?" If not, let's change it, for the best operations will be both high touch and high tech.

This is the End . . .

This analysis of the golf industry and the explanation of the formula that leads to the successful operation of a golf course has been presented in a way that I hope will enlighten the spirits of the professionals who serve the business of golf.

I have written with the hope and understanding that course owners who take these words to heart and head and hands and feet will have the opportunity to bolster their investment return.

Concluding Thoughts

YIN-YANG: *In the black, there is some white; In the wrong, there is some right; In the dark, there is some light; In the blind, there is some sight.*

Ven Abhinyana

Do or do not; there is no try.

Yoda

One's human spirit is a tapestry of his life. If one were to try to edit out of that finely woven blanket the hardships, the sufferings, the shortcomings, the days spent seeking perfection, nothing of substance would remain; for it is in the difficult times that our character grows and the fabric of what we are made of becomes strong. The journey of life is not to seek perfection but to seek acceptance that we are flawed and be comfortable with that conclusion.

Father Patrick Dolan

Index